THE AUTHOR   David Mason was born in Brighton in 1969. Having completed his degree, he gained an MA from the University of London and taught as a visiting lecturer at the University of North London. His first book, *Verdun*, was published in 2000. He now works as a manager in a central London bookshop.

SERIES EDITOR   Professor Denis Judd is a graduate of Oxford, a Fellow of the Royal Historical Society and Professor of History at the University of North London. He has published over 20 books including the biographies of Joseph Chamberlain, Prince Philip, George VI and Alison Uttley, historical and military subjects, stories for children and two novels. His most recent books are the highly praised *Empire: The British Imperial Experience from 1765 to the Present* and (with Keith Surridge) *The Boer War*. He is an advisor to the BBC *History* Magazine.

Other Titles in the Series

A Traveller's History of Australia
A Traveller's History of Canada
A Traveller's History of The
 Caribbean
A Traveller's History of China
A Traveller's History of England
A Traveller's History of France
A Traveller's History of Greece
A Traveller's History of The
 Hundred Years War
A Traveller's History of India
A Traveller's History of Ireland
A Traveller's History of Italy
A Traveller's History of Japan
A Traveller's History of London

A Traveller's History of Mexico
A Traveller's History of New Zealand
 and the South Pacific Islands
A Traveller's History of North Africa
A Traveller's History of Oxford
A Traveller's History of Paris
A Traveller's History of Portugal
A Traveller's History of Scotland
A Traveller's History of Russia
A Traveller's History of South East
 Asia
A Traveller's History of Spain
A Traveller's History of Turkey
A Traveller's History of The USA

THE TRAVELLER'S HISTORY SERIES

'Ideal before-you-go reading' *The Daily Telegraph*

'An excellent series of brief histories' *New York Times*

'I want to compliment you ... on the brilliantly concise contents of your books' *Shirley Conran*

Reviews of Individual Titles

A Traveller's History of Japan

'It succeeds admirably in its goal of making the present country comprehensible through a narrative of its past, with asides on everything from bonsai to *zazen*, in a brisk, highly readable style ... you could easily read it on the flight over, if you skip the movie.' *The Washington Post*

'... dip into Richard Tames's literary, lyrical *A Traveller's History of London'. The Sunday Telegraph*

A Traveller's History of France

'Undoubtedly the best way to prepare for a trip to France is to bone up on some history. *The Traveller's History of France* by Robert Cole is concise and gives the essential facts in a very readable form.' *The Independent*

A Traveller's History of China

'The author manages to get 2 million years into 300 pages. An excellent addition to a series which is already invaluable, whether you're travelling or not.' *The Guardian*

A Traveller's History of India

'For anyone ... planning a trip to India, the latest in the excellent Traveller's History series ... provides a useful grounding for those whose curiosity exceeds the time available for research.' *The London Evening Standard*

A Traveller's History
of South Africa

Acknowledgements
The publishers would like to thank the following for permission to use quotations in this book: Time Warner Books UK for a short extract from *Long Walk to Freedom* by Nelson Mandela; Yale University Press for a short extract from *A History of South Africa* © 2000 by Leonard Thompson; an extract from *My Traitor's Heart* by Rian Malan published by Bodley Head. Used by permission of The Random House Group Limited.

A Traveller's History of South Africa

DAVID MASON

Series Editor DENIS JUDD
Line Drawings *PETER GEISSLER*

Interlink Books
An imprint of Interlink Publishing Group, Inc.
New York • Northampton

First American edition published 2004 by

INTERLINK BOOKS
An imprint of Interlink Publishing Group, Inc.
46 Crosby Street, Northampton, Massachusetts 01060
www.interlinkbooks.com

Library of Congress Cataloging-in-Publication Data

Mason, David, 1926–
A traveller's history of South Africa / by David Mason.— 1st American ed.
    p. cm. — (The traveller's history series)
Includes bibliographical references and index.
  ISBN 1-56656-505-7 *29399697* *10/63*
1. South Africa—History. 2. South Africa—Description and travel.
3. South Africa—Guidebooks. I. Title. II. Traveller's history.
  DT1787.M38 2003
  968—dc21

                                          2003000625

Printed and bound in Great Britain

To request a free copy of our 40-page full-color catalog, please call
1-800-238-LINK, visit our web site at **www.interlinkbooks.com**,
or write to us at: **Interlink Publishing**
46 Crosby Street, Northampton, Massachusetts 01060

Contents

Preface

Once the British had acquired the Cape during the Napoleonic Wars, South Africa and its development became deeply interwoven into the history of Britain and its Empire. Until the Act of Union came into effect in 1910, South African was merely a 'geographical expression', like so many other fragmented and disunited areas. From the outset, however, the region had great potency as a paradoxical symbol, a place of enormous promise and intractable problems, a place of refuge and of looming, chronic danger, of fabulous wealth and grinding poverty. Even today, despite the drive for reform and improvement, there is a 'First World' South Africa co-existing with a 'Third World' one.

The main reason for these confused images was the fundamental historical fact that the region was the scene of an apparently unending struggle for mastery between competing African peoples, and two increasingly dominant white groups, the Afrikaner settlers (in effect another tribe, though a European one) and the British imperial authorities and English-speaking migrants. Even today with majority rule established, there are painful and controversial adjustments to be made between the 'haves' and the 'have-nots', there is profound anxiety over the long term supply of water and whether the economy can sustain the requirements of a large and needy population.

In this very well researched, clear and readable book, David Mason tells the story with great style and skill. From the earliest history to the post-apartheid era, the development of South Africa is laid out in an attractive and accessible fashion. The story has something for everybody. First there is the land itself, from the high veld to the sub-tropical coast of Kwa-Zulu-Natal; from the towering Drakensberg Mountains to the haunted desert landscape of the Karoo, from the green Arcadian vineyards of the Cape to the dusty plains and barren kopjes. Given the country's geographical and scenic variety, and its stunning natural beauty, it is small wonder that so many peoples have competed so fiercely for its land and living space. It is, of course, these same qualities that now attract the overseas tourists in their hundreds of thousands.

The history of South Africa is certainly one major pull for visitors. Where else could one discover more about characters as diverse as Shaka the great Zulu conqueror, Mahatma Gandhi, Cecil Rhodes, Baden-Powell, Paul Kruger, Olive Schreiner, Jan Smuts, and Nelson Mandela, or about historical events as fascinating as the rise of the Xhosa and Zulu peoples, the arrival of the Dutch, the Cape frontier wars, the Great Trek, the discovery of gold and diamonds, the South African War of 1899-1902, the rise and fall of apartheid and the eventual triumph of the ANC?

Apart from the beauty of much of the countryside, there are also great cities and pretty towns to savour. Cape Town is sophisticated and urbane, Johannesburg frenetic and hard-nosed, Durban sultry, Indian and spicy, Pretoria grand and executive, Stellenbosch elegant and leafy, Ladysmith quietly conscious of its historical significance during the South African War, wine growing Franschhoek was founded by Huguenots, East London by the British, and so on.

For the visitor there is almost too much to do, to see and to experience. The sheer variety of the South African landscape, its people and its towns and cities is almost overwhelming. Certainly almost every taste is catered for, from surf riding to horse riding, from mountain climbing to lazing on clean golden beaches, from seeing wild animals at close quarters to attending first rate concerts and plays, from shopping in smart city stores to buying indigenous village craftwork, from enjoying some of the best wine and food in the world to sampling an informal braaivleis – or barbeque.

As a further incentive to the traveller, due to the current exchange rate, all of this can be experienced for only a fraction of what it would cost in the West or in many other traditional tourist magnets. South Africa must be visited not once but many times. This compact and informative book will stand you in good stead no matter how often you go there.

Denis Judd
London
2003

'One Nation, Many Cultures'

'One Nation, Many Cultures' was the slogan under which the African National Congress chose to campaign during South Africa's first-ever freely held democratic elections in 1994. Although the statement might seem slightly banal on one level, on another it captures perfectly the diversities of a country that was, until recently, at war with itself to the extent that it could be described as anything but a single entity. Today, South Africa *is* a united polity and society, but the struggle to achieve this was hard fought and characterised by much human suffering and brutality.

The modern state of South Africa is comparatively new and only came into being in 1910. Both before and after this time, the region's history was dominated by political struggle, social upheaval and economic hardship. After the Second World War, the country was very much a world anomaly – a pariah state that refused to bow to the pressures of the post-colonial world order. It is only in the last ten years that the white minority conceded to the inevitability of majority rule, a move made all the more remarkable because it was not accompanied by the often expected blood bath. Since then, South Africa has been established as a respectable member of the international community as a dedicated non-aligned state, and despite the persistence of political and social fractures at home, which are only slowly being overcome, South Africa is a regional super power.

South Africa, nowadays often spoken of as one of the world's best-kept secrets, is an increasingly popular destination for tourists and travellers alike, who revel in its uniqueness and marvel at its natural beauty. This land is like no other, its people as contrasting as they are welcoming. In these pages, we will see the forces and trends that shaped South Africa into the nation it is today.

CHAPTER ONE

The Rainbow Nation: Land, State and People

The South African population is a complex mix of cultures and races, colours and creeds, outlooks and languages (eleven of which are today officially recognised). Similar diversities can be seen in the land. South Africa is a country of geographical extremes: lush bush and arid desert regions, mountains and plains, varying climates and geographical formations. It has aptly been described as the world in one country, and a lifetime is not long enough to get to know the place.

Mapping South Africa: The Physical Setting

South Africa is located at the foot of the African continent approximately half way between Antarctica and the Equator. It is bordered by the states of Namibia (to the north-west), Botswana and Zimbabwe (to the north) and Mozambique (to the north-east). It surrounds two independent states: Swaziland and Lesotho. Covering over 471,000 square miles, South Africa is a huge country that is over five times the size of Britain and home to a host of different and distinctive environments. It is a land of great danger and also natural riches and abundance. For thousands of years the physical realities of South Africa, in terms of vegetation and disease as well as climate, profoundly influenced the settlement patterns of human beings. It is, and always was, a varied place that defies easy classification.

Geographically speaking, South Africa is an aged place. Some 70 per cent of the total land surface is covered by ancient rock deposits. These are sedimentary and of the Karoo series, although to the north where the rocks are older still, the earth exudes rich mineral deposits of gold, platinum, zinc, copper, cobalt, nickel and diamond that are among the world's richest. Further to the south, where the rock deposits are younger, the land is more permeable, creating the dry sandlands of the Kalahari region.

South Africa is dominated by an arid, flat plateau which at its highest point stands 3,400 metres above sea level. Around three sides of the plateau towards the sea there is a circular escarpment of mountainous terrain, which runs for thousands of miles. The plateau is distinct from the areas beyond the escarpment. Here, on the highveld, temperatures reach an average of 27° in the summer, but the winters are bitterly cold. To the east, where the mountains reach a peak, is the Drakensberg chain, which acts as a conduit for the rains that travel in from the Indian Ocean. This creates a strip of woodland between the mountains and the sea that is both well watered and fertile, and characteristically humid. West of the Drakensberg region, the country is more arid. The savannah-like conditions of the north ebb away on the veld to rolling grasslands. In turn, these give way in the south and west to the desert-like regions of the Kalahari and the Karoo, where temperatures peak at 40° during the summer months.

The South African interior is crossed by a number of rivers and tributary streams that are unnavigable for the most part. Two rivers dominate the region: the Orange (now often referred to as the Gariep) which flows into the Atlantic Ocean, and the Limpopo, which starts its course in the north of the country before running through Mozambique and out into the Indian Ocean.

The south-west of the country, in and around the Cape peninsula, is exceptional in South African terms. Here, the climate is far more temperate and therefore ideal for a variety of agricultural practices. Comparable to the Mediterranean, a long summer season is tempered by cool autumnal and winter rains. The icy Benguela Current is tempered by the warm Agulhas current when they meet off the Cape of Good Hope. It is no surprise that it was at this place that the first Europeans settled in South Africa.

South Africa has an abundant variety of flora and fauna. The Cape floral kingdom, which is the largest in the world, incorporates 8,600 plant types from exotic orchids and brightly coloured lilies to wild

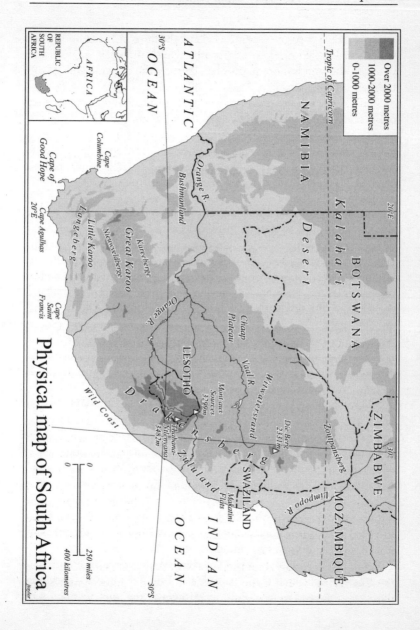

Physical map of South Africa

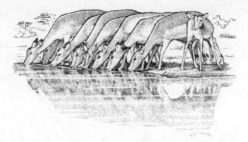

South Africa's spectacular wild life: antelopes drinking

geraniums, a thousand of which are rare. So exceptional are South Africa's wild flowers that all native flora is protected by law from destruction. In terms of wildlife, lions, elephants, rhinoceros, giraffes, leopards and cheetahs are all native to South Africa. Today, predatory big cats are to be found thriving in protected environments and nature reserves. Herbivores, such as elephants and white rhinos, are similarly sheltered, to the point where herds are so big that they do not have enough space to roam freely and often endanger themselves (South Africa is, in fact, home to the world's largest population of hippopotamuses). The rarer black rhinoceros is, however, a species under threat, for decades having been ruthlessly hunted for its horn, fabled as having great aphrodisiac properties.

Still to be found living wild in South Africa are jackals, wild cats and dogs, hyenas (of both the spotted and brown species), buffalo, large herds of wildebeest, and warthogs. More famously, twenty-nine species of antelope inhabit the country, including the adaptable kudu, gemsbok (who live in drier regions), steenbok (believed by the San to have been protected by the spiritual gods) and the national symbol, the springbok. There are also three varieties of zebra, including the rare Cape mountain zebra, the ubiquitous chacma baboon, two species of monkey (the samango and the vervet) and some 900 species of birds.

Less than a century ago, much of this wildlife had been virtually wiped out. Many species of animal were on the verge of extinction, having been subjected to the farmer's and hunter's gun for too long during the best part of two centuries. However, the implementation of a concerted policy of preservation reversed this situation. Today, South Africa's wildlife populations are protected by one of the world's best and most innovative conservation programmes, which has had the effect of stabilising wildlife numbers. South African nature reserves and national parks, of which there are over 500, are among the best managed and most advanced in the world.

The State and Economy

Since 1994, South Africa has had a multi-party political structure in place. Democratic elections are held once every five years. The first open elections were held in South Africa in 1994 and brought to power the African National Congress, which was re-elected to a second term of office in 1999. The country's constitution is one of the most progressive in the world, with a wide-ranging Bill of Rights designed to protect each and every citizen.

South Africa is a unitary state encompassing nine provinces. The country has three capitals, each home to a separate function of government (see below, pp. 155–6) although Pretoria, a traditionally conservative place, is regarded as the hub of all political life. Cape Town, the seat of parliament and the most popular tourist destination in South Africa, and Durban, a thriving port city sometimes compared to Miami, are second and third in rank and size to Johannesburg, 'the city of gold' and undoubted economic centre of the country. Other cities of note include Bloemfontein (South Africa's judicial capital), Pietermaritzburg, Kimberley (centre of the diamond industry), East London and Port Elizabeth.

By the standards of Africa, South Africa has a highly developed economy. Its basis is diverse and supported by a modern rail and road infrastructure. The economy is largely reliant on the country's vast mineral resources of gold and diamonds, iron and platinum, and in recent times this has caused some hardship, as those industries have had to weather a time of sharp downturn and commodity value loss. Nevertheless, large business interests still thrive in South Africa today, and a viable local manufacturing sector is slowly emerging. Agriculture, meanwhile, is a staple of the South African economy. Wine, fruit and cash crop exports are vitally important to the country, while the thousands of miles of coast mean that fishing is also a prime industry. Tourism plays an increasingly important role in the economy, and is today the country's fastest growing industry. Untenable before the advent of democratic rule in 1994, by the end of the twentieth century an estimated two million people visited South Africa, coming in the most part from the United Kingdom and Europe, Australia and other parts of Africa.

People: The Rainbow Nation

Between the Act of Union in 1910 and the advent of democracy in 1994, South Africa's population rose from just under six million to thirty-eight million. This growth reflected an increasing divergence of ethnicity. Today, the South African population of some 40 million people is composed of a variety of distinctive peoples.

Archaeological evidence points to human settlement, within the boundaries of modern South Africa, as far back as 115,000 BC. The later descendants of these first societies are the San hunter-gatherers and Khoi pastoralists who were the first southern Africans to come into contact with European explorers in the fifteenth century. Khoi-San

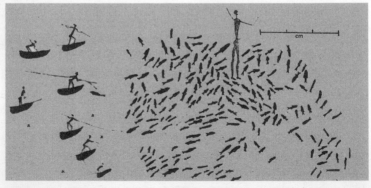

A copy of a rock painting showing fishermen in canoes from south-western Lesotho

societies led a way of life practically unaltered for some 20,000 years until alien intrusions during the course of the later 1600s. Rock paintings, the only practical documentary evidence of how the Khoi-San lived prior to colonisation of the land, depict a practical, deeply spiritual people who survived off the riches of the land and through hunting and fishing. These societies were gradually eroded – first through contact with mixed-farming Bantu-speakers from the east of the region, and later, Europeans. Over the course of time the Khoi-San were largely forced into the interior from the coastal regions of the south-west. Those who did not move were mostly assimilated into other cultural groupings. Today, there are a few hunter-gathering communities in the Kalahari-Gemsbok park and on its borders, and there are San communities elsewhere, notably at Schmidtsdrift, and they can also be found in parts of Botswana, northern Namibia and southern Angola, where their numbers are decreasing all the time.

The indigenous Bantu-speaking communities of southern Africa, the Sotho, Zulu and Xhosa predominant among them, are physically darker skinned than the Khoi-San and also have distinctive cultural traits, traditions and belief systems. It is believed that these peoples migrated into southern Africa from the north and east, although there is some debate as to exactly when or how this migration occurred. It seems almost certain that there was no mass inflow of people, but rather, small bands found their way to the region in search of suitable land for pasture. They brought with them new agricultural practices and advanced technologies and lived a more settled existence than their Khoi-San counterparts. However, these cultures too have been eroded over the years through assimilation, although tribal cultural traditions remain strong today and thrive in some areas. At present, the Xhosa, Zulu and Sotho–Pedi linguistic groups form some three-quarters of the South African population, making this a clear cultural majority within the country.

The other quarter of the population is comprised of various groups. There is the 'coloured' population, which is culturally and biologically quite diverse. The term was first coined in the late 1800s to distinguish those people who were neither 'native' nor 'white'. The term has remained in use and is not viewed in a pejorative sense in South Africa.

The coloured population descended from inter-racial relations, between Asians and African slaves, European settlers, and the Khoi-San population of the Cape. During apartheid, coloured people were classified as distinct from other races.

The white population of European descent is constituted mainly of Dutch and German settlers and sailors (who came from the late 1640s), French Huguenots (who settled in small numbers after 1685) and Britons (who formally controlled the Cape colony from 1806 onwards, later laying claim to much of the interior as well). During the 1920s and 1930s a number of Jewish refugees entered South Africa, seeking shelter from persecution in Europe. More recently, distinct communities have settled from countries such as Italy, Portugal and Greece. The most dominant of all white groupings are the Afrikaners. Identified by their own language – a variation on Dutch that evolved in South Africa – and with many of their own identifying cultural factors, the Afrikaners are the modern-day descendants of the original Dutch and German settlers. Like most other South African communities, and despite years of effort to the contrary, Afrikaners have also been greatly influenced by other neighbouring races and cultures.

Finally there is in South Africa a notable population of Asians, mostly (though not exclusively) from the South Asian subcontinent, Indonesia, and China. Many brought to Africa to work as slaves, and later in the nineteenth century, as indentured labourers, this community is in itself quite diverse and a reflection of the various places from where it originated. This is perhaps best illustrated by the variety of religions practised within the Asian community and the existence of numerous temples and mosques serving various denominations in places such as Cape Town and Durban.

CHAPTER TWO

Earliest Times: Indigenous Civilisation to c.1500

Before the advent of the modern age South Africa was a relatively insular part of the world. Its geographic location at the foot of a massive and in places unexplored continent dictated that interactions between that part of Africa and the rest of the world were strictly limited prior to the onset of European maritime adventuring in the 1400s. This was in contrast to the northern, western and eastern coasts of Africa, where contact and trade with outside cultures was established at a much earlier date.

This is not to suggest that southern Africa was completely cut off from the rest of the world. As we have seen, there was some migration on to the veld and as far south as the Cape region by Africans who travelled down from the north and east. These migrants brought to the region new ways of life which were passed on to existing cultures who could effectively do little to resist this influx.

There is, however, a problem in outlining reliably and in any great detail the major historical processes at work across the region prior to European colonisation. The pre-colonial inhabitants of southern Africa were not literate and left few records of the way in which they lived. For historians and anthropologists there are therefore a number of difficulties in constructing a reliable picture of these societies. Matters are becoming clearer due to recent technological developments and archaeological finds, yet controversy persists and even the most creditable interpretations of pre-colonial southern African history are complex in nature and open to question. One thing is abundantly clear, though: pre-colonial southern African societies were far from static.

The world's oldest human remains have been uncovered in southern

Africa. Remarkable archaeological finds, at the Sterkfontein caves, Stilbaai, and throughout the West Coast region, suggest that man originated in southern Africa some 115,000 years ago. From these it has been estimated that San hunter-gathering communities resided in the western and coastal regions of the country prior to the first millennium BC. These groups lived in small bands ranging from twenty to eighty people, who would halt at a particular location that offered a sufficient source of food and water. Temporary rights over an area would be established. When this land had fulfilled its use, or according to the seasons and availability, the bands would move on in search of new and exploitable resources. The search for food was more or less continual.

Short in stature but physically strong and imbued with great powers of endurance, the hunter-gatherers lived a mobile existence, never putting down roots for very long. They rested in easily moveable reed shelters or caves and wore animal skins as protection from the cold. They survived off a staple diet that consisted of roots, plants, insects, fish and game. Hunting was carried out using poison-tipped arrows or tools crafted from wood and stone, fishing was done by hand. The nature of their existence meant that hunter-gatherers had to endure long periods of scarcity that would be ended by feasting during times of plenty. It also meant that ties of kinship were, at best, weak. Children fended for themselves from a young age; the old and infirm would be abandoned if they were unable to keep pace with the rest of the band. The San were adept at managing their resources, making them last to provide for the entire community and until such a time as they could be replenished. The population size was also controlled to match the availability of food resources.

San culture was based to some extent on mythology that had been passed down from generation to generation, and this was expressed and recorded in oral literature and cave and rock paintings. Rock paintings, the oldest examples of which have been dated as being over 70,000 years old, were made from powdered pigmentation and ores and fixed with grease. These rock paintings, older than any found in Europe, are characterised by their boldness and simplicity. They were not merely decorative but had a spiritual significance and depicted human relationships with the environment in which they lived. The San were also familiar with the medicinal properties of plants, reflecting a deep understanding of the areas they inhabited. They told stories and acted, while traditional tribal trance dances were regularly performed to ward off disaster and danger or to help bring about seasonal rains.

Until around the 1500s the San way of life remained largely free from outside influence, although the hunter–gatherer existence was not exclusive of pastoral farming communities or mixed farmers who lived in the east of the region. Indeed, these three communities interacted, intermarried and came into regular conflict with one another. The San often turned away from their nomadic way of life and settled down as agriculturists. By the sixteenth century, though, the hunter–gathering existence was being squeezed by the spread of pastoralism and mixed farming practices. The permanent or semi–permanent settlement of land resulted in conflict and clashes between agriculturalists and the San, who lacked the weaponry to assert themselves. They were forced increasingly to retreat to less environmentally friendly areas of southern Africa.

Khoi pastoralists, meanwhile, who would move seasonally in search of suitable pasture for their cattle, had by this time become mostly concentrated in and around the watered plains of the Cape peninsula. They would exchange goods and produce with the hunter–gatherers, usually through a system of barter, but increasingly came into conflict

Rural Khoi with their animals on the Orange River in the early nineteenth century

with them over land use. Over a number of generations, they came to dominate the region and assimilated many San into their communities, either through intermarriage or patronage. It was these Khoi-San that the first Europeans in southern Africa would encounter in the late 1400s.

The eastern half of the region was dominated by Bantu-speaking mixed farmers. They started arriving from a northerly direction an estimated 300 years before the advent of the first millennium. Gradually, these migrant communities, who initially lived also in small, tightly knit communities, spread across more territory. Over a matter of centuries, mixed farmers came to settle throughout most of the eastern part of southern Africa, and in some instances, as far west as the Cape. By the year 1000, mixed farmers were spread over an area covering Natal, the Transvaal, Swaziland, parts of the Orange Free State and the eastern Cape. They dispersed with their livestock, which included the sheep they introduced to the region, and settled wherever the pasture was good. In some areas, bush land was cleared and turned over to arable farming.

The migrant farmers brought with them distinctive cultural traits, particular modes of living and different languages. Those living on the veld spoke dialects of languages that today are recognisable as Sotho, Pedi and Tswana, while settlers below the escarpment spoke a Xhosa or Zulu dialect (both language types are syntactically similar and share much common vocabulary). These communities combined sheep and cattle farming with the cultivation of sorghum millet, melons, beans and other vegetables. Land would be employed on a rotational basis and left fallow after a period of use.

Mixed farmers were mostly self sufficient, producing their own milk, vegetables and meat, and clothing themselves using animal hides. Each village would also feature people who would practise specific vocations in the dry season. There would commonly be thatchers, herbalists, potters and leather workers. There was, however, no recognisable merchant class and there were few market places across the region, reflecting the fact that farming produce was consumed or sold within its village of origin.

The migrants also brought with them knowledge of iron working which they used to construct different tools. This allowed for the development of more diverse societies that would trade these wares with other neighbouring communities. Smithing practices proliferated and village settlements often became based not only on the availability of pasture but also on the location of ores and other minerals. By the seventh century at the latest, communities had been established in the northern Transvaal that mined and smelted copper which would be used mainly for decorative purposes.

These societies were relatively egalitarian and would comprise groupings based around extended families. Settlements varied in size from under 100 people to over 1,000 (or in the case of the Tswana, some 5,000). Because communities tended to become settled in one location, average family sizes became bigger. Families would construct and reside in durable dome-shaped homesteads that were made from grass woven into a wooden or stone frame. Larger clans would often become organised into chiefdoms, with the designated chief controlling not only his followers but also use of a specific area of pasture (lands were communally owned), all livestock, and the water supply to the community.

The headship of a clan was often claimed on the basis of the number of head of cattle an individual owned. Political power and social control therefore rested on wealth, as surplus cattle could be traded or used to buy off potential rivals. The more cattle a man had the more power and influence he could acquire. Children were also a source of labour, and as more labour would allow for the growing of more food, manpower too became another form of political power. Chiefly rule, then, became dependent upon the accumulation of people and cattle, with the latter being given to people as a means of cementing their loyalty to the chief.

Chiefs were most commonly hereditary rulers who could only be deposed by a strong challenger and after a contest for power. A chief would be expected to settle all of his community's problems and any disputes. It was he who ultimately made all decisions concerning his followers. As he wielded such absolute powers, the health and vitality of the chief was closely connected with that of the community. It was believed that if the chief was sick, then so too was the society over which he ruled. Rituals and ceremonies such as tribal dances, which were believed to guard the well-being of the chief, were established as traditions, and revolved around the planting and reaping of harvests. To a very large extent, in mind, if not in actuality, the viability and happiness of these societies were dependent on the chief himself.

Life for the Bantu-speaking farmers involved deep religious convictions. Belief was based upon worship of the ancestral spirits who, it was held, influenced every aspect of life. The spirits were the ones who guided an individual in his actions and thoughts for better or worse, good or evil. Contact with the spirits was maintained as a part of everyday life and at all ceremonial occasions and they were worshipped through song and dance, and invoked when eating or drinking.

Although scientific investigation based on observation and experience did have a role to play in society, all natural disasters such as locusts, rain failure and famine were explained in terms of the spirits. Consequently, the rains failing or the spread of an epidemic would be seen as the punishment of the ancestors for existing evils in the living. Such a situation, it was believed, could only be addressed through the giving of sacrifices to the ancestors and the rooting out of all society's evil. Purges and witch hunts were therefore common practice, carried

Hollow clay pottery from Transvaal c. AD 500–600

out on the understanding that they would restore harmony and ensure a return to prosperity.

These were strictly patriarchal societies. Women were responsible for most agricultural labour as well as food gathering and preparation, water carrying and beer making, and childcare. Women were subordinated to men, with even their fates, over which they had no say, being used to cement inter-family alliances. A bride would be secured through the system of *lobola* (in Nguni; *bohali* in Sotho), a payment made by the husband's family to the wife's, usually in the form of cattle. Once remuneration had been made in this way, the husband had legal control over his wife and any future offspring. The system of bridewealth had deep political implications. Marriage was often used to settle disputes or subjugate one chiefdom to another on terms more or less agreeable to both parties. Moreover, the richer a man was, the more wives he could afford to buy. It was a neat way of consolidating wealth and future prosperity.

Education was similarly vital to the cementing of the political and social order of clan life. The chief would use education to cultivate for himself devout, life-long followers. Boys and girls were brought up in accordance with prevailing cultural norms and would be inculcated with a particular view of how society was controlled. Initiation schools, where adolescents would be segregated from their homes and families, were designed to train young men as brave soldiers and breed loyal brotherhoods which would be prepared to defend to the death the honour of the chief. Female schools taught girls the skills needed to run an efficient home and how to be a virtuous wife.

In general terms, the mixed farming existence, although settled, was not always an easy one. The onset of drought, or the effects of local conflict and warfare, which was usually a result of a serious dispute over cattle ownership, could force individuals and families into a hunter-gathering mode of life or a client relationship with another chief. It was also often the case that villages would have to move to find better pasture that could support more people and enlarged herds. Nevertheless, these were quite complex societies, with established political systems and economies that were often as successful as they were diverse. Prior to the penetration of the region by white settlers during the early nineteenth century, the farming-based African societies of the eastern region were mostly gaining in power, wealth and numbers. They would continue to do so until challenged by a new type of settler with a new tool of political power – the gun.

CHAPTER THREE

Colonisation
c. 1500–1800

The First Europeans

In 1487, five years before Christopher Columbus sailed to the New World of the Americas, the Portuguese explorer Bartolomeu Dias led a two-ship expedition around the Cape of Good Hope. Having navigated the Cape peninsula, Dias was forced to seek shelter from a storm some 170 miles to the east, at Mossel Bay. He then sailed on for another 150 miles before his frightened charges revolted, refusing to travel any further away from Europe.

Dias's mission was to find India, and to capture for Portugal the markets of the east, believed by contemporary European explorers to harbour untold riches. Although the voyage had been thwarted by his men, it had proceeded far enough to convince Dias that, in fact, the way east to India *could* be prised open. His belief undiminished, Dias returned to Lisbon to convince his nation's rulers that another expedition should be despatched forthwith.

This was the first recorded European sighting of southern Africa. Yet, it would be over a decade before the sea route from Europe to India (via the Cape) was finally opened up by another Portuguese explorer, Vasco da Gama. Da Gama's brief was to bring substance to the recently signed Treaty of Tordesillas, which had carved the world into separate Spanish and Portuguese spheres of influence, giving the latter theoretical control over the continent of Africa and the far-off lands of India and China. He was to secure the Cape route before sailing out into the Indian Ocean.

On 4 November 1497, ninety-three days after he set sail, Da Gama

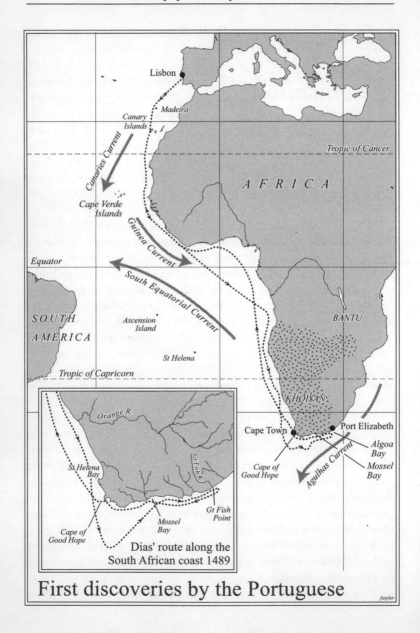

First discoveries by the Portuguese

landed some 100 miles north of the Cape peninsula, at St Helena Bay. Here the expedition rested for a little over a week, making tentative incursions inland. Da Gama then proceeded around the Cape and, following in the footsteps of Dias, anchored at Mossel Bay, bartering sheep and cattle from the local inhabitants. Relations remained cordial in this first extended meeting between the indigenous population of the region and Europeans. However, Da Gama's real work was only completed some seven months later when he landed on Indian soil. The importance of the Cape, nevertheless, as a landmark on the route to India and the east had been established. Subsequently, Portuguese expeditions rounded the Cape on an annual basis, as their fleets established control over the Indian Ocean, and as trade was extended further east, eventually reaching China (in 1513) and Japan (in 1543). For the Portuguese, however, southern Africa was to remain largely uncharted territory: a place they initially could not (and later, would not) penetrate.

The biggest problem with the region was its relative inaccessibility. The seas in and around the Cape were not easily navigable for sixteenth- and early seventeenth-century sailors who were inexperienced in dealing with, and often ill-equipped to survive, the difficult conditions particular to that part of the world. A good many ships were wrecked as they attempted to round the Cape. In consequence, the passage around the southern tip of Africa became a huge challenge to many of the earliest expeditions to the east, an immense danger to be overcome rather than a convenient or welcoming stop-off.

Furthermore, those parties who either chose or were forced to disembark there, found little to enamour them to the area. The very basics of life – fresh water, meat and vegetables – were not easily procurable, nor was there any trace of marketable or exotic commodities, like the cinnamon and other spices Da Gama had found and brought back from India. The local population, too, was mostly unwelcoming, or more properly put, resistant to the likelihood of exploitation. There were numerous recordings of landing crews being ambushed before they could begin to barter for food and water. In 1510, a party of fifty that included the Portuguese Viceroy to India, was attacked and slaughtered in an operation most probably designed to protect local cattle. Under such circumstances the possibility of picking up cheap slaves, which was a preoccupation of all voyagers to the east during this period, remained remote. So the Portuguese established bases elsewhere, along a 2,000-mile stretch of the south-east and east African coasts, from where they could protect and further their interests in the Indian Ocean and, by moving inland, more successfully seek out the riches they desired.

The emerging seafaring nations of Europe were slow to reach the Cape. Initially, the French, Dutch and English had not challenged, nor been much interested in, Portuguese advances in the east. Instead, attention was focused on Spanish exploration of the New World in the west. However, the obvious commercial benefits to be had in the east, coupled with a growing sense of boldness and curiosity on the part of these nations, meant that by the last decade of the sixteenth century, they too were traversing the Cape route. The first English ship anchored at Table Bay in 1591, eleven years after Sir Francis Drake had rounded the Cape. The first Dutch fleet arrived in 1595, and like the English before them, enjoyed better relations with the local inhabitants than most of their Portuguese predecessors, managing to exchange a few head of cattle for some European metalware.

By the early 1600s, French and, to a lesser extent, Scandinavian fleets had joined the Portuguese, English and Dutch in sailing the region, although no immediate challenge was yet posed to Portugal's mono-poly of trade east of the Cape. As far as southern Africa was concerned, there was one abortive attempt at 'colonisation' in late 1619, when an English commander acting without official sanction of any kind claimed Table Bay in the name of King James. Nothing was done to substantiate the move, however, and it was quickly forgotten. It would be some years before any European nation showed further genuine interest in the area. In the meantime, the Cape and surrounding coast acted merely as a new place for European ships to pause on outward or homeward bound journeys.

The purpose of shipping stopping off at the Cape was simply to refresh and re-stock. Once a crew had bartered for cattle or sheep and replenished supplies of water, there was little more for them to do. The fact that interactions with the indigenous population were always kept to a minimum meant there existed little understanding between the two cultures. Such ignorance, and the irrationalities and even fear attendant on this, persuaded most Europeans not to linger around the Cape for longer than was absolutely necessary.

With the Portuguese firmly established on the eastern coast of Africa, Dutch and English merchant ships were the most frequent visitors to southern Africa in the early to mid-1600s. Fleets from both nations shared access to Table Bay, co-existing but never co-operating to make the place more hospitable to their needs. Nor did anyone show much initiative in exploring away from the coastal area as the hinterland was viewed with a great deal of suspicion. A mark of the frequency with which Table Bay was used can, nonetheless, be seen by the fact that Dutch ships would use the point to drop off messages for compatriot ships sailing in the opposite direction. The beginnings of the trans-formation of the Cape, from a mere staging post on the route to the east into a permanent base for European merchant interests, evolved out of the misfortunes of a crew of shipwrecked Dutch sailors, forced to spend a long and gruelling winter at the Cape.

THE DUTCH

In 1602, competing Dutch merchant-traders who for so long had worked against one another amalgamated their resources into a united concern, the Vereenigde Ooste-Indische Compaigne (VOC) or Dutch East India Company. Granted a charter by the Dutch States-General that same year, the VOC was given an absolute monopoly on Dutch trade east of the Cape, which was rapidly building around Indonesian spices. The administration of this expanding network of interests, which the VOC was also required to oversee, was carried out from Batavia (modern-day Jakarta) from where the VOC was expected to orchestrate its operations while keeping expenditure low and profit margins high. It was an exercise in attempted cost cutting that partly explained the decision in 1652 to establish a permanent camp at the Cape.

In 1648, the VOC ship *The Haarlem*, one part of two Dutch fleets to round the Cape en route for Java that year, failed to navigate typically rough seas at the southern tip of Africa. The ship was wrecked and all surviving crew members forced to seek refuge on land close to the site of the future development of Cape Town. To survive, the men were forced to rely on instinct and any resources that could be extracted from the surrounding environment. Records show that the experience was a far from easy one. However, the crew adapted quickly and were able to do enough to keep themselves alive until the following year, when they were picked up by a fleet travelling back to Europe.

During their time at the Cape, the men had co-operated with the local population in order to secure fresh meat. The climate also proved conducive to the growing of some fresh fruit and vegetables. All of this was reported back to VOC officials in the Netherlands, who studied the testimonies of *The Haarlem*'s crew in some detail. If the episode highlighted one fact, it was that Europeans could survive for lengthy periods in this part of the world, previously considered hostile and therefore unpromising. If this were the case, what was to stop the Company establishing some sort of outpost at the site? Such a base, once a basic local infrastructure was put into place, would serve as a means of overcoming the problems that afflicted every crew of every ship that sailed to the east: the unavailability of proper medical care, the lack of fresh food and drink, and the need to repair ships and rigging that often broke in the hazardous seas off the Cape.

More importantly, in the view of the VOC's directors, improved mortality rates, a cheap and regular source of supplies and the chance to maintain fleets better, would save enormous sums of money. The crew of *The Haarlem* had also been quick to stress the importance of the Cape from a strategic point of view. Certainly, there existed a need to protect the trade route to the east from the fleets of other nations; a base at the Cape, halfway between Europe and India, would adequately serve this purpose.

So it was that in 1652 the VOC sent three ships, carrying ninety men, to the Cape in order to establish a Dutch settlement there, to be governed from Batavia but which would be ultimately answerable to the VOC's directors in Amsterdam. The expedition was instructed to lay markers to aid navigation of the area; to construct a hospital; to build a fort; and to develop essential agricultural practices. In all of these respects, this first concerted European attempt at settling on southern African soil was an experiment with no guarantees of success. The group had no means of knowing whether or not its efforts would endure.

The commander of the expedition was the thirty-three-year-old Jan van Riebeeck (1619–77). Born in the Netherlands, Van Riebeeck had been employed by the VOC since 1640, serving in Batavia, Japan and Formosa. A controversial figure, he had been accused of private profiteering and sent back to Europe in 1648. A careerist in as much as he was looking to overcome this disgrace and rejoin the service at the earliest possible opportunity, Van Riebeeck was a vociferous supporter of the plan to establish a base at the Cape, a stance that eventually led to him being sent to oversee the project.

The development did not get off to the best of starts. A small earth fort was erected and vegetable gardening instigated on a small scale. However, other arable practices were slow to develop, and were hindered by VOC policies and a lack of manpower. Livestock could be bartered from local Khoi-San, but relations grew increasingly uneasy as the question of grazing rights around the nascent settlement became a point of contention. The earliest expeditions away from the coast were considered to be disappointing. Investigations turned up no evidence of valuable mineral or gold deposits and the local terrain was viewed in a sinister light, as it contained strange and unknown flora and fauna. It was widely believed that the interior was home to the unicorn, and there were widespread fears among early European settlers, which would not fully abate until the 1800s, that all of the animals of the region were not only bizarre but highly dangerous as well. All of this meant that the settlement evolved around the coast, fenced in literally and metaphorically; a Dutch outpost on the edge of an apparently forbidding continent.

From the outset, Van Riebeeck was beset by financial constraints as the VOC was reluctant to invest too heavily in the settlement, and by the unsuitability of many of his charges for the job in hand. Reflecting in later life, Van Riebeeck wrote that he had been:

> . . . landed on a dry and barren waste, without a place to live, and with only a parcel of light materials . . . without a single man possessed of any kind of skill – but with sickness in abundance – without a single herb for our refreshment – and thus with some 90 weak, unskilful, sea-worn and scorbutic men, we had to commence work, at which . . . they were so raw that the Commander had to set to work himself as engineer, excavator, gardener, farmer, carpenter, mason and blacksmith.

Under the circumstances, it was not surprising that the settlement was not immediately able to serve its intended purpose as a haven for Dutch shipping on the way to Batavia. Indeed, when the first fleet visited the emerging station in early 1653, it had to provide rice and other supplies to the expedition, although in return it was able to obtain a small supply of fresh vegetables, water and some firewood. For the first few years, however, the settlement remained on a precarious footing, as Van Riebeeck worked hard at increasing productivity among his men and establishing the emerging Cape Town as a viable, self-sufficient community.

The Establishment of a Settler Community at the Cape

The settlement was to overcome this period of uncertainty, although it would be some time before the Cape could compare in stature to other similar European colonial stations in Africa, the Caribbean and Asia. That the Cape settlement did not perish during its formative years was due to two factors: the ecological make-up and population patterns particular to the region; and the willingness of the VOC to encourage individuals in agricultural enterprises.

In the first instance, and as proved by the experience of *The Haarlem*, the Cape carried little threat to the health and well-being of Europeans. The locality was not known to harbour diseases that would threaten the mortality either of humans or domestic animals. Furthermore, the climate was extremely pleasant and compared favourably with that of southern Europe, and so the land was suitable for a variety of agricultural practices and successful pastoral farming. Added to this, the set-up of indigenous societies was not an immediate barrier to the establishment of a workable settlement. The population was not concentrated, but rather lived in scattered communities that were politically quite fragmented. Thus, there was no local political body in existence able to thwart colonisation during its initial stages, nor contest ownership of, or access to land.

Secondly, the VOC was keen to encourage a diversification of interests among the colonial population. The VOC was eager to obtain regular reliable supplies of commodities that it could sell through its system of commercial monopolies at a fixed rate. As a means to this end, the administration in Batavia decided to encourage its employees and ex-employees to settle at the Cape and cultivate land (which was also subject to a monopoly), and to sell their produce to the VOC. To stimulate the local economy further, ·the Company simultaneously instigated a programme of franchising single commodity concessions for imported goods to men based locally. In turn, the franchise owner would be expected to act as a broker for the VOC within the Cape community.

The process of land settlement was begun in 1657, when nine individuals were granted land rights outside the fortified perimeter of the colony. They divided into two groups, each to farm the twenty-eight acres of land granted them by the VOC. Although these were the first of the so-called free burghers, in reality these men only had a modicum of liberty (they were, for example, still subject to VOC rules and regulations), and their agricultural practices were hedged by a number of restrictions. The farms could only be used to cultivate essential foodstuffs that could not be secured via barter from the local population, and that were needed to sustain the new colony and, more importantly, supply VOC ships. They could only trade with the local authorities, at prices fixed by the VOC. The farmers were not permitted to buy cattle or sheep from the Khoi-San at more than the rate paid by the VOC, and all interactions with Africans were governed by the strict observance of local laws. They were not able to act in a manner liable to undermine official monopolies, nor undercut these monopolies by offering produce for sale at a cheaper rate. Moreover, despite being amnestied from land tax for the first twelve years of their occupancy, the farmers were only granted leases on the understanding that they remained *in situ* for at least twenty years, and on condition that they passed on to the VOC one-tenth of their annual yield. If they wished to leave their farms, they would have to return to the VOC in order to work out the remainder of their contracts.

The returns for the first nine burghers were less than spectacular, though none starved or was forced from the land. Over the next few years, they were joined on the land by new men and some families, most of whom were ex-VOC employees of German or Dutch descent, some of whom had opted to be freed from their contracts. Over time, viable communities emerged that were distinct from, but intrinsically linked to, the expanding urban community that was evolving around the fort and harbour at Cape Town.

Cape Town remained at the centre of the colony, and its importance as the social and administrative centre of the settlement grew as the colony expanded in size. It was also the hub of all commercial activity with the only European market in southern Africa. Burgher farmers would ride there in ox-wagons in order to sell on the products of their labours to the VOC. Sheep and cattle could be exchanged or bought, as could slaves who had been imported into the Cape to work as labourers, and agricultural tools and machinery. Cape Town was also the only place to purchase cloth and domestic accessories, as well as non-essential foodstuffs (such as coffee and tea) and other imported goods (such as firearms, which were a far more integral part of every burgher's existence).

The extension of the colony was at the expense of local indigenous societies. The settlement of land by burgher farmers had an

A view of Table Bay in 1675 showing a Khoi-San family and the Dutch castle

immediate impact on the way the local Khoi-San population lived. The new colonial farms and communities could only be constituted by expropriating land previously worked or settled by the Cape Khoi-San. As already noted, these societies were not organised in a manner that could immediately stand up to, and effectively resist, such encroachment. In consequence, local communities were forced to retreat in the face of settler advances, but more often than not, could not do this and at the same time maintain their social and political equilibrium. Many clan leaders found their authority undermined by an inability to resist burgher advances, a situation that would worsen once the colonists began to help themselves to Khoi-San cattle and sheep stocks.

Undoubtedly, the relative ease with which the indigenous population of the Cape was initially rolled back served merely to encourage further waves of white settlement. VOC officials were not slow in encouraging ever more of their employees to opt for free burgher status. There was also a drive to encourage immigration from the Netherlands, but this floundered in its earliest years because the criteria for entry would only allow for 'men of good conduct and sound Protestantism, subjects of the Dutch Republic'.

THE HUGUENOTS

The VOC's immigration drive was given a boost after 1685, when 200 Huguenots, or Protestants, who had fled to the Netherlands from France following the revocation of the Edict of Nantes, were granted a free passage to the Cape. Provided an oath of allegiance to the Netherlands was taken prior to departure, each Huguenot family was guaranteed effective ownership of a parcel of land to farm and given a loan with which to purchase materials. The migrants were treated as free men although they could only practise their religion within the confines of the Dutch Reformed Church. The VOC was determined that the Huguenots would not remain as an obviously distinct social and cultural community and so they were deliberately dispersed throughout the already established Dutch burgher settlements. Furthermore, laws were passed decreeing that Dutch was the official language of the Cape, again as a means of promoting Huguenot assimilation into the majority Dutch settler community.

It did not take longer than a generation for full assimilation to occur. There was no resistance to adopting a new language and church, and many Huguenots married into the Cape Dutch community. The Huguenots also proved themselves to be industrious folk and contributed greatly to the early development of the colony's economic life. They brought with them good knowledge of farming techniques and sound working practices that suited the local climate and resulted in their plots flourishing. Such endeavours bore fruit most quickly in the local wine industry.

The Development of the Cape into a Colony

Within twenty-five years of the establishment of the Cape settlement, there were more free burghers than VOC men living at the Cape. By the end of the century there were some 1,100 burghers within the colony, half of whom were dependant children. Family sizes were increasing all the time and the fertility rate among settlers would remain high over the next century. In this way the Cape developed into a settled and functioning colony, with an ever-diversifying social and economic composition. This was facilitated by the immigration into the colony of artisans and merchants from European countries such as Germany, Scotland and England.

The VOC was concerned that the colony should not expand so quickly as to jeopardise its grip on the reins of power. It therefore attempted to limit the area of settlement away from the fort at Cape Town to a radius of thirty-five miles. This policy was successful for as long as there was enough land available to meet the requirements of the expanding free burgher community, while the only market in the region was at Cape Town itself, and for as long as that market could absorb the total surplus output from settler farms.

The farmers working within this boundary initially concentrated on producing marketable cash crops. Some, but not all, would undertake a little livestock rearing. Farms were of similar size, and each would be worked by perhaps a dozen slaves, as well as casual Khoi-San labour during the harvest season. By the early eighteenth century, farming practices had been expanded to include wine production and wheat growing. The introduction and employment of improved agricultural methods meant there was less under-production across the colony – something that had characterised early settler farming at the Cape – although crops still frequently failed and droughts were an intermittent threat that farmers could do little to avoid. Nevertheless, by the 1700s, there were clear signs of the potential of the colony as a producer of agricultural produce, as well as other commodities such as wine, that could be exported at great profit.

Simultaneously, however, the VOC's stringent land policies were beginning to unravel. The practices of price fixing and closed markets meant that, even after a bumper harvest, a farmer might not necessarily be able to earn enough to support himself and his family for the year. This situation was exacerbated by the obvious corruption of senior local VOC officials, many of whom cultivated large estates as a means of generating personal profits that often accumulated into fortunes. These men could manipulate the market to ensure that their products were sold before those of the settlers, or alternatively sell to passing ships without going through the proper, official channels. Furthermore, they would use VOC employees to work on their land as a means of cutting costs. Needless to say, bribery was endemic. The worst offender in all of these respects was the Governor, Willem Adriaan van der Stel (1664–1733). Succeeding his father in 1699, Willem was a nepotistic man who set up his sons as wealthy burghers, and he was determined to wield his authority as a means of making his fortune. He built up the largest estate in the colony and lived in the most ostentatious of residences. Unfortunately for him he was neither subtle about what he was doing nor clever enough to hide the truth. This was too much for many other burghers of independent means who raised objections in Batavia that were to result in Van der Stel's recall in 1707.

But the fact that so many burghers struggled to make ends meet had the more significant effect of putting pressure on land availability. In order to be able to sell more a burgher would have to grow more. For this, extra acreage was needed which could only be acquired by breaching the boundaries of the colony. This process of further expansion, once started, was difficult to reverse, as the VOC had no effective means of policing the colony's frontier. The VOC was therefore forced to relax its land policy, and recognise the rights of white farmers to settle under licence land beyond the thirty-five-mile radius. Only in this way could the VOC hope to maintain control of the settler population.

Of course, the further expansion of settler communities into the interior was disastrous for indigenous people, now faced with another wave of encroachment onto their land and the further loss of pasture for grazing. By this time, however, some Khoi-San had recognised that the environment around them was changing for good and that, for better or worse, they had little choice but to interact with the newcomers. Subsequently, old VOC edicts were overturned, as colonials and locals bartered goods: the colonials gaining the cattle that would afford them a better chance of financial success; the locals, the firearms that would allow them a means of surviving in this new society.

CULTURAL DEVELOPMENTS IN THE EARLY CAPE COLONY

The settler societies that took root away from Cape Town did not develop in a monolithic fashion. Rather, the opening up of the interior presented the opportunity for material advancement and personal profit. Some were able to thrive under such conditions; others found it difficult to compete with their neighbours. Consequently, in a relatively short time, there developed an increasingly complex society marked by differences of wealth, social status and, more and more, skin colour.

Those settlers living beyond the old colonial boundary became known as *trekkers* or *trekboers*, denoting them as migrant farmers. The earliest *trekboers* rapidly developed a strong sense of their own uniqueness and came to distinguish themselves from the colonialists of Cape Town. They were frontiersmen who survived on their wits, by hunting and trading with Africans, and through their own hard work. Mostly, their outlook was underpinned by a pronounced sense of their past history which identified their Dutch origins and strong religious beliefs (many were Calvinist Protestants, although they rarely had a formal place to worship in the early days of settlement in the interior).

The strongest indicator of the evolving cultural separateness of the frontier communities was the language they used. The dialect of Dutch southern Africa, the *taal*, during the course of the 1700s was turned into a distinctive idiom, later known as Afrikaans. Words and phrases from other languages such as Khoi and Bantu, English and Portuguese, as well as slave tongues like Malay, were incorporated into the *taal* and used on an everyday basis.

Customs and traditions from other cultures were also adopted by *trekboer* communities. Many men of European descent chose to practise the local African way of polygamy. Nearly all *trekkers* abandoned European styles of dress either wholly or partly, finding indigenous forms of clothing both more suitable to the frontier environment and easier to craft. There was also a degree of inter-racial mingling. The realities of life dictated that, at least occasionally, all *trekkers* would have to do business with the local Khoi-San. Moreover, not all *trekkers* were white. A small number of freed slaves and some Cape coloureds left the coastal region for the interior and enjoyed practically the same freedoms as white *trekkers*.

Equality between the races was, however, undermined by the existence of slavery, which was practised by free Africans and coloureds as well as by whites; also, VOC laws passed at the Cape gave legality to ideas of racial differentiation. Within the colony, it was decreed that society was stratified into a hierarchy that saw at the top VOC officials, followed by free burghers, slaves, and lastly 'hottentots' (a prejudicial term applied by Europeans to the local Khoi-San population). This classification put whites, who were all in the top two classes, ahead of Africans and coloureds, who were the only races to fill the lower two classes. Although some blacks and coloureds had achieved burgher status, such thinking closely reflected the fact that all slaves and most labourers were black, while the overwhelming majority of landowners were of European origin.

There was also a blatant and increasing disregard among the *trekkers* of existing patterns of African settlement and modes of life. In their quest for cattle and suitable pasture and agricultural land, the settlers dispossessed the Khoi-San of their livestock and limited their access to land. A common practice was to curtail Khoi-San liberty almost entirely by forcing individuals and families to work on settler farms. Not all Africans were subjugated in this way, but all lost lasting security of tenure on land that had been theirs since time immemorial.

THE EXPANSION OF THE COLONIAL FRONTIER IN THE EARLY 1700S

As greater numbers moved away from the coastal region, less land and livestock were available in the area immediately bordering Cape Town. *Trekkers* were consequently forced to migrate further inland in search of suitable land for cultivation and pasture. In the first decades of the eighteenth century there was a marked shift of population eastwards across the Hottentots-Holland mountains. In this region, some 150 miles from Cape Town, the village of Swellendam was established. In the opposite direction, to the north, grew the village settlement of Tulbagh. In between these outposts and Cape Town, *trekboers* occupied land that best suited their own requirements.

Once settled, a farm became the property of the farmer, who could keep his estate in virtual perpetuity, provided an annual fee was paid to the VOC at the Cape. This process of expansion was limited only by the unsuitability of some lands, like the arid expanse of the Karoo, which served to restrict northward movement of the *trekkers*. Some-times, but only occasionally, new settlers were deterred by the hostile reactions of local Khoi-San, who would raid settler stock or burn crops. In response to such resistance, *trekboer* communities would form their own militia attachments, known as commandos, to protect their land and property against any such attacks.

Farms began to grow in size as a means of supporting larger family units and increasing herd sizes. Population growth mirrored the increasing area inhabited by Europeans. As settlements spread and increased in number, so it became easier to subjugate indigenous people who resisted the expropriation of land by *trekboers*. Further-more, the further away settlers moved and the more their numbers multiplied, the harder it became for the VOC to assert effective poli-tical control over these communities. In reality, the only factor still tying the *trekboers* to the Cape was the need to use Cape Town for trading in agricultural and pastoral commodities, and for sourcing liquor, tobacco and other products which they could not yet produce themselves.

SLAVERY

A major problem for both the VOC and the free burgher population in the formative years of settlement at the Cape was finding a cheap and reliable supply of labour. Settlers required both casual and permanent labourers to work all year round on their farms. Similarly, the VOC constantly needed people to herd cattle, build municipal utilities, and erect and maintain defence works. A preoccupation of the entire European community was the production of enough food to sustain the colony and supply visiting ships. Simply put, the population of the colony was not large enough to fulfil all these endeavours. Too few immigrants were entering the Cape during this period to help ease the labour shortage and those who did come expected to better themselves materially, and so would not readily work for a wage or engage in menial tasks.

As the area of settlement increased so the need for labour grew. One obvious solution was to employ by force more of the local Khoi-San population. However, VOC laws placed restrictions upon the employment of the indigenous peoples of the colony, which meant such practices could only successfully take place in the frontier regions, away from the prying eyes of Cape Town officialdom. But even when Khoi-San could be employed, many were resistant to working as forced labour and consequently burghers found them to be unreliable and likely to run away at the earliest possible opportunity.

Another solution was to import slaves from other parts of the Dutch empire, where slavery was a common VOC practice. Van Riebeeck championed the move but was not wholly encouraged by the Batavian administration, which feared that once the practice was introduced, burghers would be less likely to labour for themselves. However, an appeal to the VOC directors in the Netherlands proved more fruitful and in 1657 the first slaves were imported into the Cape. Thereafter, the VOC bought slaves primarily to meet its own needs but would regularly hire out or sell on all surpluses to the burgher population.

Once introduced, the number of slaves imported quickly rose as the burgher population came to depend upon and, ultimately, expect bonded labour. In a few years, the entire economy was based upon the trade, with longer-term consequences for the development of the colony and attitudes towards race among the European community. In the 150 years of slavery at the Cape, some 63,000 slaves were imported from east Africa, Madagascar, Indonesia and South Asia. As long as the trade lasted, it acted as a reliable indicator of the material prosperity of the colony. The more slaves employed in the Cape, the greater the level of local agricultural activity. At the height of the trade, the slave population achieved parity with the number of free men. All burghers able to generate even a modest income could afford to buy and maintain a small indentured labour force.

Indentured labourers were the mainstay of the colony's economy. From a young age male slaves toiled on VOC and burgher farms, in the vineyards and on public works. Women would work as domestic servants in burgher households or in official residences. Children born to indentured women were classified from birth as slaves. Under Dutch law, a slave owner had absolute authority of ownership over each of his slaves who, in turn, had no recognised legal rights whatsoever. The experiences of slaves at the Cape were characterised by brutality and regular humiliation. The only genuine constraint on owners was the fact that slaves were a relatively valuable commodity. The law did allow for the punishment of burghers found to be ill-treating their slaves, but in practice this rarely happened. Rather, the local courts would condone torture and physical punishments if it felt this was justified. Judges often needed little excuse to find any such justification. Minor infringements of the law would result in legally sanctioned whipping, branding, or the loss of an ear. More serious offences, such as an attempted escape, could lead to manacling, scourging of the body, or breaking on the wheel. Many were banished to Robben Island, seven miles off the coast from Cape Town, a location that was used as a prison until the late twentieth century.

Slave families were often broken up as children were sold on to another master. Many slaves adopted a deferential approach to their owners, but even for those who did not, rebellion was hardly an option as slaves were kept in small, solitary units and had little contact with the world outside their working environment. A small percentage of Cape slaves were permitted to keep their own livestock, or would be paid a meagre cash wage by their owners. Most, however, worked merely for food and shelter and were kept quiescent with regular tots of brandy. Under local laws, slaves who converted to Christianity were entitled to their freedom but few were granted this status even after conversion and this practice was scorned in official circles.

In reality, slaves were socially ranked with the Khoi-San population. The only strata of society lower than slaves and Khoi-San were convicts and political prisoners, shipped to the Cape from Batavia. However, these men and women would at least be set free once their sentences had been served. The same could not be said of the enslaved population. Moreover, although viewed in a similar light as slaves by the white population, in the eyes of the law until 1775 the Khoi-San remained a technically free people, merely deprived of the rights of citizenship enjoyed by the settler population.

Slavery acted as a catalyst for the brutalisation of, and discrimination against, all blacks in the Cape. As there were few effective controls governing the treatment of slaves, maltreatment became a commonplace. The effects of this upon the community at large were diffuse.

Violence and discrimination on racial grounds were increasingly practised at every level of society, and during the eighteenth century, prevalent racial attitudes were to be reflected in legislation that affected the lives of free as well as indentured blacks. The most symbolic act in this respect was a law passed in the 1760s requiring all Khoi-San and slaves to carry a pass signed by their employees, verifying the fact they were gainfully employed. Meanwhile, throughout this time, the Cape administration developed a profitable sideline trade in slave exportation.

LOCAL RESPONSES TO THE COLONY

As we have seen, prior to 1652 the Khoi-San reaction to Europeans was marked by ambivalence. When circumstances necessitated, they would act in defence of their interests and property. On other occasions, they would freely barter with visiting sailors, exchanging livestock and fresh foodstuffs for metal goods, tobacco, alcohol and other wares. Disputes would often arise, mostly as a consequence of visiting sailors making demands which the Khoi-San either could not, or would not, meet. Such encounters might result in armed conflict or the loss of life.

After the advent of VOC rule at the Cape, more enduring relations developed between the colonist and indigenous populations of the area. But these were never static and hardly ever predictable. In some instances, settler farmers formed mutually beneficial working relationships with Khoi-San; in others, friendships were forged based on trust and respect. For the most part, however, the attitudes and actions of the Europeans precluded this from happening. Little respect was ever shown by the newcomers towards the Khoi-San, and the exclusion of the latter from the land and access to natural resources was in no way negotiated. This was a source of growing resentment among the Khoi-San, yet effective means of fighting back were not readily to hand. Revenge was only gradually and intermittently exacted.

During the later part of the eighteenth century two common forms of Khoi-San reprisal were enacted throughout the growing area of European settlement: attacks on livestock, and the burning of fields, crops and settler homesteads. Such attacks would invariably be in response to the loss of all or part of a herd of cattle or the unavailability of land for grazing pasture. Most actions of this type occurred in isolation, although the increased frequency and scale of them sometimes gave the impression that the Khoi-San were engaged in a concerted war of guerrilla tactics. Some successes were recorded: tracts of land were recovered and lost cattle recaptured. These victories were mostly pyrrhic, however. Burghers, formed into heavily armed commando units, would seek an immediate and deadly revenge for any such reverses.

The VOC reacted to Khoi-San attacks on settlers by fortifying outlying farms and properties. Fences were erected, but this merely exacerbated an already serious problem, as these barriers often cut off not only white farmlands, but also access to undisputed pasture. Conflict, or more properly put, warfare, rumbled on throughout the 1660s, climaxing only in 1677. During this time, the VOC employed a strategy of 'divide and rule', signing treaties with certain chiefdoms which, once confirmed as allies, would be employed against other communities that persisted in resisting the advancing colonial tide.

This helped the VOC eradicate much of the insecurity that had come to characterise the daily lives of many free burghers. However, for the Khoi-San of the Cape, the consequences were disastrous. Numerous (though not all) chiefdoms and many more family units were split apart, as entire communities were uprooted. The displaced population dispersed, some moving towards the Cape (where they were assimilated into the colonial system), others migrating northwards. Many Khoi-San chose to act as herders to settlers' cattle, or were more humbly employed alongside indentured labourers as farm hands.

Many pastoralists who headed north into the Karoo region were reduced to hunter-gathering techniques as a means of survival. Later, during the 1730s, as the boundaries of the Cape Colony caught up with these refugees, there was a re-engagement of earlier hostilities. The outcome, however, was the same as the *trekboers*, backed by the VOC, were able to establish control over the local environment.

This entire process, sparked by an obvious reaction on the part of the indigenous population to the advent of a new, uncompromising settler community in and around the Cape, in the space of a generation confirmed the inferior social and political position of the Khoi–San within southern Africa.

Away from the Cape

The earliest phases of settler expansion away from the Cape were limited in a way that meant that throughout much of the region of southern Africa indigenous modes of life remained unaffected by the advent of European society, at least for the time being. Khoi–San, living north of the Berg River and St Helena Bay, were not as immediately subjugated as their brethren further to the south. In the opposite easterly direction, colonial expansion was slower and restricted by difficult terrain, poor communications and problems of supply. In the 1710s, Swellendam remained a colonial outpost. It would be another sixty years before the eastern boundary of the colony reached the Sundays River, and not until 1812 did the Great Fish River fall within the same cordon. Expansion in this direction, if not rapid or even inevitable, was steady as the search for land was extended further away from the Cape. However, this meant that for much of the 1700s, local mixed farming communities continued to dominate much of the region and, in some cases, to thrive due to the existence of profitable trading links with the Portuguese on the eastern coast of the continent.

Meanwhile, wherever they could, *trekboers* were moving on to the best pasture and assuming control of vital natural resources. This had a detrimental effect on Khoi societies, which in such circumstances struggled to maintain their way of life. The slow loss of land and livestock by theft or trade meant that larger chiefdoms became untenable. As bands of Khoi became smaller so they became easy prey for *trekkers*, who were always in need of labour. Once employed in this fashion, of course, the Khoi like the San before them were dependent on the white population for the means of survival.

Forced dispersals, quasi–enslavement and death at the hands of commando units, exacerbated by a series of smallpox epidemics (to which the Khoi had very little collective immunity) meant that by the late 1770s there were no surviving independent Khoi communities living in or near the area of colonial settlement. The only surviving, nominally independent black or coloured societies lived at the northern extremities of the colony. The best known example would be the Bastaards (or Oorlams, later Griqua) people. Of mixed racial origin, being the children of Khoi–San women and settler men or slaves, these people adapted to their environment, practising Christianity and speaking the Dutch *taal*. As a consequence, many were able to establish themselves as successful farmers and acquire property. Others, however, fitted into the colonial order by working on settler farms as, or alongside indentured labour.

Colonial Fissures

There emerged over time a divergence of interests between the settler communities and VOC officialdom. Hardly perceptible at first, this was to become more pronounced during the course of the eighteenth century.

The VOC was steadfast in its commitment to maintaining the Cape as a viable station on the route to the east. This meant ensuring that productivity levels remained healthy while keeping expenditure in check. To do this, it continued to rely on monopolies in trade and land. Strategic considerations were also a top priority.

However, the VOC found that as the colony grew it had less effective control over the settler population in terms of how the *trek-boers* governed and policed their own communities. There was only scope for enforcing VOC laws in certain areas some of the time, and in other areas none of the time. As an example, the VOC had little effective means of forcing free burghers to pay the fees due on their land, and many simply did not bother ever to honour these obligations.

Eager to keep the peace, the VOC was mostly prepared to compromise on, or turn a blind eye to, any such shows of independence. There were also common cultural bonds and mutual interests, especially against the Khoi–San, that fostered a sense of fraternity between the official and non-official elements of white society. Despite appearances, though, there occurred throughout the 1700s a shift in the real balance of power within the colony, away from the VOC, to the more numerous, more spirited free burghers. The VOC was not in a position to transform itself to keep the pace of change in a rapidly evolving environment.

Moreover, there were fundamental differences between the culture of Cape Town, which was inhabited by officialdom and a well-to-do mercantile class, and the interior. There were in Cape Town hospitals, churches, educational institutions, municipal buildings, fine houses and other trappings of a relatively comfortable colonial town. By contrast, the interior was mostly deprived of even the most basic infrastructural developments. There were few enough decent roads, no schools, few churches, and people lived in huts or hastily erected dwellings that rarely featured basic home comforts. Over time, this reality would reinforce ideas of differentiation that were almost impossible to check or reverse.

Easterly Expansion: The Trekboers Opposed for the First Time

The easterly expansion of the colony occurred only slowly during the eighteenth century as *trekker* families moved further away from the Cape in search of suitable pasture. The VOC claimed as of right any lands settled by burghers, loaning it back to the *trekboers* in exchange for a yearly due. Most people who settled in this way found themselves living in great isolation, often a day or more's wagon ride away from their closest neighbour. They lived by their own rules, ignoring authority when they pleased and following codes of conduct that suited only themselves.

These loan farms averaged 600 hectares each, which was expected to be enough to facilitate farming on a profitable scale. Some farmers did prosper; sheep farming on the southern Karoo was especially rewarding. Other enterprises, however, were blighted by failing crops, drought and a more general inability to extract decent yields from the land. Labour was also in short supply. Those Africans who could be employed on settler farms were bound by a form of apprenticeship from a young age, working the land in exchange for shelter and food.

The main barrier to unfettered colonial expansion in the east was the cohesiveness of the societies indigenous to the region. The first settlers to reach the region were prone to negotiate with African societies over land and access to natural resources, and compromises were often reached. However, as *trekker* numbers increased, so cordiality became less frequent. Inevitably, the Nguni-speaking Xhosa farming communities of the eastern Cape and Transkei acted to defend their control of the land. The term 'Xhosa' was originally used by local Khoi and meant 'angry men', perhaps a reflection of the fact that these tribes were politically well organised and certainly formed tighter social units than the Khoi-San to the west. Better placed to fight back than their Khoi counterparts, the Xhosa could not be removed from their environment either easily or quickly. Conflict, once started, was to last until the middle of the nineteenth century.

Initial skirmishes between settler commando units and Xhosa regiments escalated into warfare as the Xhosa attempted to halt the progress of white farmers across the Fish River. The problem became so pronounced that, in 1778, the Governor of the Cape visited the region in person in order to broker a deal between the two parties. This attempt at getting both sides to recognise the Fish River as a natural dividing line between their respective societies had little hope of succeeding as it conceded too much from the Xhosa point of view, but less than enough to satisfy the growing land hunger of the settlers. Furthermore, the Governor's tour, far from cooling the situation, merely stoked the fires of conflict. The following year, the fight for land and cattle stocks re-ignited, and this time, the *trekboers* were overwhelmed by a determined and highly organised adversary.

In the event the *trekkers* had been easily thwarted. Despite appeals to the authorities at the Cape, no help had been forthcoming, and the notion developed among the settlers that, in fact, they were being left to their own devices and could not rely on the VOC for military aid in establishing themselves around the Fish River. This caused deep-seated resentment, but also a determination to strike out alone as a means of overcoming the Xhosa. An already independently minded community, the *trekboers* of the east now closed ranks.

They spent the next decade struggling to survive in an environment of great hostility and much insecurity. New settlers, however, were not put off by the region's instability; the desire for large tracts of land was too strong for that. As *trekker* numbers increased so their ability to match the Xhosa was augmented. Raids against Xhosa chiefdoms became a regular occurrence. In turn, the Xhosa would respond by attacking settler property and livestocks. By the 1790s, the situation had spiralled to the point where the colonial authorities felt compelled to intervene. A commando unit was despatched from Cape Town with instruction to impose a truce on the region but, in the circumstances, had neither the power nor the authority to bring about any such settlement.

The advantage appeared to lie with the Xhosa, who were able to soak up militia pressure and in turn, use guerrilla tactics of their own to good effect. Taking advantage of political unrest at the Cape (see below, p. 47–8), in 1795 a local group of *trekboers*, calling themselves Patriots, rebelled and proclaimed the independent Republic of Graaff-Reinet. This was a response to the lack of affirmative action taken by the VOC against the Xhosa. It resulted in all-out local rebellion, with a ban on tax payments to the VOC and the election of a political assembly. The rebellions spread to other regions of the colony, notably Swellendam. However, the Patriots' protests did little for their cause, and more pertinently, did nothing to diminish the effectiveness of Xhosa defences. The situation was an intractable one; resolution was still a long way off.

The Company in Crisis

The Patriot rebellions were the culmination of a period of crisis for the VOC that had begun in the 1770s and would lead to the eventual ending of VOC rule over the Cape. In essence, this crisis stemmed from the inability of the VOC to modify its structures of power as a means of meeting the changing nature of life in the colony. It had less effective political control over much of the burgher population and the area of land under settlement. It maintained economically restrictive practices that benefited ever fewer people, selling imports at a high price while purchasing local produce at a low rate. Further, the VOC was increasingly outmoded in its cultural and social outlook.

The root cause of all the VOC's problems was the fact that it could not deliver economic satisfaction on a regular basis. The VOC was only as popular as the colony's free citizens were affluent. This affluence depended on trade margins being profitable and land and labour both being available in quantity. As we have seen, on the last two counts burghers were being forced further afield in the hope of attaining farms of the requisite size, as well as the work force to toil on them. However, the bigger the colony became, the more the colonists impinged on indigenous ways of life, resulting in conflict and more political problems for the VOC. Trade remained good when a decent price could be fetched for exportable goods and commodities, such as wine, wheat and meat. However, with no protective mechanisms in place, the Cape's export trade was wide open to the vagaries of the world market. When depression set in, as it did in the 1770s, this lowered prices and thus incomes. This was another major source of discontent among the burgher population.

To keep the colony solvent the VOC attempted to levy a land tax on settlers, but the move was neither popular nor widely observed. Matters came to a head in 1779, when a group of influential Cape colonists petitioned the VOC's directors in the Netherlands. A deputation was despatched to rail against official corruption, demand fair political representation for the non-official community, and an end to VOC-sponsored restrictions and monopolies on private enterprises.

Hopes were high that the directors' response would move some of the way to meeting these requests. In the event, it took the VOC four years to post a reply that did nothing to meet the petitioners' demands. So another appeal was sent, this time to the Dutch States-General which, although quicker to respond, would only concede equal burgher representation on the Cape's Council of Justice.

At this point, possible confrontation was headed off by an upturn in the local economy. The political fallout from the French Revolution in Europe resulted in France sending a garrison to the Cape to help the Dutch protect their regional interests against possible British intrigue or attack. This influx of men stimulated the local economy. Simultaneously the VOC, perhaps trying to buy its way out of trouble, launched a massive programme of defence building. These two developments combined to generate an economic boom that, although short lived, temporarily deflected the discontent that was simmering among the burgher population. However, once depression hit in the later 1780s, the rumblings against the Company grew louder and it became harder for the VOC to maintain any semblance of legitimate authority.

In this respect, it was not helped by the dissemination of new ideas, filtering in from the outside world. The recent revolutionary movements in Europe and America, and before these, the Enlightenment, propounded ideologies that in some ways justified the cause of the Patriot-burghers against the perceived authoritarianism of the VOC. Added to an already volatile mix, such ideas merely heightened the tensions already prevalent within Cape society, and in some circles resulted in a liberal backlash against the VOC.

MISSIONARIES

During the 1790s European missionary societies were making their presence felt throughout southern Africa. After one aborted attempt at activity in the 1730s, the first mission station was established by the Moravian Church in 1792, some 100 miles east from Cape Town. The Moravians were soon joined in southern Africa by the Congregationalist London Missionary Society. By the early nineteenth century other British, French and German Protestant groups had been joined by the Dutch Reformed Church in a joint, though hardly united drive to 'Christianise the Africans'.

Controversy surrounds the political and cultural impact of the work of these societies. Many historians argue that they acted as mere agents of imperialism, working to undermine indigenous cultures and traditions as a means of opening up these societies to a 'European' and, therefore, more civilised way of life. Whatever the merits of this argument, it does not diminish the impact of missionary work in southern Africa.

The London Missionary Society was the most active of all these groups in the nineteenth century, and was headed in the early 1800s by two men who did much to ameliorate the lot of Africans in southern Africa. John Philip (1775–1851) arrived at the Cape in 1819 and was immediately vocal in his criticisms of the ways in which white settlers treated local Africans. He was politically active both locally and in London against the extension of white settlement in the east. As a prominent member of the anti-slavery movement, he did much to whip up the hostility of Cape settlers, who came to see him as an outright meddler. Robert Moffat (1795–1883), David Livingstone's father-in-law, was active in the northern Cape and north of the Limpopo River. Fluent in the Tswana dialect, Moffat's work centred on teaching local communities the ways of Christianity as well as improving their material conditions. He was responsible for translating the Bible, and produced the first works printed in a southern African language.

Wherever missionary stations existed, they became a beacon for African refugees, who had been left without land and forced to scrape a living working on settler farms. The missions would provide education, shelter and food. Through religious discourse, the missionaries would attempt to interpret anew the world for peoples who, in a short space of time, had been stripped of the certainties (and even uncertainties) that had previously governed their lives. Rates of conversion were never high although this rarely stopped missionaries from trying, but even if they had not been converted, Africans could take advantage of the facilities offered at the stations.

The Fall of the VOC and the First British Administration

By the mid-1790s, the VOC was facing financial ruin following the recent depression. The Cape was close to economic collapse (owing an estimated £10 million), a situation exacerbated by the decreasing political legitimacy of the VOC throughout the colony.

This state of affairs did not go unnoticed in Europe, where the revolutionary wars were threatening to overturn the established political order. In 1794, France marched into, and occupied, the Netherlands. The move alarmed the British, by now the dominant world sea power, for a number of reasons. Prime among these was the very real threat that the Cape would fall into the hands of the French. With British trading interests in India firmly established, such a move would seriously threaten communications with the east and undermine Britain's ability to defend these concerns.

It was therefore decided that Britain should pre-empt the French and send a force to occupy the Cape. In June 1795, a British fleet sailed into Table Bay and forces were sent ashore to wrest control of the Cape from the VOC. With little means of effective resistance, the VOC did not take long to relinquish its authority. The change in government was neither challenged nor mourned. With not much credibility to draw on, the VOC had minimal support and, in the event, the local white population accepted the change with little or no fuss.

The new governors, however, were not heralded as liberators, but rather were treated with considerable caution and some hostility. As a means of counteracting such sentiments, the British acted quickly to dismantle the most unpopular aspects of VOC rule. The first British Governor of the Cape ended all trading monopolies while promising 'to adopt every measure which may appear to promote the prosperity of the Settlement'. Prices began to rise, production levels increased, and the merchant classes of Cape Town expanded in both number and affluence. The administration also promised to guarantee existing property rights and, for the most part, did not meddle with the legal system although torture was made illegal.

The British also grasped the nettle presented by the breakaway republics of Graaff-Reinet and Swellendam, offering the rebels amnesty for their past actions if they acceded to British rule. These terms were not accepted, so the Governor brought to an end any prospect of further negotiations and cut off supplies of ammunition and other essentials to the rebels. The tactic worked and the rebel republics were brought to heel by 1797.

The period of the first British administration of the Cape was short-lived, however. Bowing to the logic of legality, which dictated that the British occupancy had no basis in law, the Cape was returned to the Dutch in 1803, following the 1802 Anglo-French peace of Amiens. Although their brief tenure at the Cape had been an undoubted economic success, the British left somewhat maligned by the local white population. The Dutch descendants resented British ideological tolerance in religious and educational matters as much as the

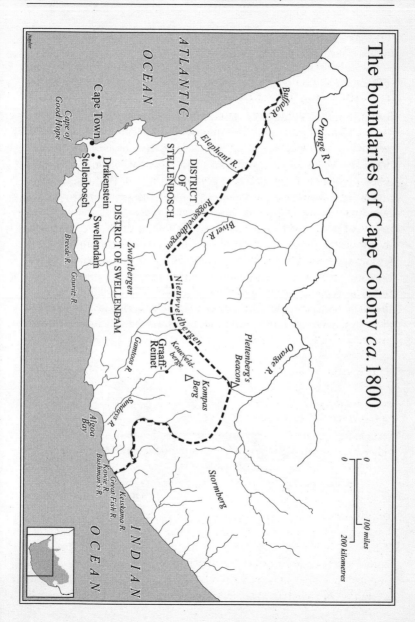

The boundaries of Cape Colony *ca.* 1800

ATLANTIC OCEAN

Cape of Good Hope

Cape Town

Stellenbosch

Drakenstein

Swellendam

DISTRICT OF STELLENBOSCH

DISTRICT OF SWELLENDAM

Zwartbergen

Breede R.

Gouritz R.

Gamtoos R.

Sundays R.

Algoa Bay

Graaff-Reinet

Koueveld berge

Kompas Berg

Nieuwveldbergen

Elephant R.

Roggeveldbergen

Buffalo R.

Orange R.

River R.

Orange R.

Plettenberg's Beacon

Stormberg

Keiskama R.

Great Fish R.

Kowie R.

Bushman's R.

INDIAN OCEAN

0   100 miles

0   200 kilometres

humanitarianism they espoused, which seemed to favour unnecessarily the black majority of the region.

LEGACY OF THE VOC

For 143 years, the VOC governed a colony that had during that time spread from Cape Town, 500 miles towards the Fish River in the east and 300 miles to the north. The impetus for this expansion lay almost exclusively with the free white subjects of the colony. This reality forced the VOC to play 'catch up', in a race that left it increasingly impotent to control society, affect political change and enforce the law. Under the circumstances a settlement evolved that was in part volatile, sometimes unruly, and mostly prejudiced in outlook.

The VOC's unwillingness to loosen its hold on the reins of power was increasingly difficult to justify once its outdated economic policies began to unravel. Yet it did not adapt to changing circumstances or try to reform itself in any fundamental manner. In the end, the VOC was unable to resist its inevitable fall. The society it left behind was economically unstable, politically naïve and racially intolerant. The longer-term consequences of this would resonate over the next two centuries.

CHAPTER FOUR

Conflict: Developments in African and European Southern Africa
c. 1800–1870

The Batavian Administration, 1803–05

The new Dutch republic, which had been confirmed in 1803 and assumed responsibilities for the Cape that same year, was determined to rule the colony in line with the ideological liberality that underpinned its outlook. It was to be a reforming administration, tolerant and constructive in approach, with an overarching plan to overhaul the ways in which the Cape was governed.

It did not succeed in all its original aims. Slavery, which was viewed by the Batavians as an abomination, remained in practice when investigations highlighted the fact that the colony's economy was utterly dependent upon indentured labour. Attempts at extending justice to the African majority also floundered in the face of settler protests. However, a basic educational system was extended throughout the colony, central government was opened up to incorporate greater burgher representation, and local government was changed with minor judicial and administrative powers devolved to frontiersmen. The supremacy of the Dutch Reformed Church and Dutch language were also upheld.

The Batavians achieved a lot in a short space of time. However, their reign was curtailed in 1805 when the continuing uncertainties of Europe, this time due to the activities of Napoleon Bonaparte, convinced the British government once again to occupy the strategically sensitive Cape. Southern Africa, variously permutated, would remain a part of the British empire for a further century and a half.

TIME OF CHANGE

The nineteenth century was a time of radical change for southern Africa. Geo-politically, the region changed beyond recognition with the expansion of the colonial frontier. Starting at the Cape, British imperial authority was strengthened and then extended into the interior. Within the ever shifting boundaries of the region there were established a number of separate settler states. Seismic shifts also occurred in the composition of African societies, culminating in the emergence of a number of formidable black nations. The interactions between indigenous, settler and colonial powers were both overlapping and complex, intensified by rivalries concerning land ownership and access to valuable natural resources. It is these interactions, rivalries and attendant conflicts that shaped both the region and its peoples during the 1800s.

African Societies

THE *MFECANE*

Since the arrival of European settlers in southern Africa, indigenous societies had been ravaged by disease (notably smallpox), famine (due to rain and crop failure) and war (both intertribal and against settlers) and there were further migrations northward in search of pasture, coupled with intermarriages into the coloured population of the Cape. A process of similar, yet greater, political and social change was triggered throughout the interior in the early decades of the nineteenth century.

This process is known as the *Mfecane* (in Nguni) or the *Difaqane* (in Sotho) meaning, literally, the crushing. During the time of the *Mfecane*, which peaked during the 1820s and 1830s, long-established African chiefdoms were either defeated, assimilated into other polities, or forced to flee their area of habitation. In some cases, tribes were destroyed entirely. This was at the expense of stronger tribal nations who emerged out of the chaos of these wars.

Although the finer details of the *Mfecane* are somewhat sketchy, a broad outline framed by mass human suffering stands out. Central to

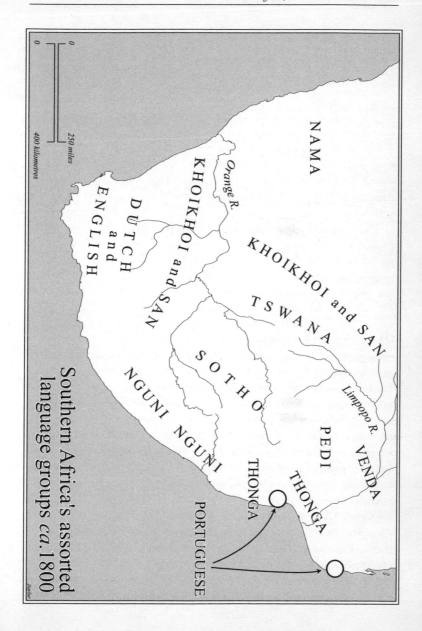

Southern Africa's assorted language groups *ca.*1800

NAMA

KHOIKHOI

Orange R.

DUTCH and ENGLISH

KHOIKHOI and SAN

KHOIKHOI and SAN

TSWANA

SOTHO

Limpopo R.

NGUNI NGUNI

PEDI

VENDA

THONGA

THONGA

PORTUGUESE

0
0
250 miles
400 kilometres

the process was the expansion in the 1820s of the Nguni-speaking Zulu kingdom across the low veld of Natal. Militaristic and increasingly aggressive in posture, the Zulus for a time conquered all before them, forcing other Nguni speakers to migrate north on to the highveld. This mass human tide had a ripple effect, causing further displacement of populations and, in turn, a shortage of land and livestock. New chiefdoms such as the Swazi and the Sotho emerged out of this confusion, while others re-formed and relocated much further to the north (the Tswana and Pedi, for example). Once started, the *Mfecane* produced a series of cyclical wars, both among Africans and between Africans and whites, that petered out only slowly and at great human and material cost.

The causes of the *Mfecane* are much debated. Central to the entire process was the social realignment and emergence of a strong Zulu nation in the early 1820s. As will be seen, this new nation was built on military conquest and, to a much lesser extent, power gained through the exploitation of trading opportunities presented by the presence of Portuguese colonialists to the east and, less markedly, the British to the south. More recently, historians have also highlighted a number of other factors that undoubtedly facilitated the *Mfecane*. Significantly, an era of intermittent drought from the late eighteenth century caused widespread occurrences of food shortages and famine. This put immense pressure on numerous communities, who began to compete with one another for land or to migrate across territory in search of new pastures and water supplies. Other factors of note include the knock-on pressure of refugee influxes into the region as a result of white colonisation, and the increasing demands being made across the region for labour, either to be assimilated into the Cape colony, or for the Portuguese slave markets, centred on Delagoa Bay.

If the causes of the *Mfecane* are blurred, its immediate consequences are more clear cut. Those African rulers best placed to capitalise on the unfolding crisis did so, expanding their societies in size, while using this position of strength to acquire goods and cattle which, in turn, were used to bolster the number of their adherents through the extension of patronage. As the number of refugees increased, the easier it became to secure followers in this manner. Enemies were dealt with ruthlessly and

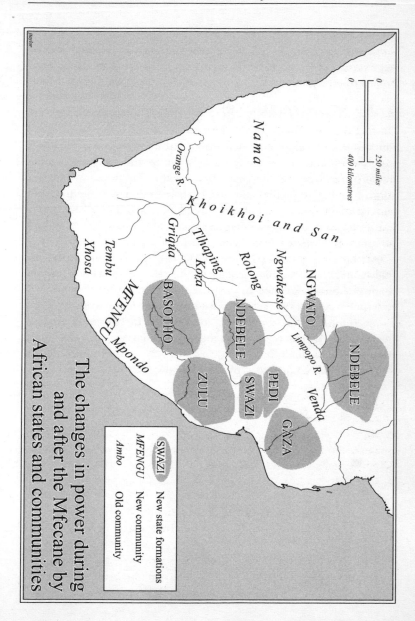

The changes in power during and after the Mfecane by African states and communities

SWAZI	New state formations
MFENGU	New community
Ambo	Old community

the vanquished saw their land conquered and their people absorbed. To some extent, then, the *Mfecane* evolved into a self-fulfilling process, with the strong becoming stronger still while the weak and needy were forced to capitulate.

THE RISE OF THE ZULU KINGDOM

During the first decade of the nineteenth century, the Nguni tribes situated in the region of modern day KwaZulu-Natal were experiencing environmental problems in relation to the land and natural resources. This created internal friction within the tribes over the use and availability of pasture and water. Such tension was intermittently exacerbated by the arrival of Griqua raiders, searching for labourers to force back to the northern Cape, and slavers from Delagoa Bay, seeking to spread their network of clients ever further south.

At the same time, two local chiefdoms, the Mthethwa and the Ndwande, were absorbing smaller Nguni clans of the region, as they both acted to consolidate and expand their territory and resources. It was not long before the Mthethwa and Ndwande were in direct competition with one another for local power. In 1817 the Ndwande won out, but despite the death of the Mthethwa paramount chief, their rivals were not annihilated.

A Mthethwa commander, by the name of Shaka (c.1787–1828), had

The legendary Shaka Zulu

avoided involvement in this defeat, and instead, turned his attentions to building up a new kingdom, the Zulu, centred on his own ancestry. Shaka, demonised by history as a cruel and bloodthirsty tyrant, was the illegitimate son of a minor Zulu chief. Neither loved nor cared for as a child, he endured a harsh and often humiliating upbringing (Shaka, translated literally from Zulu, means 'beetle'). However, he was a brave character, a trait quickly recognised by the Mthethwa chiefs, who appointed him to the head of a regiment. Having learnt much militarily from his apprenticeship with the Mthethwa, between 1817 and 1820 Shaka increased his followers by absorbing or eliminating neighbouring tribes. In late 1819, showing tactical cunning and amazing ruthlessness, Shaka provoked the Ndwande into attacking the Zulus. Having been unable to break through a resilient defence, the Zulus ambushed the retreating Ndwande army on the Mhlatuze River, inflicting a resounding defeat. Thereafter, the Zulus under Shaka were the undisputed authority in the region, shortly to be organised into a powerful, centrally controlled state.

The power of the Zulu nation, which was in Shaka's hands exclusively, rested on a central political authority and the militarisation of the state. Representatives of defeated or assimilated chiefdoms acted as royal agents to Shaka's court. They were expected to carry out his will and provide regiments for the Zulu army. They would be replaced if they did not conform to the wishes of Shaka, or moved to another area specifically to carry out his orders. They had no control over their chiefdom's regiments and no effective means of influencing the way in which they were deployed.

Each regiment would live together, barracked in military camps, forbidden to marry until they were no longer of fighting age or ability, and unable to return to their homes during the harvest season. Most regiments would be initiated together and so developed a strong sense of fraternity and unity of purpose. Shaka's regiments were noted for their braveness and loyalty. They were disciplined and highly efficient. Each regiment had its own distinguishing uniform and carried different colours on its shields. The weapons they employed broke with Nguni tradition. Long spears, usually launched through the air at some distance, were dispensed with. In their place short stabbing swords were used that were far more effective in close combat. This also meant that soldiers could move faster when in battle. To this end, they were strictly forbidden from wearing sandals during active service. Regiments were also issued with large shields, which were highly effective against flying spears and a formidable barrier that, when fitted together, allowed groups of soldiers to close ranks.

Shaka asked a lot from his men but the rewards were usually high. Each regiment was properly fed and well looked after. However, failure to carry out orders to the letter and incidents of cowardice were dealt with ruthlessly. In this way Shaka cemented the loyalty and obedience of his charges and could depend upon those qualities for a considerable time. Expeditions of conquest were undertaken on a regular basis as a means of keeping regiments battle sharp. For the most part, Shaka employed a standard tactic of attack: deploying a central regiment that would be protected by a flanking regiment on either side. Reserve units would never be far behind. This horn-shaped formation enjoyed great success as the Zulu army conquered all before it.

The Zulus were ruthless in pursuit of victory and renowned for their bloodthirstiness. Suspected and actual rivals would be wiped out, entire villages razed, and women and children were often among the victims. Through a series of comprehensive victories against societies settled between the Tugela and uMzimkhulu Rivers which were achieved in just such a style, the Zulu nation under Shaka was both consolidated and made rich. Of course, the dislocation this caused throughout the 1820s as refugees fled in a westerly and northerly direction increased the overall insecurity of the region. In turn, greater numbers fell prey to the Zulu war machine. The costs, in terms of human life, were perhaps without precedent at the time in this region of the world.

For a decade Shaka's rule went unchallenged. However, over the course of time, the strain of maintaining a permanently active militia state began to show. With all able-bodied men on service, agricultural and homestead-based work rested on the shoulders of women, the old and very young. This was a situation that could not go on indefinitely. While it did, however, it caused increasing resentment and placed great strain on the fabric of Zulu society.

But perhaps more pertinently, Shaka's system could only be

sustained by keeping the army active and victorious. After a while, the Zulus had conquered all they could realistically conquer and captured an optimum level of bounty. Furthermore, by eliminating all forms of opposition, Shaka perpetuated the need to maintain the material and military aggrandisement of the Zulu nation, while his arbitrary methods allowed no scope for dissension or negotiation. Something had to give. In 1828, on the eve of a planned raid east of the Fish River and into the Cape colony, rebellion came in the form of Shaka's half-brother, Dingane (c.1795–1840), who assassinated the chief aided by another of his brothers and a servant. After a brief power struggle, Dingane succeeded Shaka, thus bringing to a close one of the bloodiest eras in southern African history.

THE REACTION OF OTHER CHIEFDOMS

Not all chiefdoms that scattered before the advancing Zulu tide were subjugated. Those that had a degree of internal social cohesion were able to sustain power elsewhere. Some Ndebele clans, as an example, were able to establish themselves across the Limpopo River, in an area today incorporated into Zimbabwe, after they had resisted Zulu attacks in 1821. The Pedi similarly moved in a northerly direction where, initially at least, they could maintain unity. In both cases, the example of the Zulu state was reproduced, albeit on a smaller scale, as these peoples devastated communities that lay in their way and took the opportunity to capture livestock and pick up new patrons. Thereafter, they settled down into a peaceful way of life. Other tribes such as the defeated Ndwandwe tried to emulate the Zulus with little success. The Swazi confederacy was better placed both geographically and militarily to ward off not only the Zulus, but also other refugee chiefdoms.

Undoubtedly, the shrewdest chief operating at this time was Moshoeshoe (1786–1870), a Sotho-speaker, who rejected the prevailing tactics of bloodshed and conquest in favour of a defensive diplomatic stance. Throughout the 1820s, Moshoeshoe courted refugees and communities that had scattered, encouraging them to join him on his shielded mountain-top base of Thaba Bosiu, the Mountain of Night, in Lesotho. Most of those who came under his protection were Nguni-speakers, mixed with a smattering of Khoi-San and Sotho-Tswana.

Thaba Bosiu was blessed with a natural spring and space for storage and thousands of people. It could not be readily breached from any angle and was therefore practically impregnable. From this base, Moshoshoe was able to protect those people who agreed to come under his tutelage. Patronage was secured by loaning to families cattle that had been earlier raided from weaker communities. As his followers grew in number, so Moshoshoe was able to extend this network of patrons and expand control over land for miles around. A centralised state slowly began to take shape. The process was not without complication, and Moshoshoe's followers on a number of occasions were forced to defend themselves from attack. However, Moshoshoe's reluctance to go to war, coupled with his willingness to negotiate with rivals whenever possible, served merely to augment his standing and draw more followers to Thaba Bosiu. By the mid-1830s he had an estimated 25,000 people under his rule, living productive lives as farmers and generating regular surpluses of maize and grain.

Moshoeshoe's life was a long one (he lived into his eighties) but his progressive attitudes never diminished. His outlook remained tolerant and he actively encouraged public debate within society. He embraced missionary activity among his people, believing that the education this provided was key to the future advancement of the nascent Sotho state. He never went so far as to convert until he was on his deathbed, as he understood that polygamy cemented his nation through the inter-marriage of his relatives into sub-chiefdoms. However, he was contemptuous of witchcraft and other similar traditions which, he believed, had an unhealthy hold over his people.

The Transformation of African Society

The *Mfecane* created powerful new nations which, for nearly two decades, thrived by employing ruthless military tactics involving conquest, great destruction and immense loss of life. The 'crushing', once started, took on an impetus of its own as refugee communities moved across land in a bid to re-establish their societies. Some aped the strong-arm tactics of the Zulus; others crumbled in the face of such a challenge and were either assimilated or annihilated. But nobody could escape, as

African society in the eastern half of southern Africa was transformed. Much of the land was depopulated or rendered unworkable. In order just to survive some resorted to the practice of cannibalism. However, the new nations that, on one level, had affected this revolution, on another did little to diminish the social inequalities that had previously prevailed. Nor were they the harbingers of a fairer political system. The old hierarchical structures of power were, if anything, reinforced by the *Mfecane*.

THE XHOSA

The state of semi-permanent conflict that had characterised *trekker–* Xhosa relations across the Fish River in the late 1700s continued into the nineteenth century, eventually drawing in the imperial forces of the British colony. The longer the situation remained unresolved, the more intractable it became. The Xhosa could score temporary victories by employing to their advantage a numerical superiority and effective guerrilla tactics. However, the *trekkers* could retaliate with modern weaponry and a ruthlessness that could quickly negate any such gains. Furthermore, neither side had available to them the resources needed to sustain the sort of lengthy campaign that would ensure a final victory.

When the local *trekker* community rebelled in the mid-1790s, it brought a short period of respite to the frontier conflict. The Xhosa responded to the rebellion by retiring to their villages. This hiatus abruptly ended in 1799, however, when local Khoi servants started to abandon settler farms, formed themselves into roving bands and started a campaign aimed at restoring lost ancestral lands. The move caused enormous disruption within the settler community, compounded by the sanctions imposed upon them by the British.

The Xhosa seized the opportunity presented to them and attacked the *trekboers* with a ferocity that betrayed twenty years of frustration and anger at continual incursions on to their land and against their cattle. Farms were captured, settler homesteads razed to the ground and other properties smashed. The Xhosa made common cause with the Khoi rebels, who utilised guns captured from the *trekkers*. The two communities extended their original aim from merely rolling back the settler advance into the more forthright goal of completely defeating the *trekboers*.

There was little that the latter could do. With each and every Xhosa–Khoi attack, the border between the two communities became more blurred. Raids deep into the Graaff-Reinet district caused many *trekkers* to abandon their holdings entirely. The campaign was sustained for three years until most settlers had been driven out of the region. At this point, however, the Khoi rebels reverted to their earlier objective of claiming back ancestral land. This split the alliance with the Xhosa. Into this breach stepped representatives of the Batavian administration who, in one of the regime's last acts, negotiated a truce with the rebels.

The victorious Xhosa could not rest easily on their laurels. There was every chance that the settlers would return to reclaim their land, bolstered by reinforcements and modern weaponry with which to establish themselves. The new British administration at the Cape was not prepared to allow the situation to re-ignite. Instead, it chose to pursue a hard-line policy, designed to bring law and order to the region via a system of strong governance.

The theory was more difficult to put into practice, however. For the next half a century they were never sure which tactics worked best. Furthermore, they would discontinue a particular course of action rather too soon if it did not pay dividends: government agents, local treaties, buffer zones, frontier passes were all tried and, for the most part, dropped after a short period.

The first British attempt at stabilising the frontier came in 1811 when a line of fortifications was built along the banks of the Fish River. The aim was to contain the Xhosa to the east bank of the river. The project was an outright failure, however, as the Xhosa continued to occupy land far beyond the west bank of the Fish. British officers in the region interpreted such defiance as proof of expansionist tendencies within Xhosa ranks. This was spurious at best. Nevertheless, the new British Governor of the Cape, General Sir John Craddock (who served at the Cape from September 1811 to October 1813), was sufficiently impressed by these dispatches to decide to act against the Xhosa. In 1812, a British army that included in its ranks *trekboers* and Griquas marched against the Xhosa, managing to expel an estimated 20,000 from the west bank of the Fish. The force showed little restraint in its actions and used the operation to raid Xhosa cattle.

Earlier Xhosa gains were wiped out at a stroke. The local balance of power now lay with the settlers, who returned to the region in notable numbers. Hundreds, if not thousands, of Xhosa were meanwhile left destitute, homeless and without the means to sustain themselves.

But, once again, the victory was not absolute. As soon as the colonial troops were withdrawn, the Xhosa began to move slowly back towards the Fish, as determined as ever not to be driven off land they claimed as their own. By 1818 they were grouped and ready to launch an offensive deep into settler territory. A force of some 10,000 was able to re-take extensive tracts of land, but overstretched itself by laying siege to the settlement of Grahamstown. Unable to capture the town, the break in the Xhosa advance allowed enough time for the British to raise a strong military detachment which, in three months, was able to push the Xhosa back some 150 miles to the Kei River. Despite pleas for leniency from Xhosa chiefs, the counter-attack was characteristically ruthless and bloodthirsty and resulted in the capture of 30,000 head of Xhosa cattle.

Thereafter, the Xhosa were cleared from all land between the Keikamma and Fish Rivers. The Cape administration deployed patrol units to keep the territory neutral, that is to say, free of Xhosa communities. Only now was the corner turned, as the British began the arduous operation of bringing the eastern frontier under effective control. As part of this process, in 1820, 5,000 British immigrants were settled in the area in a concerted effort to tip the local demographic balance towards the white population (see below, pp. 73–4).

These actions were still not enough to crush the Xhosa. They were provoked by both the patrols and the settlers, and time and again attempted to reclaim land through invasion and the use of limited military campaigns. However, the more resources and people the Cape administration moved into the eastern Cape and frontier regions, the less chance the Xhosa had of victory. Their numerical advantage was dwindling and they simply could not hope to match the superior weaponry available to the British settlers, local garrisons and the *trekboers*.

A brief period of relative calm was abruptly shattered in the early 1830s when *trekboers* violated the neutral buffer and headed into Xhosa territory, seeking decent pasture in a time of drought. The Xhosa were provoked into defending their land and attacked settler farms to the west. Moving on a broad front, the Xhosa forced many settlers to retreat in panic. A concerted counter-attack was launched and, as usual, reprisals were characterised by brutality. A Xhosa chief named Hintsa (c.1790–1835), who hitherto had been an irritant to the British who believed him to be the head of all Xhosa chiefs, was captured under the pretext of meeting to negotiate a settlement and murdered when he attempted to flee. The British then declared the area between the Kei and Keiskamma Rivers to be neutral and annexed it to the Cape as Queen Adelaide Province. However, a mixture of mistrust of the *trekboers*, a vociferous humanitarian lobby at home and an unwillingness to take formal control of such a troublesome region, convinced the British to abandon the interest and opt instead for a series of treaties with local chiefdoms, aimed at bolstering their independence and opening up trading links. The settler communities were outraged but powerless to affect the decision.

The move was in no small part a reaction to the growth in the ivory trade over which various Xhosa settlements had great influence. From virtually nothing in the early part of the century, ivory exports from southern Africa – the result of poaching and big game hunting that would, over time, greatly threaten the local elephant population – were by the 1830s worth millions each year. This was enough to make the colonial administration, ever with an eye on profit margins, sit up and take note. Furthermore, it was believed that commerce was another means by which to bring stability to the region. Wagon routes, serving regular markets, were constructed to meet the local settler and African demand for consumer goods and equipment. Trade in the direction of the Cape, not only in ivory, but also agricultural produce and other goods, was also encouraged. In this way, the economy of the east was spurred on and showed signs of steady growth throughout the 1820s and 1830s.

THE FINAL DEFEAT OF THE XHOSA

The treaties binding the Xhosa to friendly relations with the British imperial administration certainly stimulated trade and helped maintain order for a few short years. However, these alliances continued to rankle with local merchants and farmers who felt their economic interests were not protected to anything like the same degree. Further still, they resented their inability to expand their farms into Xhosa territory and access pools of locally based, exploitable African labour.

It was a line of argument that found sympathy in some official circles, where it was realised that more land and cheap labour added up to greater profits in agricultural industries. However, without some sort of pretext the treaties could not be broken. Only continual Xhosa cattle rustling of settler herds offered an excuse for the severing of relations, although this was not of sufficient scale to warrant such a move.

The murder in 1846 of a Khoi policeman by Xhosa men who were attempting to free a colleague from arrest proved decisive. The Cape government used this as an excuse to launch a punitive attack upon the Xhosa, so starting the War of the Axe (so-called because the man who had been arrested was supposed to have stolen an axe). The colonial forces asserted themselves with such ferocity as to belie the fact that this was a war over something as relatively inconsiderable as the loss of one policeman's life. In defence of settler–merchant demands, the Cape forces unleashed a scorched earth campaign that lasted for months, leaving countless Xhosa communities in a state of absolute destitution, starving and without land. By a long way, this was the bloodiest of all the frontier wars. The treaty system had been brought to an abrupt end.

Thereafter, Cape forces occupied all Xhosa land in the region of the Kei–Keiskamma Rivers. The bullish new head of the Cape colony was Sir Harry Smith (1787–1860). A headstrong character with a pronounced sense of his own importance, Smith was the type of person to inspire awe in mere mortals as well as prime ministers and princesses. His career had been an illustrious one and he had been involved in numerous campaigns around the world (he was a veteran of the wars against Napoleon, had laid siege to Washington, DC, and more recently, defeated the Sikhs at Aliwal in India). Upon arrival in southern Africa, he insisted that the occupation of Xhosa land be formalised, and so in late 1847, the Cape annexed the region as British Kaffraria (later, Ciskei). But this was not the end of the affair. Smith continued to stir up the situation, using every opportunity to humiliate

Sir Harry Smith

Xhosa chiefs and provoke some sort of reaction. He also acted without regard for Xhosa culture and custom. His attempted removal in 1850 of one paramount chief, Sandile (1820–1878), sparked a Xhosa rebellion that quickly spread to include Khoi peasants and other Africans on the run from work within colonial society. In this way, the Xhosa were able to contrive one final campaign aimed at reversing the erosion of their territory which had proceeded, in fits and starts, for decades.

The chances of success were not good from the start. Despite showing characteristic bravery and endurance, the Xhosa were no match for the combined force of sheer numbers and greater weaponry that the colonials had at their disposal. The final frontier war lasted close on three years, but the longer it went on, the more misery was inflicted on the Xhosa. In the end, their lands were opened up to white settlement. The Xhosa had finally been conquered.

THE CATTLE KILLINGS

The misery of defeat was compounded in 1856 when the Xhosa community imploded as a consequence of a self-inflicted mass culling of cattle and the wanton destruction of grain supplies. On one level, the cullings were a response to a deadly lung sickness that arrived from Europe and had, by the end of 1855, spread to affect some two-thirds of all Xhosa stocks. Yet other reasons for the killings are not hard to discern. Beaten and embittered, despairing of the future, the Xhosa were for the most part looking for hope and seeking an explanation for the recent land losses and the arrival of the cattle disease. Many turned to the ancestors and came to the same widely held conclusion that the land was polluted and could only be cured through some form or other of ritual purification.

This was indeed a society gripped by desperation, willing to attach plausibility to any notion that offered a glimmer of hope. In April 1856, a teenage girl named Nongqawuse (*c.* 1840–98) offered salvation, when she relayed details of an encounter she had with two male spirits. They told her:

> You are to tell the people that the whole community is about to rise again from the dead. Then go on to say to them all the cattle living now must be slaughtered, for they are reared by defiled hands, as the people handle witchcraft. Say to them there must be no ploughing of lands, rather must the people dig deep pits (granaries), erect new huts, set up wide, strongly built cattlefolds, make milksacks, and weave doors from buta roots. The people must give up witchcraft of their own, not waiting until they are exposed by the witchdoctors. You are to tell that these are the words of their chiefs.

Nongqawuse's vision was retold far and wide and given much credence. She had further visions that suggested the whites would be forced into the sea if the Xhosa community purged itself of witchcraft, identified as the root cause of the malaise affecting society as a whole. The sacrifices the Xhosa had been asked to make through Nongqawuse promised ancestral intervention leading to redemption. The slaughter promised a return to prosperity, with lands being fully restored, cattle reappearing in great numbers and grain pits being filled.

A majority of chiefs readily believed the prophecy and encouraged their people to slaughter their herds. Great pressure was exerted on those who refused to comply with the vision. Some, but not many, effectively resisted this pressure. In total, an estimated 90 per cent of Xhosa are thought to have destroyed their cattle and razed grain stocks.

A strange euphoria gripped the Xhosa as the cullings started, reflecting a belief that salvation was on the way. Carrying out the vision to the letter, people did not farm or labour, but rather, waited for salvation, for their cattle to return and for the white man to leave. Days and then months passed yet nothing miraculous happened. Hope turned to desperation. The idea spread that those holding on to their livestock were preventing Nongqawuse's prophecy from turning to reality and so more beasts were sacrificed. But there was to be no extraordinary regeneration of the Xhosa. Tens of thousands, faced with starvation, were forced to migrate west into the Cape colony to find work as waged labourers. Those who chose to stay were faced with inevitable starvation. It is thought that some 40,000 Xhosa died in this way following the cattle killings.

This was suicide on a mass scale. By 1857, with some 80 per cent of cattle stocks wiped out, the population of British Kaffraria had fallen by 68,000 to just over 37,000. This effectively broke Xhosa society and was far more damaging than all the previous wars with the settlers. Many of those who survived the disaster were left with no choice but to enter colonial society as a way of earning the means of survival. Others fled to the mission stations and found solace in a new religion. Entire chiefdoms disappeared and with them went centuries of tradition and culture. The Cape administration, meanwhile, encouraged Xhosa assimilation within the colony and opened up ex–Xhosa land to white settlement. With effective opposition to colonial expansion in the east obliterated, the government proceeded over the course of the next few decades to limit the amount of land available to Africans for agricultural activities in the region.

AFRICAN SOCIETIES ADAPT TO COLONIALISM

As the case of the Xhosa illustrates, African communities during the nineteenth century were faced with a stark choice: adapt to colonialism or face extinction. Traditional indigenous ways of life, everywhere across the region, were eventually exposed to colonists and their political and social systems. The pressure to conform to these systems was enormous and grew with time.

Those communities that were either slow or reluctant to adapt found themselves brought into increasing conflict with settler society.

Resistance was ever more difficult to achieve as the white community increased in size and became reliant on the use of weapons to which Africans did not always have access. It became far easier to fit into the new political order than to stay outside it. Those who chose to resist colonialism found life incredibly tough. Even the strongest of polities such as the Sotho under Moshoshoe came to the realisation that it was easier to have some dealings with the settlers, especially in terms of ensuring continuing access to certain natural resources and, as importantly, to material resources such as guns.

Commercially, there were benefits to be had from the colonial system. The high demand for ivory made many Africans rich beyond imagination. The Zulus especially exploited all such trading opportunities to the limit, responding to the demands of the market and using this to their material advantage. However, the majority of southern Africa's indigenous population did not benefit from the extension of colonialism. The loss of land and curtailing of traditional forms of subsistence forced more and more people into wage labour, working for whites in exchange for a paltry wage. Those who did not end up on farms or plantations would drift to urban areas, where they worked as casual labourers and lived as proletarians. Many Khoi-San and after 1857, Xhosa, headed for the growing settlements of Cape Town or Port Elizabeth. Even poorer members of the relatively prosperous Sotho and Zulu nations ended up in the towns, employed perhaps as dockers or artisans or domestic servants. For the most part, African communities remained segregated in the towns in their own quarters.

The numbers of Africans living and working in urban areas increased markedly during the 1800s. Their lives were characteristically harsh and governed by laws that restricted freedom of movement. A proclamation of 1809 required all Africans to register as living at a fixed abode. Failure to do so resulted in classification as a vagrant and possible prosecution. A pass made of wood or metal and worn on a necklace was also compulsory. This would prove gainful employment. Without a pass, Africans were not allowed to travel. There was no way of escaping from such subjugation within the colony and only on the missions was the pass law not enforceable.

The British at the Cape

The second British occupation of the Cape in 1805 was confirmed under the terms of the 1815 Vienna peace settlement that followed in the wake of the final defeat of Napoleon's French empire. For possession of the colony, the British paid the Dutch government £6 million in compensation. In a relatively short space of time, the Cape was assimilated into the British imperial system which was soon to be the biggest and most powerful in the world. This had major social, economic and political ramifications for the region as southern Africa was opened up to new ideas and a quite different style of government.

The British interest in the Cape was primarily strategic as the point lay on the way to India. Until the opening of the Suez Canal in 1869, the Cape route was the only passage to the east from Europe and so was carefully guarded. Other than this consideration, the British government scarcely concerned itself with the region until the discovery of diamonds in the 1860s and gold in the 1870s. In the formative decades of British rule in southern Africa there was a steady trade with the region but little capital investment of note.

On re-taking the colony, the British immediately acted to reverse the political liberality that had characterised the brief period of Batavian rule. The first permanent Governor to the Cape, the Earl of Caledon (who served from May 1807 until September 1811), restored autocratic rule, governing via proclamation and ensuring that political authority reverted to the central administration. He then set out on a programme of internal development, designed to bring the Cape into the modern world.

Civic amenities, where they already existed, were extended through local investment; where they were lacking, they were introduced. An efficient mail service was established, linking Cape Town to the interior and to the outside world. Old roads were mended and new ones built, bridges were erected over waterways. Cape Town was the place that benefited most from this programme of development; a decent sewerage system was introduced, water piping fitted and street lighting extended throughout the town. Long Street, the highly fashionable residential area, was lined with the type of houses that would not have looked out of place in Georgian Bath or Dublin. A number of hospitals were invested in, churches and new museums opened and libraries built. By the 1820s, Cape Town was a thriving settlement, increasingly cosmopolitan in composition (the town's first mosque, used by the free coloured population, had been opened as early as 1800) and featuring a boys' college, a commercial exchange and a number of banking houses. Educational standards were higher in Cape Town than in the rest of the colony where schooling opportunities for most remained few and far between.

The early British administrators of the Cape concentrated their efforts on making the colony economically viable and self-sufficient. As a consequence of this, the pace of colonial expansion slowed as the government was reluctant to take on more responsibilities, and thereby more costs. Instead, attention was focused not on the settlement of more land, but rather, the better employment of land already under white ownership. New industries such as sheep farming and wool production were developed, financed mostly by credit raised on the Cape Town exchange.

Slowly, the rural economy of the Cape was transformed, as farmers responded to the opportunities presented by a market free of trading restrictions. By the 1830s the value of Cape lands had increased, surpluses were being generated in cash crops and exports were on the rise. There emerged a wealthy class of farmers, small in number but increasingly powerful as a lobby. However, there was a commensurate rise in the number of indigenous farmers who were being forced from the land due to rising costs.

In the 1820s the government and major landowners entered into a mutually beneficial political alliance that was to endure for some considerable time. The government was assured of farmer backing for as long as it acted to uphold the social *status quo*, especially in relation to the African population, and keep commerce free from restriction. The government was willing to oblige, for it realised that agricultural success was key to the prosperity and therefore viability of the colony.

Within a matter of decades, the British had radically altered Cape society through a programme of various reforms that were designed to bring the region into line with the rest of the empire. This caused much friction throughout southern Africa, as well as points of social conflict, that went unchecked for many years. Other measures, however, were designed to transform the Cape from a political backwater into a progressive colony.

ECONOMIC CHANGE

For a long time, the merchant classes of the Cape had yearned for greater freedom in terms of trade, and as we have seen, mounted a campaign against the restrictionist policies and monopoly practices of the VOC. The British inaugurated a change in economic and trade policies that suited these local interests. During the first decades of British rule, the Cape was opened up to greater commercialisation. There was major investment in the internal communications infra-structure which acted as a great fillip to local industry. New industries were introduced, such as merino sheep farming, that proved most successful. Existing industries, for example wine production, were boosted by the opening up of new markets in Britain and throughout the British empire. Overall, export levels increased, directly benefiting Cape merchants and landowners.

Foreign capital investors took a while to become interested in southern Africa, although more capital flowed into the region under the British administration than it ever had done under VOC rule. Furthermore, the British treasury could occasionally be persuaded to inject sums of money to stabilise the local economy.

The major effect of the rolling back of the old VOC market regu-lations was to expose southern Africa, quite suddenly, to the vagaries of the world market. Consequently, the Cape economy would slump periodically in line with downturns in European or world trade. This would have an impact upon export levels of products such as wine. Furthermore, gluts in the world market for commodities such as wheat would adversely effect the profit levels of southern African agri-culturalists, for they operated in a market that was scarcely protected. Such crises would often result directly in further migrations into the interior.

IMMIGRATION FROM BRITAIN

The early British administrators of the Cape were keen to encourage immigration from Britain, as a means of 'Anglicising' southern Africa and also of stimulating local economic growth and diversification. Initially, immigration from the metropolitan country was sluggish, and there were very few non-official Britons resident at the Cape in the 1810s. In response to this situation, and also as a means of alleviating rising unemployment in Britain, the Cape government planned and executed a programme of British immigration, resulting in the settlement of 5,000 people in the newly created district of Albany, situated along the eastern frontier of the colony.

The 5,000 were carefully chosen from some 90,000 applicants in what has been described as 'the first modern attempt at a government-sponsored settlement colony'. Migrants were split off into parties led by wealthy patrons, and settled on small farms set beside villages that were meant closely to resemble home. The social composition of each party was carefully engineered to reflect each class of British society. Hence, the patrons were of the gentry, while there was a smattering of traders, artisans, farmers and labourers throughout the remainder of each group.

The experiment failed largely because the social mix was not sufficiently broad. There were not enough labourers and farmers and perhaps too many artisans and petty merchants. Furthermore, the size of the farms, which were each limited to 100 acres, was not sufficiently large to be economical and much of the land settled was unsuited to intense agricultural practices. Simply put, these smallholdings could not compete with neighbouring *trekboer* farms that might be 4,000 acres large and worked by slaves (the Albany settlers were not permitted to use indentured labour).

The settlements did not get off to a good start. The immigrants barely had time to acclimatise and reap their first harvests before droughts were followed by floods, rendering all their earliest efforts a waste. They also had to contend with an unstable political situation as the Xhosa attempted to overturn their exclusion from the area between the Keikamma and Fish Rivers.

Within three years the experiment had mostly failed. Around

two-thirds of the immigrants had moved away from Albany, drifting towards the towns at Grahamstown or Port Elizabeth. Here, many turned to trade and did rather well, or worked as artisans, earning a decent enough living and finally achieving the material comforts for which they had come to Africa in the first place. In both locations, the presence of the immigrants bolstered the local economies and helped turn these developing towns into successful centres of commerce. They were also key in building up urban society and culture away from Cape Town. These Britons were responsible for establishing many a school or library in interior towns, and brought with them ideas and skills that affected the course of nineteenth-century southern African arts and literature, architecture and scientific investigation.

Those who chose to stay on the land were able to increase the size of their holdings with relative ease. In the main, these families turned to sheep farming and wool production, industries that were to thrive in the eastern Cape districts. However, this was hardly the result expected by the colony's governors who had invested much time and money for a small return. The 1820 settlers were the last of their kind. There would be no further efforts to encourage mass migrations from Britain to the Cape, although the idea would be discussed from time to time.

EARLY ADMINISTRATIVE REFORMS

The Anglicisation of southern Africa in the early 1800s was not restricted to the immigration programme. The administration also overhauled the structures of government to reflect British systems and procedures more closely.

British men, or British appointees, acceded to posts both locally and in the colony's government. English replaced Dutch as the official language of the Cape and was used on government business and in the courts. Some Dutch customs were replaced, although Roman-Dutch law remained the basis of all policy with British legal procedures being used to test court cases (circuit courts toured the interior from 1811). The British also introduced a system of primary education and built schools throughout the colony, where instruction was in English. They also broke the Dutch Reformed Church's monopoly on religious practice, allowing other Protestant churches to establish parishes throughout the Cape.

THE ABOLITION OF SLAVERY

The abolition of slavery in southern Africa illustrated perhaps more than any other reform the extent to which the region had been integrated into the British imperial system. Although the outlawing of slavery did not happen overnight, and was much resented within the Cape, especially among those of Dutch descent, the Cape government was compelled to introduce the legislation in line with the rest of the empire.

Like the Batavians before them, the British initially upheld slavery throughout the colony and for the similar reason that it was quickly recognised that the success of the local economy was utterly dependent on indentured labour. Moreover, the early British administrators of the Cape were committed to ensuring a steady supply of cheap labour for the white farming communities, and so, enforced pass laws designed to tie Africans to an employer and make freedom of movement more difficult (see above, p. 69). This legislation was only removed in 1828, partly in response to the virulent campaigning of the humanitarian lobby in Britain.

The path to slave emancipation throughout the British empire was traversed only slowly. The anti-slavery lobby had a difficult job on its hands overcoming those with a vested interest in the maintenance of the trade. In 1807, the British parliament passed legislation prohibiting the shipment of slaves, either to British colonies or on British ships. Simultaneously, attempts were also made to improve conditions for slaves throughout the empire. Technically, this limited the further expansion of the industry, although in reality it was still able to flourish, as the new laws could only be patchily enforced. In the Cape colony these edicts were ignored. Later legislation, however, was harder to ignore. In 1816, laws were passed requiring all colonial administrations to introduce slave registers. This was followed in 1823 by the setting of a legal minimum standard for working hours, food and clothing for slaves, as well as outlawing the use of punitive measures against slaves outside of the law courts. A Guardian of Slaves was employed in each colony to oversee the implementation of these standards. Three years later, all slaves were extended official protection and allowed to buy their freedom (an allowance that was rarely taken advantage of, simply because few slaves had the means of paying off their masters).

This battery of measures culminated in the 1833 Abolition Act. At a stroke, all slaves within the British empire were freed from bondage and the trade was outlawed. Owners were entitled to compensation for each of their slaves. However, the Act did not anywhere change master–servant relations immediately as it was hedged with a system of so-called apprenticeship designed to last for five years, which effectively kept many ex-slaves tied to their former owners in return for a meagre salary. Nevertheless, the fact remained that indentured labourers could no longer be kept against their will.

In southern Africa, the emancipation of slaves was very unpopular, especially among the Dutch-speaking community, resulting in many choosing to migrate away from British rule (see below, p. 78). However, all ex-owners were well placed to continue to exercise social and political controls over former slaves. Liberty was no guarantee of a job, and so many freed slaves remained employed by the same people, either as 'apprentices', poorly paid labourers or tenant farmers. Others took refuge with missionaries, while fewer still were able to establish themselves as subsistence farmers or sharecroppers. The abolition of slavery created a short-term labour shortage throughout the region that further exacerbated resentment against the British where it already existed.

Political Developments

The early British Governors of the Cape were autocrats, answerable only to the London government. Initially, there was little opposition within the colony to such a system. The colonial population was to a large extent used to this form of government, and the new economic policies of the administration gave it an amount of space within which to operate in the political sphere. However, such undemocratic means were slowly eroded as the twin demands of political reform and fairer representation grew. In this respect, the small increase in the number of

Britons resident in southern Africa was decisive; they were, after all, used to nominally democratic forms of government.

It took a considerable time for reform to occur. London was wary of giving away too much political power too soon, fearing that an autonomous southern African parliament would be difficult to influence and would become dominated by men hostile to the majority black population. There was support for such a stance within the Cape itself, as many liberals did not trust powerful ex-slave owners who had the means to dominate local political life under a supposedly more representative system.

However, authoritarian rule was never going to appeal to the liberals for very long and during the course of the early 1800s opposition to the local form of government became more pronounced. This was partly contained by the granting of certain concessions. In 1827, freedom of the press was granted following the earlier suppression of non-official publications. Shortly thereafter the right to political assembly was proclaimed.

The setting of precedents in other parts of the British empire had an impact on southern Africa. In 1840 a model for colonial self-government in two stages was instigated in Canada, with a representative assembly being followed after an appropriate period of time by a fully responsible, locally elected body. The implications of this development for the white settler society at the Cape were obvious.

The Canadian model was favoured in London for it afforded local men the time thought necessary to acquire basic parliamentary and administrative skills. The British were careful to ensure that this indeed happened, and so it was not until 1852 that the Cape was granted a representative form of government. Two houses of representation, an upper and a lower, came into existence, both elected by a franchise that was limited by income. In order to meet the franchise qualification, a man – for only men could vote – had to reside permanently in a property worth a minimum of £25 and earn £50 per annum. In theory there were no racial restrictions on the franchise.

Representative government worked well and effectively did little to alter the real structures of power in the colony. British political paramountcy remained in place as the Cape government stayed loyal.

Indeed, the local administration was happy with the set-up and reluctant to accept fully responsible government when the time came, for this meant not only greater accountability, but also more expenditure across a region that was increasingly volatile. Nevertheless in 1872, the Cape administration was forced to accept responsible government. A liberal, non-racial constitution was enacted, following a British government pronouncement that stated:

> All Her Majesty's subjects at the Cape, without distinction of class or colour, should be united by one bond of loyalty and common interest, and we believe that the exercise of political rights enjoyed by all alike will prove one of the best methods of attaining this object.

However, only a few black or coloured residents of the Cape had sufficient means to qualify for the franchise and the fact that there was no theoretical colour bar to the corridors of power did not translate into practice. Between 1872 and 1909, when the Cape parliament was ended, only white representatives were ever returned. Some of the more liberal features of the constitution were also rolled back during the 1880s and 1890s.

The Great Trek

In the 1820s the Dutch-speaking population of the colony stood at 43,000, compared to 8,000 English-speakers. Under the circumstances, it was perhaps only natural that British reforms and pronouncements would cause a certain amount of resentment and that cleavages within white society at the Cape should open up. The Dutch-descended settlers, independently minded and used to living according to their own rules and within the precepts of their own belief systems, were very much vexed by what they saw as British interference in their lives. They disliked the imposition of English as the officially recognised language within the colony, thought legislation to protect the welfare of slaves was misguided, and were generally suspicious of British culture. The *trekboers*, who were now usually referred to simply as Boers, and whose own distinct Afrikaner culture was at an advanced stage of development, felt isolated from, and threatened by the British. This was not without longer-term political consequence.

Simmering resentment against British modes of rule boiled over in 1836 with the beginning of a mass migration of Boers away from the Cape and into the interior. Over the next six years, some 15,000 Afrikaners would join this exodus which differed in intention from any of the previous migrations of whites across southern Africa. It was a confusing occurrence, for the most part arduous, as families and communities packed up their belongings onto roughly constructed ox-wagons and headed in a north-easterly direction. Everything went with them including livestock and servants and chests crammed full of belongings, as the search for new homes and a new start out of the reach of formal British controls led the *trekkers* on to the veld and towards the region that would become known as Natal.

Those who went had certain traits in common. There were few professional men on the trek for professional men were able to make a good living under the British. Rather, those who went were mostly tradesmen, herders or agriculturalists, self-reliant and steady folk used to looking out only for themselves and their families. Most were churchmen, Calvinists of the Dutch Reformed Church, including some fundamentalists known as Doppers.

In essence, what became known as the Great Trek was an outright assertion of self-interest. There was a widespread feeling among the *trekkers* that British rule, despotic in nature, was infringing certain rights inherent to the burgher way of life. Since their arrival, the British had done nothing but meddle in local politics and the social sphere.

In some respects this was true. The British administration was far more organised than VOC rule. In consequence, some areas in which the Company had governed only ineffectively were rendered workable by the British. The example of land tenure is pertinent to those who joined the trek. Previously, rents due to the state from farms had gone unpaid for years or, in numerous cases, had never been paid at all. The British put in place procedures to regulate land tenure and tried to claw back monies owed. This was widely resented by *trekboers* who saw it as a direct attack on their right, their *God given* right, to land and pasture.

On another level, the Boers were perturbed by the increasing competition in the agricultural trade that resulted from the opening up of southern Africa to greater commercialism. They also disliked the British approach to matters such as education, and felt uncomfortable with British legal procedures and courts. Many believed their religion to be under attack from the demonopolisation of the Dutch Reformed Church throughout the Cape (although the Dutch church itself did not condone the trek). Another point of contention was the reforms to the structures of government, which left the Boers without any genuine representation, either at regional or colony-wide level. In the minds of many thousands, all of this added up to a concerted attack on a hitherto unfettered way of life.

The emancipation of slaves was the last straw for many, an act that symbolised all that was wrong with British rule. Most Boer farmers were entirely dependent for their livelihood on the use of indentured labour. This they justified as being part of the natural order of things: blacks were simply lesser beings than whites, never to be placed on an equal footing. Emancipation ran contrary to this distinction which, it was held, was ordained by God. Of course, such thinking was often used to justify the maltreatment of slaves. It was difficult to convince some of the very irrationality that underpinned this strongly held belief; it was part and parcel of their cultural make up, socially acceptable and defensible on quasi-religious grounds. The abolition of slavery was also proof positive that life had been better before the advent of British dominion of the Cape.

So, many Boer communities decided to escape from the perceived injustices of British rule, feeling they had been left with no other choice. Economically weak, politically voiceless and socially fractured in their isolated settlements, any kind of uprising against the administration would have been a hopeless cause. The decision was made, therefore, to head into the interior in an attempt to regain lost liberties.

Not all of the *trekkers* were idealistically motivated. Many joined the exodus because it afforded the opportunity of escaping from debts and creditors; most were in some kind of economic trouble. However, all who left the Cape during this time believed that they would be better off when their journey came to a halt. Some were motivated purely by the hope of finding suitable pasture, which was increasingly in short supply in and around the Cape, and others, by the desire to start up their own viable farming interests. There were those who were determined to claim large tracts of land which they later hoped to sell off at a substantial profit. Almost all of the participants in the trek believed they would find what they were looking for. Most thought they would simply move on to and occupy vacant plots. Those who understood that much land would already be in use saw no good reason why they could not come to an agreement that would allow them the space they sought.

There were four separate paths out of the colony followed by parties of *trekkers*, each starting from a different place. One of these was led by Piet Retief (1780–1838). A popular yet unimposing figure within the Boer community, Retief had worked as a builder prior to setting up as a cattle farmer. Before leaving from Grahamstown he published a declaration. In this, he spoke on behalf of those following his lead, stating:

> We are resolved, wherever we go, that we will uphold the just principle of liberty; but whilst we will take care that no one shall be in a state of slavery, it is our determination to maintain such regulations as may suppress crime and preserve proper relations between master and servant... We quit this Colony under the full assurances that the English government ... will allow us to govern ourselves without its interference.

Retief's resolution, couched in moderate terms, reflected his belief that the authorities of the Cape had acted erroneously in respect of racial relations. The only way of addressing this situation was to go far away, to a place where the Boers could govern themselves in accordance with their own susceptibilities.

The trek was slow and patchy, characterised by human hardships of the worst kind. Typically, a convoy might cover as much as five miles a day, but often the pace of the trek was dictated by the availability of water and good pasture. Some groups of *trekkers* were well organised, at least to begin with. Others parties found themselves enveloped in chaos and moved without either much direction or conviction. Most *trekkers* were quickly disabused of the notion that they were moving into a country of plenty. Lands would be settled and temporary communities established, but mostly these were contested by indigenous peoples. Problems arose over the Boers' determination to assert ownership over land, rather than settling for mere occupancy. This led to almost perpetual conflict in places, but also had the effect of forcing groups of *trekkers* into tighter, more cohesive units. A *trekker* victory against the Ndebele in 1836 at the Battle of Veg Kop – in retaliation for a trek party being prevented from pushing northward – resulted in some 400 Ndebele casualties but only two for the Boers. This was immediately interpreted as a sign of divine intervention and another justification for the righteousness of the trek.

A number of settlements sprang up in the south-western corner of the Transvaal area, the largest being Potchefstroom, founded in 1837. Other smaller groups found themselves settled in more vulnerable areas, east and north from this point. The majority of *trekkers*, however, concentrated themselves in the Natal region. Hemmed in by the Indian Ocean on one side and the Drakensberg Mountains to the north, Natal was home to the formidable Zulu nation. It was a far from easy ride into the area but this was nevertheless where Retief led his party. Once there, the Boers struggled to establish themselves in an area where there was little free land and, as so it turned out, little hope of accommodation with local African societies that were well organised and defensive of their property and trading links.

Nevertheless, the region was favoured by many Boer leaders. The land was fertile and suitable for settlement and the sea offered excellent trading opportunities. Both facts encouraged men like Retief to believe that they had found their promised land. The Zulus, however, had other ideas. Their chief, Dingane, was approached by Retief, who wished to negotiate a mutually beneficial land agreement. Dingane, the younger half-brother of Shaka, was a fickle and somewhat arrogant despot, adept at manipulating his friends and foes alike as a means of getting his own way. He was especially ambivalent towards the white man and was both suspicious of the *trekboers* and alarmed by their arrival in such large numbers. Aware that a neighbouring state of white settlement might well threaten his power and influence, Dingane refused to grant any land concessions to the Boers. Retief, having come so far, was determined to

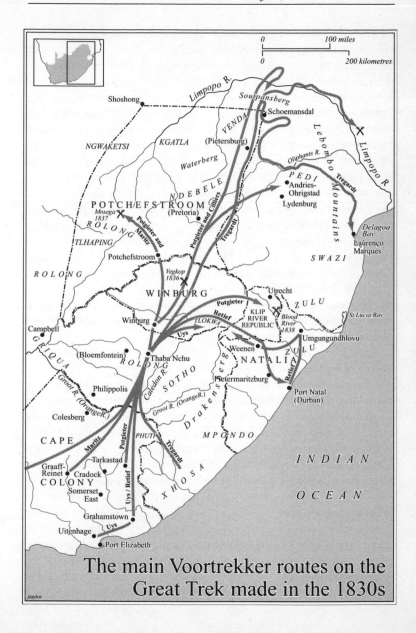

The main Voortrekker routes on the
Great Trek made in the 1830s

negotiate a formal and enduring settlement with the Zulus and continued his quest for favourable terms.

SLAUGHTER AND REPRISAL

Conflict between Dingane and Retief became inevitable once *trekkers* started to rustle Zulu cattle. Retief attempted to head this off and return 300 head of cattle to the Zulu chief, believing that such a gesture would open up the way for a negotiated settlement. However, the demeanour of Retief's party, who were openly armed and increasingly agitated, served merely to heighten Dingane's suspicions and he decided to eliminate the Boer leader and his followers.

In February 1838 the two men met at Dingane's kraal of Umgungundhlovu, 'the Place of the Elephant'. Retief brought with him a contract that, he believed, once signed by Dingane, would bind him to recognise Boer land claims. The piece of paper meant nothing to Dingane. He happily signed the agreement. Once this had been done, Retief and his men let down their guard and Dingane had them shackled and taken to his place of execution. Here, Retief and his party, which totalled 100 including thirty black servants, were executed one at a time.

Thereafter, Dingane chose to pursue a strategy of annihilation as a means of dealing with the influx of new white settlers. A Boer camp on the Tugela River was ambushed and razed to the ground, resulting in the killing of some 281 Boers, nearly 200 of whom were children, and a further 200 servants. Thirty-five thousand head of cattle and sheep were carried off. The Zulu army then turned its attention to the small, white settlement of Port Natal, burning it to its foundations. Dingane then attacked two strong Boer commando units that had gathered in the interior, defeating one and sending another fleeing on to the highveld. The surviving Boers concentrated themselves close to the smouldering site of Port Natal.

Immediate calls to avenge the Zulus were not heeded until reinforcements were sent in number from the Cape. These duly arrived in November 1838. A wealthy and stubborn farmer from the Graaff-Reinet district, Andries Pretorious (1798–1853), assumed control of training a commando fit to beat the Zulus. Composed in the main of

The Zulu king, Dingane

Boers, the unit was joined by some Englishmen from Port Natal and a number of Khoi-San and local African allies.

The coming battle, Pretorious told the commando, was a holy war against a heathen enemy. Confidence was high and an oath of allegiance was sworn beforehand in which it was affirmed that the day of victory would be forever kept as a holy day. Revenge was to be exacted methodically and in proportion to the earlier massacres.

Pretorious drew his force into a defensive camp on the Ncome River. Protected by the steep banks of the river, he ordered his men to draw their wagons into a circle (or *laager*), a tactic that had previously worked to such good effect at the Battle of Veg Kop, affording them the means of thwarting any Zulu advances. Dingane was provoked by the camp and decided to attack the commando in early December 1838, feeling justly confident that numerical superiority would bring him a decisive victory that would finally drive the Boers from the region.

The chief had miscalculated on a number of levels, however. His army had no means of attacking the formidable defences of the *laager*, and the Boers' gunfire was especially effective at picking off row after row of Zulus. Furthermore, even those attacking units that could escape the torrent of bullets could not negotiate the river banks, and so were thwarted as they attempted to approach the camp. An estimated 3,000 Zulus are believed to have died that fateful day, falling heaped up in a ditch that ran parallel to the Ncome. The conflict became known as the Battle of Blood River so red was the water stained. There were no Boer casualties recorded.

This was a turning point on the Great Trek, an event much mythified but which nevertheless held out hope that viable new settlements could be established away from the Cape. Blood River also confirmed to many of the *trekkers* the righteousness of their mission, as the victory was seen as ordained through God's own will. In the aftermath of the battle, fresh waves of *trekkers* headed into Natal, or tried their luck across the Orange River.

The Zulu nation was split by the defeat. Dingane attempted to deflect from the tragedy by attacking the Swazi, but this did not work in his favour and he was forced to flee when his brother Mpande (1798–1872) led a rebellion against his rule. Further in-fighting lessened the ability of the Zulus effectively to resist white incursions into their territory. Afrikaners exploited the opportunities which this presented to them, establishing themselves on farms and forming themselves into cohesive communities. This had the effect of forcing Africans off the land or into inequitable tenant relationships with white settlers who, increasingly, occupied land on a large scale. Perhaps the major consequence of the Great Trek, aside from the further subjugation of African polities, was the mass increase of the area of southern Africa now settled and effectively controlled by white people.

THE MYTH OF THE GREAT TREK

In the early twentieth century the Great Trek assumed its place at the heart of the pantheon of Afrikaner nationalism. It was discussed as a purely ideological flight from persecution, symbolic of all the hardship and struggles inherent in the evolution of the Afrikaner race. Few Afrikaners questioned the fact that it was a seminal event in their history.

However, the reality was very different. The trek was not an exclusively Boer affair. About a third of the estimated total of participants were black, and along the way, various *trekker* parties were assisted by Khoi-San or African tribes such as the Rolong. A number of Britons also joined Boer commandos or offered protection to *trekker* groups in times of need. More pertinently, perhaps, this was not the mass migration of an entire culture, as suggested by the mythologists. Only a minority, perhaps not even one-third, of the Afrikaner community actually left the Cape. It was only the poor and dispossessed who left, while the majority were happy enough to stay living under the British administration. Eventually, in years to come, they would assume political control of the Cape.

The Emergence of Natal, the OFS and the Transvaal

As the *trekker* parties moved further away from the Cape, into vast tracts of lands populated by enormous herds of wild animals that were often thousands strong, there followed in their wake traders and missionaries who would take the same tracks pioneered by the Boer parties. The influence of both groups was to have a decisive effect on the development of southern Africa over the next thirty years.

The traders established trading routes and markets as the interior was opened up and linked to the major centres of commerce at Cape Town, and on the coast at Port Natal and Port Elizabeth. This boosted local industries that were invested in as a means of meeting the growing needs of the export market. Two industries in particular flourished in the middle to late 1800s. Wool exports rose ten-fold between 1845 and the late 1860s, as more farmers turned to sheep rearing in the eastern Cape and Natal. The demand for hunting products such as ivory and skins also spiralled, to be met by a determined breed of men who worked with improving technology and ever more ruthlessness in their search for exotic commodities that could fetch a high price in Europe and America. Vast tusks, imported into the Cape by rugged Boers or African hunters, would be sold on at a handsome profit prior to export. Officers of the Indian army meanwhile, throughout the middle to late 1800s, were stopping off at southern Africa in increasing numbers to indulge a seemingly insatiable appetite for big game hunting – a pastime that would thrive well into the twentieth century before its ecological consequences were fully realised.

The missionaries often smoothed the path of traders through their efforts to spread European culture and influence. More mission stations were opened up offering solace for tribes unsettled by the further extension of communities of white settlement. Convert numbers remained low and many missionaries did more harm than good simply because they had little genuine understanding of the people they were dealing with, or the conditions that had forced them on to the stations in the first place. Nevertheless, the influence of the missions spread, as the Bible was translated into more vernacular languages, and great efforts were made to educate Africans in European values. A few missionaries spurned dogma, working instead towards righting perceived injustices and helping African societies come to terms with the new settler communities.

NATAL

In the immediate aftermath of the Battle of Blood River, some 6,000 Afrikaners are believed to have headed for Natal. The Cape administration chose to stand back from the situation for fear of provoking further conflict. Instead, it left the *trekkers* to their own devices.

The area was divided into districts, each with its own commando militia and local council (overseen by a magistrate) which were both there to enforce the law. Each Boer family was entitled to settle a portion of land. A claim would be made, after which a certificate of ownership would be issued by the district magistrate. A commission would then inspect the farm to make sure that its tenancy was not disputed, before granting a deed. Only then would rent be payable to the government. This was a far from simple process. Often, a claim would be lodged to a parcel of land that was then left unoccupied. Others would later lay another claim to a part or all of the land, resulting in disputes over the deed. Demarcating lines between properties were also often less than clear, leading to further confusion.

Nevertheless, the region became subject to white control relatively quickly. Although it was for a long time bereft of a powerful, central authority, a constitution was agreed upon in 1839 by a body of twenty-four elected men, known as the *volksraad* (or people's council). In the following year, the Afrikaner republic of Natalia was declared and immediately recognised by the Cape colony, which was keen to foster good relations with the new state as a means of maintaining an informal interest in the region.

Although elected by a white male franchise, the *volksraad* did not have unconditional support. Pretorious disliked the constitution and powers bestowed upon the *volksraad* and clashed with its members early on. He withdrew his support for the body and many others chose to follow his lead. Furthermore, the *volksraad* had no effective means of bringing the Boers under control. The experiences of the trek had done nothing to diminish their strong-headedness, and so, Natalia was a disorderly place, where the local authorities found it difficult to impose their will or any regulations they chose to enact.

Natalia was a racially divided state and Africans had little chance of thriving within its loosely defined boundaries. They had no rights to citizenship which were reserved for people of European descent (specifically, Cape-born Dutch speakers) and so no means of entering into the political decision-making process. Furthermore, African claims to land were almost always overlooked and their right to occupancy was liable to be overturned. Afrikaner rights to land usage, meanwhile, were asserted by force if necessary, and the local black population was subjugated on to the new farms as waged labourers. A system of pass laws was quickly introduced and imposed on the African population of Natalia. As a means of creating a sufficiently large pool of labour to work the land, legislation was enacted which was aimed at forcing blacks on to the farms.

The British administration of the Cape was uneasy about all such developments, which ran contrary to its prevailing philosophy of establishing more equality between the different races of southern Africa. This unease grew with time, as more Africans headed towards the republic in the wake of the dislocation caused by Mpande's rebellion against Dingane. While the British had been happy for the *trekkers* to establish their own republic they were perturbed by their bullying tactics in relation to the local black population. It was feared that slavery would be imposed on Africans who, in the eyes of the British at the Cape, were and would remain subjects of the Queen.

Perhaps more worryingly, the existence of the republic posed a potential threat to the small British trading community centred on Port Natal since the 1820s. Cape strategists also had concerns about the fact that Natalia had clear access to the sea, a possible future threat to British naval interests along the coast of southern Africa. A watchful eye was therefore kept on the early development of the republic. It became increasingly clear that the Cape government, acting on instruction from the home government, would intervene if the Natalians behaved in a manner likely to destabilise the region or the security of British interests in southern Africa in any way.

It was not long before just such a course of action became necessary. In 1841, Africans migrating into the republic were challenged by local commandos, acting at the behest of the *volksraad*. The recently introduced pass laws had quickly turned a labour shortage into a labour surplus and the Natalian government felt compelled to remove this new influx from its jurisdiction. A 'reserve' was set aside to the south, on lands settled by the Mpondo people. This act stirred up much resentment among those being forced to move on to the reserve, and there was every chance that the Mpondo would fight in defence of their territory.

This was too much for the Cape government. In 1842 British recognition of Natalia was withdrawn and a small force despatched to protect Port Natal, shortly to be known as Durban, and aid the Mpondo in defence of their land. These developments confirmed the

Natalians' worst fears, namely, that the British were once again going to subject them to *their* laws and customs.

Having come so far, the *volksraad* was not prepared to let this happen. A Boer force encircled Durban, which had still not fully recovered from Dingane's previous attack, and put the port under siege. British military detachments could do little to assist the settlement, and it was only after reinforcements arrived from the Cape that the Boers were forced into submission. Thereafter, the Cape annexed the republic, renamed it Natal, and swept aside the flimsy Afrikaner government. British strategic and commercial interests in the region had been safe-guarded. Military efforts were then stepped up to secure Natal for the British. Although the *volksraad* continued to meet until 1845, it had ever less authority, as Boers reacted once more to the arrival of British rule by heading out of the republic.

Over the next few years they would be replaced by British migrants who started to drift into Natal from the Cape. With these men came financial investment by the Cape government and further speculation in land. This generated an economic boom across the region in the 1850s which most benefited local wool farmers. Maize production throughout the region was extended on the back of this upturn and was followed by the end of the decade by the establishment of a sugar plantation industry.

FURTHER AFRIKANER DISPERSALS

Those Afrikaners who left the Natal region headed out on to the veld. Here, they became scattered across a wide region, ranging from the Orange River in the south to the Soutpansberg Mountains, hundreds of miles to the north. There were concentrations of Boer settlements, notably around Potchefstroom, the Winburg colony, and in the region of the southern Caledon River. For the most part, however, families lived in small isolated villages and attempted to establish themselves as farmers.

These settlements rarely enjoyed much sense of stability. There were clashes everywhere with chiefdoms over pasture; with the Pedi, Venda and Ndebele to the north, and with the Sotho and Griqua community to the south. With conflict over pasture came a whole array of other disputes and skirmishes, most notably over cattle. This disrupted trade routes across the region and left many people unable to sustain themselves adequately.

The more isolated Boer communities became, the harder it was for them to put down roots as safety could only be had in numbers. The further north settlers went, the more difficult it became for them to obtain, and then maintain, grazing lands. Only where Afrikaners were concentrated, as at Potchefstroom, were they able to settle effectively. South of the colony of Winburg, the Boers came into conflict with Moshoeshoe's Sotho, a fight that became more devastating the longer it went on. However, here too, *trekkers* were more prevalent and so better placed to sustain such a campaign.

AN UNSTABLE INTERIOR

The annexation of Natal may have solved a particular set of problems for the Cape government. However, the resolution was not absolute. Those Boers who now chose to migrate once more took with them the same desires to live an unfettered way of life. The threats inherent in this, to British trading interests and the majority black population of southern Africa, still remained. It soon became clear that the logic applied by the Cape government in Natal would also have to be applied elsewhere across the region.

The trick now was to uphold peace in the interior while keeping costs in check. As a means to this end, the imperial government sent more administrators to the Cape, and then in the early 1840s, developed a system of treaty agreements. These treaties tied independent African states such as the Griqua and the Sotho to friendly relations with the Cape colony. The treaties were administered by locally based British agents, who could also keep a watchful eye on the emerging colonies of white settlement. The system was designed to keep to a minimum the need for direct military intervention in the interior, which was a costly drain on resources that the Cape governors wished to avoid.

Following conflict between Boer migrants and the Griqua community, the first resident British agent was established at Bloemfontein in 1846, on land purchased from a Cape farmer. This area, sandwiched between the Orange and Vaal Rivers, was much disputed and the British agent was not able to improve the situation. It was left to the swashbuckling Harry Smith to try to impose a settlement. Following the annexation of British Kaffraria (see above, p. 65), Smith immediately headed northwards, determined to quell the unrest across the Orange River. It did not take him long to reach the conclusion that the situation was intractable. In 1848, he therefore chose to annex the entire region to the Cape, impulsively and with little thought for the fact that this ran contrary to his paymasters' designs.

This was the Orange River Sovereignty, an area approximating in size to England, and incorporating numerous chiefdoms both large and small. The British aimed at reaching accommodation with all of these in pursuit of their stated aim of protecting them from further *trekker* aggression. To the Boers this was a highly provocative gesture. A thousand-strong force, led by Pretorious, attacked the British agent in Bloemfontein, forcing him to retreat towards the Cape. Smith reacted by raising a force to meet Pretorious head on. The clash at Boomplats resulted in Pretorious and his men being pushed back across the Vaal River.

None of this was welcomed at the Cape or by the colonial administration in London who saw in the annexation nothing but added (and unnecessary) expenditure and responsibility. Nevertheless, Smith's act amounted to something of a *fait accompli* and was reluctantly accepted. However, this was merely the beginning of a whole new chapter of problems. The British were unable to put into place an adequate system of administration, and so struggled to impose either their will or the rule of law. Investors were further put off by the instability that characterised the region. In this part of southern Africa frontier law prevailed. The trade in firearms was rife; the chosen weapon of defence, for Boers and Africans alike, was the gun. This further undermined the British in their quest to bring the region to heel.

The local British agency set about demarcating the sovereignty into districts in the hope of establishing clear boundaries between tribal and settler areas of pasture. This became almost impossible to police. Settlers continued to try to establish large farms in the region, taking no notice of district lines. Different African communities, notably Moshoeshoe's Sotho, recognised boundaries only when it suited them and all the communities had a tendency to stray over the limits of their own areas. There was then much resistance to a policy that was practically ignored by those whom it was designed to control. Moshoeshoe became increasingly resistant to the Sotho incorporation into the sovereign territory, a stance that brought the entire treaty system into question. One British agent was withdrawn from the region, tired and beaten and his successor had no better luck in bringing stability to the sovereignty. The Sotho adopted a concerted policy of raiding Boer farms and homesteads and the situation became increasingly dangerous. By the early 1850s, the patience of the British was running short.

The British Withdraw

In a piecemeal fashion, the British decided to renege on their responsibilities in the Orange River Sovereignty, and at the same time in the area north of the Vaal River – commitments enshrined in the treaty system.

Across the Vaal River, the Boers had set up a *volksraad* in 1849. This body was dogged by dissent and in-fighting in its formative phase but, nevertheless, the first steps towards the formation of a cohesive white settler state had been taken. Following the defeat at Boomplats, it was to this region that Pretorious migrated, and when the time came to negotiate with the British, he was able to exploit prevailing Boer disagreements and assert himself as the senior representative of this community. He met with agents of the Orange River Sovereignty in 1852 at the Sand River. The ensuing convention cemented a British withdrawal of responsibilities north of the Vaal River.

In exchange for a guarantee of free trade, the British gave to the Boers of the region 'the right to manage their own affairs without any interference on the part of the British government'. The British further agreed to retreat from 'all alliances whatever and with whomsoever of the coloured nations to the north of the Vaal River'. In effect, the British had given the settlers a free hand to deal with the black population of the area.

Although the Convention was never formally ratified, the British government had by the terms of the agreement recognised the independence of a new state in the Transvaal, known to the Boers who ran it as the South African Republic (SAR). Here, they would have the scope not only to govern themselves freely without any unwanted interference but, more pertinently, could enact in law the philosophies central to their very existence. Needless to say, this was to result in direct conflicts with local chiefdoms, notably the Tswana, who bitterly resisted subjugation and assimilation into the settler polity.

Two years later a similar arrangement was reached over the Orange River Sovereignty. The British agent at Bloemfontein met with representatives of the local Afrikaner population and relinquished formal control over the region. A trade arrangement was followed by the abandonment of all treaties with black rulers north of the Orange with the one exception of the Griqua community headed by Adam Kok (1811–75), maintained as a sort of buffer state ally. The state which emerged in 1854 from this convention was known as the Orange Free State (OFS).

The British withdrawal from formal involvement beyond the boundaries of the Cape colony was thus completed in a few short years. This had been achieved at the expense of previous promises that were made in order to ensure the fair treatment of African peoples across the whole of southern Africa. This ideal had proved almost impossible to put into practice in the face of Afrikaner hostility, and so was sacrificed in favour of agreements that served to uphold essential commercial interests.

If this was a grand design it initially worked out to Britain's advantage. Both the SAR and the OFS were heavily dependent upon the Cape colony and the ports of Natal for trade in a variety of goods. Most importantly of all for the white settlers, all firearms and ammunition had to be secured through the Cape. But the states were also dependent on the British for foodstuffs, cloth and other domestic commodities.

Longer-term issues hampered the early phases of both governments. They had problems enforcing the law, were administratively ineffectual, and had relatively little control over the lands which they occupied. However, in both cases, theoretical control was established over local Boer populations, as well as the means of dominating smaller African societies. The larger African states, however, for the time being maintained control over their land and established trading links, bringing into question the overall effectiveness of early settler state rule.

In outlook, the early leaders of the SAR were conservative men and this reflected upon settler society. For years the SAR was left in a chronic state of underdevelopment, bereft of an infrastructure and without the most basic of amenities. There were no towns of note. Rather, most people continued to settle in small village communities, isolated and often miles from their nearest neighbours. There was little for people to do. Religion remained central to the lives of almost all settlers and small churches sprang up across the region, acting as the focus for all social activity. There were few educational opportunities as schools simply did not exist, and there were no libraries.

Politically, the SAR was shut off from the outside world and characterised by a degree of inconsistency. To become a citizen of the emerging republic, one had to pass a series of strict criteria pertaining to religious and ideological belief. Even if these were met, acceptance would come only slowly, if at all. Nor was there much semblance of democracy. Despite a weighty constitution made up of 232 articles, citizens had no basic guarantee of rights. The governing *volksraad* met only occasionally, and then could change laws unilaterally. This was a recipe for chaos, and unsurprisingly no one took much notice of new decrees or laws.

By contrast, the OFS rapidly evolved into a relatively stable society. A constitution, influenced by British traditions and loosely based on the American model, was introduced. This provided for equality before the law as well as freedom of the press and of political assembly. Blessed by a fertile environment, the state's economy rapidly evolved around agricultural practices and sheep and cattle farming. The OFS also benefited from the fact that many of its villages lay on the trade route to the north and so a number of markets and trading stations emerged across the region. Bloemfontein was built up as a thriving capital town, and educational institutions were opened there. Perhaps most significantly of all, in the 1850s and 1860s, the black and white communities reached a degree of understanding that allowed both to live in relative tranquillity, with each maintaining a modicum of independence over their lives.

By the late 1850s, a pattern of colonial settlement had emerged across southern Africa, with four colonies established throughout the region. Between these, there were several common bonds. Trade was the most important of all as it resulted in the development of an infrastructure of roads, bridges and mountain passes that linked the region. It also encouraged the development throughout the interior of numerous towns that acted as market and administrative centres. The establishment of the Afrikaner states also resulted in a compromise between the Boers and the British which, while it lasted, was to foster common interests and stimulate economic growth and social cohesion throughout the colonies.

The Shaping of the OFS, Transvaal and Natal

Over the next few years southern Africa enjoyed a short period of relative peace in consequence of the final defeat of the Xhosa, the temporary satiation of Sotho land desires (following a short war against the OFS in 1858), and a period of consolidation within the Zulu nation. There were still conflicts between whites and African polities over land and cattle, but on a relatively manageable scale. The abeyance of Afrikaner–British tensions further helped to stabilise the region.

It was during this time that the new settler states of the SAR and the OFS began to establish themselves as viable institutions. From the British government's point of view this fundamentally solved a whole host of problems that involvement in the interior had created. There had never existed a strong desire to have formal influence in southern Africa outside the Cape. With the withdrawal from the interior complete they could now focus their attention wholly on the Cape.

The experience of involvement away from the Cape colony had shown the British that they had little to gain but much to lose from becoming involved in regions that were costly to administer and beset by conflict. The path they chose to pursue from the early 1850s amounted to a compromise with the Boers. In return for recognition of the two new republics, the Afrikaners fully acknowledged the Cape colony and the British right to be there. This agreement was hedged to favour wider British interests. By allowing the SAR and OFS the freedom to govern as they wished the peoples within their own borders, the British assumed control of the external defences of both states. Britain also had enormous influence over their respective foreign policies. Moreover, British economic and trading influence across the whole of southern Africa was not threatened. This is not to suggest that Anglo-Boer rivalries disappeared entirely; there were still frictions between the communities and these would come to the surface intermittently. In the main, however, the compromise that existed between the settler states and the British endured for some years.

In the early 1860s there were two significant developments that, in time, affected the whole of southern Africa. One pertained to the entrenchment of racism in the settler states, and moves to segregate Africans to their own separate land holdings in Natal. The other revolved around the joint economy of the region, which went through a period of diversification and, for the first time, began to attract foreign investment. The two matters were linked by the question of land.

Investment was not yet on a large scale as many foreign banks were still wary of a region that was unstable and had no apparent natural or exploitable resources. However, it was clear that there was a profit to be had from agricultural ventures. Thus, wool production in Natal and the Cape, wheat production in the OFS, and tobacco cultivation in the SAR, all attracted backing which served to boost an economy otherwise sluggish in terms of growth.

New industries were also developed. Taking advantage of the humid coastal climate particular to Natal, large-scale plantations were started by Cape merchants keen to diversify into new markets. Sugar production was by far the most successful plantation venture, mostly due to the fact that it was worked by indentured labourers, imported from India on short contracts that paid very little. From here sprang a new southern African culture. Most of the Indian men and women who arrived in Natal in the 1860s were low caste Hindus from Madras. When their contracts expired after five years many chose not to return home, but to stay on and create a new life for themselves in Africa.

Throughout the four colonies, land was still the basis of both power and the economy. Much land was owned by absentee landlords, or held by speculator companies. Many absentee landowners found it more profitable to rent out their land to African farmers, who would use it to suit themselves. Many found this to be more profitable than engaging in arduous agricultural work.

In the Transvaal and the OFS, a system known as sharecropping or 'farming-on-the-halves' emerged, whereby poor white farmers would rent out to an African tenant a proportion of their holding in return for a high percentage of the sharecropper's harvest. This allowed for a diversification of crops and gave to the land holder access to crops he did not have to produce himself. The sharecropper, meanwhile, would hopefully produce enough to sustain himself and his family, selling off to local traders any surpluses that were generated.

Africans and settlers were learning to co-operate and co-exist with each other. However, both of the Boer republics were societies built upon racist ideals (the SAR more so than the OFS). In both states, political power remained a white-only domain. Both rejected the example of the recently introduced Cape system of representative government, which had an open franchise and, in theory at least, an equality of opportunity in the political sphere. Indeed, to some degree, the OFS and SAR both gave constitutional expression to racist ideas and enshrined in law the denial of basic political rights to blacks. Article 9 of the SAR constitution stated that 'the people desire to permit no equality between coloured people and white inhabitants, either in church or state'. Such discrimination was more blunted in the OFS, but existed nonetheless. In both republics, discriminatory measures were established early on as a fact of everyday life.

In Natal, a colour-blind franchise was introduced by the British in 1856, when responsible government was extended through the region. However, despite influxes of British immigrants, the Natal white community was far less liberal in outlook than its Cape counterpart. Here, the settlers had no time for the ideal of equality, and resisted all measures introduced by the British to protect African interests. Racist attitudes were as clearly discernible at the surface of Natal society as they were in the Boer republics. The locals organised themselves to

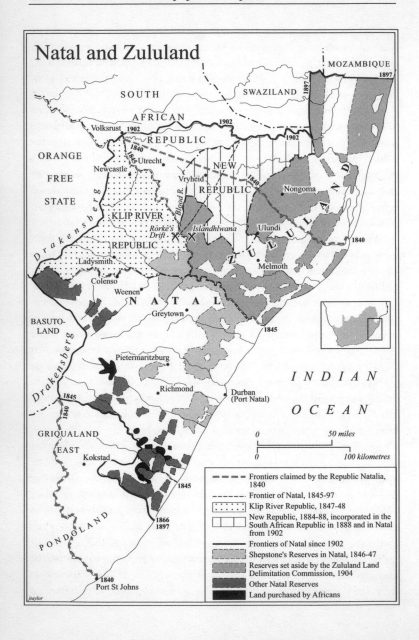

Natal and Zululand

MOZAMBIQUE
1897

SOUTH

AFRICA

SWAZILAND

Volksrust 1902

REPUBLIC

1902

1902

ORANGE

1840

Utrecht

NEW

FREE

Newcastle

Vryheid

REPUBLIC

Nongoma

STATE

KLIP RIVER

Rórke's
Drift   Islandhlwana

Ulundi

1840

REPUBLIC

Ladysmith

Melmoth

Colenso

Weenen

N A T A L

Greytown

1845

Pietermaritzburg

I N D I A N

Richmond

Durban
(Port Natal)

O C E A N

GRIQUALAND

1845

EAST

Kokstad

0   50 miles

1845   0   100 kilometres

1866
1897

- – – – Frontiers claimed by the Republic Natalia,
         1840
- - - - - Frontier of Natal, 1845-97

P O N D O L A N D

Klip River Republic, 1847-48

New Republic, 1884-88, incorporated in the
South African Republic in 1888 and in Natal
from 1902

Frontiers of Natal since 1902

1840   Shepstone's Reserves in Natal, 1846-47

Port St Johns   Reserves set aside by the Zululand Land
                  Delimitation Commission, 1904

Other Natal Reserves

Land purchased by Africans

jtaylor

oppose local African polities and, in the early 1860s, to campaign against the arrival of migrant labourers from South Asia.

Ultimately, the local white settlers had their way. In the 1860s laws were passed excluding blacks from the franchise. A crude system of pass controls, applicable to all Africans, was introduced shortly thereafter, but this was not far-reaching enough. The settler population of a few thousand wished to exclude the tens of thousands of Africans of Natal from the best lands, which had already been parcelled out among the white population. Bowing to just such pressure, the Natalian administration introduced southern Africa's first officially sanctioned segregationist scheme.

The architect of this programme was Theophilus Shepstone (1817–93), Natal's Secretary for Native Affairs. The son of missionary workers, Shepstone had migrated to southern Africa from England in the early nineteenth century. A talented linguist and administrator, he was employed as an interpreter during the settler–Xhosa conflicts of the 1830s before becoming the resident agent for Native Affairs in Natal in 1845. The system that was to bear his name, which he developed after being promoted to the position of Secretary in 1856, allowed for the separate administration of Africans, according to their own customs and traditions, in specially set aside 'reserves'. Shepstone believed that Africans should be allowed to live by their own laws and unfettered by the rule of the white man (the colonial administration did, however, attempt to outlaw witch-killings and other traditions it found 'repugnant'). This was convenient inasmuch as it justified the removal of local communities resident on lands claimed by settlers.

The reserved lands were not of the best quality, but totalled nearly two million acres, enough it was thought to allow for comfortable subsistence farming. The administration of the reserves was paid for out of a locally raised hut tax on African homesteads, and implemented by tribal chiefs. These chiefs were subject to approval by Shepstone, who never hesitated to relieve unruly or unco-operative chiefs of their duties.

The scheme was defended on humanitarian grounds by Shepstone and others, who spoke of it as a way of protecting indigenous culture from the sometimes pernicious influences of European ways. In truth, it was a means of ensuring the dominance of a small minority population over a far larger majority. This reality was illustrated by the policing of the reserves, which criss-crossed Natal like a checkerboard. Strict curfews were maintained and the pass laws upheld to keep track of Africans outside of the locations. This was indeed a sinister harbinger of things to come.

CHAPTER FIVE

Diamonds, Gold, War: South Africa in the late nineteenth century

The economic advancement of southern Africa up to the later 1860s, had occurred only in fits and starts. Stable industries were in place prior to this time, such as wool, wine, wheat and sugar production, but these were mostly locally owned concerns. As previously noted, the region had trouble attracting foreign capital investors, and those who came were reluctant to stake too high a claim in a place that had a reputation for conflict and instability. Those British investors who endowed capital at the Cape in the early 1860s were impatient for a quick return. Their shuffling of money between banks resulted in a financial crisis that crippled twenty-eight Cape banking houses between 1863 and 1865.

One major deterrent to foreign investors was the fact that southern Africa seemingly had no exploitable stocks of valuable natural resources. There had been occasional gold rushes across the interior but these came to nothing. There was, in fact, much speculation over gold during the 1860s but this was to be overshadowed by the discovery of another rare and valuable commodity: diamonds.

This find greatly altered the course of southern African history. In the longer-term, diamonds were one part of an equation that, by the early twentieth century, had transformed the region from a disparate collection of neighbouring colonies, which varied in size and power, into a cohesive nation. Ruled as a British concern, this new state was politically united and run by the white minority in defence of their distinctive interests and to the detriment of the African majority. In the more immediate term, the mineral discovery was partly responsible for a change in the approach of the British government to southern Africa.

In the last decades of the nineteenth century, British colonial administrators slowly abandoned their preference for informal dominion, and instead adopted a more wholly interventionist approach towards their colonial possessions. In respect of the Cape this was to lead to a reversal of policy and a return to direct involvement in the interior.

There were a number of reasons, none exclusive of the other, for this new approach. In a wider context, imperial strategists became increasingly jittery about protecting existing colonies and trade routes. The way to India still needed securing, and in response the naval base at Simonstown on the very tip of the Cape peninsula was subject to heavy investment. There was also increasing competition in Africa from rival European states. By the final decade of the century there was a determination that the Germans in particular should not steal a march on trade with the southern African interior. Moreover, the re-emergence of the old conflicts over land and resources slowly but surely saw the Cape government drawn back into the politics of the interior. In this, it was partly concerned over the appalling treatment meted out by the Boer republics to Africans, and partly by an understanding that integration of the four colonies into a single political unit was the best means of achieving economic and social progress.

Without the discovery of diamonds and later, gold, it is impossible to say whether this desire to see a united southern African state would have emerged. The discovery of these two minerals in such large quantities across the interior, however, resulted in a shift in economic dominance, away from the Cape and towards the Boer states. British imperial agents were always likely to respond to such a chance.

Southern Africa Transformed

The so-called Mineral Revolution, the consequence of the discovery of diamonds and gold, totally transformed the face of southern Africa. The region was changed at every level, in town and country, among black and white, rich and poor. In the course of a few decades, the area developed a core industrial base. There was investment and infra-structural change on a scale that previously would have been unthinkable. The demands of capital and the need for labour tolerated no obstacle, physical or human. Those societies who stood in the way of the new order were defeated and brought under control. The landscape was forever changed, as armies of men and machinery cut into the earth's surface, going ever deeper in order to yield nature's riches.

Diamonds

Diamonds were discovered in 1867 at the point where the Harts River flows into the Vaal. So began the metamorphosis of southern Africa from a tired, somewhat quarrelsome region, into a major contributor to the world's economy, despite its internal political and social fractures.

The earliest excavations were limited to shallow digs, centred on the settlement of Klipdrift, on the north bank of the Vaal. The land of the diggings was contested, claimed not only by both Boer republics but also by the Griqua chief Nicholas Waterboer (1819–96). In 1870 local diggers joined forces and proclaimed their own government, intending to close off the trade to outsiders and further speculation. The British government pushed the Cape administration into exploring the legitimacy of all these claims, and if need be, to supersede them. This it was reluctant to do, but eventually in 1871, the administration annexed the territory, known as Griqualand West, to the Cape on the pretext of 'protecting' the Griqua from the Boers (in accordance with its earlier treaty with Adam Kok). The OFS, which believed it had legitimate claims to the site, was compensated by the sum of £90,000.

The first digs were quickly exhausted. As the miners went deeper into the earth, however, they discovered deeper-lying deposits. The fear spread that the diamond supply might run dry as nobody was yet sure just how deep the deposits were. So, in 1876, laws were introduced to restrict the size of individual claims and prevent the unbridled expansion of the industry.

The diggers encountered problems early on that slowed progress and required further capital investment. Primarily, the process of digging and sifting for diamonds was a laborious operation that required not only great patience but also a reliable and, preferably, cheap labour force. This could be raised from local African communities, but soon competition for such labour was high and wages were forced up. Furthermore, the deeper the digs went, the more dangerous and expensive they became. Walkways collapsed, pits flooded and pulleys snapped under the strain of their loads. Expensive machinery needed to be bought and then maintained, and advanced forms for processing digs, once introduced, gave advantages to those diggers who could invest in the newest technology. In such circumstances, only the strongest could survive, especially once an ancient volcanic deposit was uncovered (the Kimberley 'Big Hole'), suggesting that the supply of diamonds, if not inexhaustible, could be mined for some decades to come.

THE CHAOS OF KIMBERLEY

The spot on which the first diggers settled in rows of tents grew at a rapid rate into the town of Kimberley. Formed in the late 1860s, by the start of the following decade the town was the second largest in the whole of southern Africa, and temporarily accounted for some 80 per cent of the region's total exports.

This spectacular rate of growth was caused by an influx of migrants from the rest of southern Africa and abroad. By 1872, there were an estimated 50,000 people at Kimberley, the majority of whom were

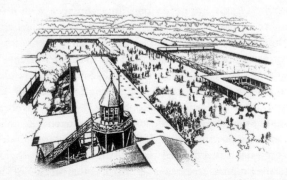

The De Beers compound at Kimberley with its watch tower, wire netting and the communal bath on the right

African labourers. In these early years, the town was governed according to 'diggers law', meaning there were no formal law enforcement agencies active in the area. Crime, especially robbery, was rife and murder not uncommon. Criminal gangs formed and organised local rackets that often revolved around bars and prostitution. Strong liquor offered the only form of entertainment to men used to a rugged existence.

Around this chaos there emerged a number of needs that were fed by the introduction of other industries. Railways were quickly constructed to ferry men and diamonds to and from the digs and bring consumer goods and food to the region. This greatly benefited the economies of neighbouring regions. Demolition and dynamite concerns established themselves and did well, as did engineers and wagon builders. Middlemen emerged to organise labour and broker work forces for deployment at the digs. A veritable array of tertiary industries evolved, providing clothing, alcohol, firewood and transportation facilities. The more cash that was generated at Kimberley, the more these industries proliferated. It was a boom economy and many exploited it while the going was good.

THE MINING MAGNATES

The most lucrative claims were quickly bought up by speculators with sufficient capital backing. There was a tendency for these to be taken over, in turn, by stock companies operating on a large scale and often backed by foreign investors. This was significant, for only miners with capital behind them could afford to compete at the mines after a few years. The deeper the digs went, the more costly the outlay became. Skilled labour had to be imported from abroad, from California, Australia or Europe, to fulfil specific roles at the mines. Earlier digs had to be shored up, an expensive undertaking if a plot had collapsed or been flooded. New chemical processes were introduced and machinery imported, again at enormous cost. The independents could not afford this and were gradually squeezed out.

The crunch for many arrived after 1875, when the world market became saturated and the price of diamonds began to plummet. The value of the stone was based on its rarity, but since the Kimberley discovery diamonds had become more commonplace. Many read the signs and sold up their interests while the going was good. Others, however, became stuck with claims that, however productive, looked unlikely to turn a working profit ever again. Many individuals chose this time to give up their plots to whoever would buy, others joined forces with fellow diggers and formed larger conglomerations, hoping to weather the downturn. Those smaller claimants who decided to sell were usually eager to get out as quickly as possible and a number of magnates were happy to relieve them of their pitches.

One such speculator was Cecil John Rhodes (1853–1902). One of the most powerful men of his time, Rhodes was an empire builder in more senses than one. He dreamed of annexing for Britain much of the rest of the world not already incorporated into the empire (including most of Africa and all of the United States). The son of a domineering clergyman, Rhodes was born in rural Hertfordshire. As a boy he suffered equally on the one hand from a stifling home life, and on the other from poor health. He was diagnosed as having tuberculosis when only sixteen years old. His brother had recently migrated to Natal, and on medical advice, Rhodes' parents decided that he too should head for Africa in an effort to be cured of the disease.

Rhodes' rise was meteoric, despite his being an awkward, somewhat immature youth. Before his twenty-fifth birthday he had earned millions from the diamond industry at Kimberley, a wealth he would later use to buy himself political power at the Cape as a means of furthering his increasingly pronounced political ambitions (he would assume the premiership of the Cape colony in 1890). Backed by wealthy European bankers – he would eventually earn the attention of the Rothschilds – Rhodes had set about buying disparate, seemingly worthless pitches whenever the opportunity arose. Over time, he accumulated enough claims to give him a substantial stake in the Kimberley mines. His virtual monopoly was confirmed in 1889 when he bought out his closest rival, Barney Barnato (1852–97). This left the way open for his company, De Beers Consolidated, to exploit the inevitable upturn in demand for diamonds. Rhodes also took over the marketing of Kimberley diamonds world-wide, ensuring that prices were not depreciated unnecessarily due to the market being flooded. De Beers also branched out into other areas of the industry, providing ice and pumping facilities to digging concerns. If Rhodes' strategy proved one thing, it was that the diamond industry could be run more efficiently by larger organisations.

LABOUR

The Kimberley boom created a massive demand for labour that was, initially at least, insatiable. People from all over southern Africa regardless of skin colour rushed to the digs, all hoping to turn a quick profit. More dedicated speculators arrived from further afield: Britain, Europe and the Americas. Only a percentage of these people had any kind of claim to a dig. The rest ended up labouring on terms dictated by the claim owners.

In the earliest days of the Kimberley digs Africans migrated to the region and entered into labouring contracts of their own accord. While the initial boom period lasted, the demand for labour outstripped availability, and so it was very much a seller's market. Good wages could be had on favourable terms, guaranteeing a tidy sum at the end of a contract. Furthermore, individual labourers could play one potential employer off against another in order to secure a better salary. People of the Pedi, Sotho and Tsonga tribes, the latter travelling from Mozambique, could earn up to 25 shillings per week cash. Most were happy to work for between three to six months, before returning home with most of their wage in their pocket.

With time this situation altered entirely. The downturn in the market that resulted in the mines being run both more efficiently and as a monopoly meant there were fewer labouring jobs to go around. Africans were still applying to work at Kimberley in their thousands, however, spurred on by the notion that easy money could be had. This created a surplus of labour which, in turn, led to a depreciation in wage levels.

This was not the only change. White workers resented competition from black workers, who had a tendency to undercut them in the job market. The demand was therefore voiced for the introduction of stringent controls over African workers. This hit a political chord, for the governments of the Boer republics, the Cape and Natal, all to some degree felt there was a need to stem the human flow towards Kimberley. In consequence, the diamond industry quickly became subject to racial divisions.

The first step was the introduction of worker passes which required labourers to register before commencing work at the mines. Fixed-term contracts, which practically could not be broken, were also made compulsory. While both of these measures were originally applied to *all* labour, regardless of colour, white workers were reluctant to comply with such edicts, and as it was whites who held the majority of skilled or semi-skilled jobs on site, the mine owners did not force the issue. However, both terms were strictly applied to Africans.

Security problems were to result in the housing of mine workers in compounds. This was a response to diamond smuggling, initially a relatively easy occupation and so a massive problem for the mine owners. As the mining companies were able to exert great authority throughout Kimberley, they dealt with smugglers on their own terms. Those caught would be locked up, placed in solitary confinement, and not released until they had excreted any diamonds they had swallowed. At first, the companies would strip search employees as they left the mines, but this procedure was easily circumnavigated and did little to decrease the illicit trade. When strip searches were stepped up in 1884 white workers went out on strike at what they perceived as unfair treatment. Thereafter, strip searches were confined to black workers.

In 1885, De Beers decided stricter measures were needed to overcome diamond smuggling and introduced compound housing. This was a most unpopular move. Although the compounds were designed to hold all mine labour, few whites would be housed in such a way. Once again, the issue was not forced. When black workers stopped work in protest, however, the strikers were summarily dismissed and replaced by new recruits. Thereafter, all black mine workers would live in closed quarters with their liberty mostly curtailed.

There were, of course, other benefits for the mine owners in having the majority of their labour force organised in this way. They had almost complete control over workers' lives. In a political sense, potential problems could be closely monitored: agitators could be picked off and protest movements curtailed before they spread. There were also financial advantages to the compounds. Accommodation costs were low and food could be provided more cheaply, yet a percentage of every wage could be deducted for these provisions. The compounds also provided the means of strictly disciplining the African work force. The De Beers compound bore a close resemblance to a prison. It had a watchtower, high fences and netting surrounds to prevent diamonds being thrown out of the site. Conditions were appalling. Those who lived within the parameters of the compound were, in fact, treated no better than common criminals.

By the late 1880s, the division of the diamond industry along racial lines was complete. While Africans were confined to working in unskilled jobs for decreasing wages, whites were working almost exclusively in 'skilled' jobs as technicians, engineers, foremen or machine operators. For this, they commanded higher wages and the respect of the bosses. Increasingly organised, white workers demanded protection for their status and a colour bar to thwart the progress of blacks at the mines. This they achieved through the manipulation of prejudices prevalent at the time throughout Kimberley and, more generally, southern Africa.

Despite these worsening conditions, black migrant workers continued to seek employment at Kimberley. In the twenty-five years from 1871, hundreds of thousands of Africans found work at the mines, in what has been described as the 'first large-scale enlistment of the black populations [of southern Africa] into the white cash economy'. This begs the question: why were so many prepared to work at the mines, for increasingly poor wages?

There are a number of answers. Foremost, many Africans saw mine work as a way of furthering their agricultural interests. Wages could be used to buy farming equipment, new stocks of cattle, or pay off creditors following a poor harvest. Some younger men used their earnings to buy cattle for *lobola*, thereby smoothing the transition to manhood. Many invested their wages in firearms and ammunition, to be used for hunting purposes or as a more straightforward means of protection. Similarly, cash was the easiest way of obtaining other consumer goods from local markets.

More pertinently perhaps, wages earned at the mines could be used to fulfil financial demands made by the colonial governments. In Natal and the Cape, the administration demanded from African communities annual hut taxes, payable on each homestead. These taxes put added pressure on farmers, for it was yet another obligation to be met out of harvest profits, which had to be paid regardless of harvest failure or cattle sickness. Under such circumstances, a family head would often migrate to work at the mines, or send a younger family member, in order to make up this shortfall. Often, a family would become dependent on such additional income, and the short-term solution would become a permanent arrangement.

POLITICAL IMPLICATIONS OF THE INDUSTRY

The Kimberley finds had a diffuse impact on the whole of southern Africa. The infrastructure of the region was developed and the economy grew at an unprecedented rate (thereby becoming more viable from the point of view of foreign capital investors), combining to ensure the closer commercial integration of the whole region. There were also enormous political implications. The manner in which the British had acquired the mining region caused much disquiet among the Afrikaner populations of the OFS and the SAR, who believed the mines rightfully belonged to the Free State. This was a belief held by most Afrikaners, and so for the first time, Cape Boers openly voiced solidarity with their cousins on the veld. One consequence of this sense of injustice was that the Boer republics acted in an obstructionist manner in terms of allowing the free flow of labour to the mines by introducing strict pass controls. In the early 1870s, this temporarily threatened both the productivity and profitability of the mines. It therefore became clear to the British administration that their new economic interest would need to be protected politically. They were also faced, for the first time, with the possibility of a political backlash from the Cape Dutch population.

The Confederation of South Africa

In 1875, the British Colonial Secretary Lord Carnarvon (1830-90) unveiled a policy that proposed to link the Cape, Natal and the two

Afrikaner republics into a single political entity. His rationale was straightforward. Such a state would be strong enough to pay for its own administration and defences out of mineral revenues. It would assimilate all white settlers under one flag and so reduce tensions between English and Dutch speakers. Finally, it would bring to an end any notional disputes over ownership of the mineral find.

Rather than relieve unrest among the Afrikaner communities, however, the proposal merely fuelled suspicions. The idea quickly evolved that the scheme was aimed at facilitating maximum British exploitation of southern Africa's new-found wealth. It was also seen as a means of establishing British political controls absolutely over the region. The reaction against the scheme was most loudly heard in the SAR.

The lobby in favour of confederation was equally loud. Some settlers and administrators, mostly of British origin it should be noted, saw it as the only means of bringing to an end, once and for all, disputes over who actually owned the site of the diamond mines. The same people were also keen to be able to claim, pre-emptively, any further such finds. There were widespread and much believed rumours of huge gold deposits in the eastern Transvaal region, lands governed by the SAR. In the event of such a find, whoever controlled the gold-yielding region would have enormous political influence over the whole of southern Africa.

Many merchants, officials and mine owners from the Cape and Natal were also aware of the more urgent need to secure access to wage labourers from the north. Almost all British economic interests in the region were dependent on African labour. Without this, the diamond mines, plantations and wool industry would struggle to turn a profit. In defence of these interests, Carnarvon and others were prepared to intervene politically against any obstacles that were put in the way. Confederation aimed at creating the right political environment for the protection of essential economic concerns and for encouraging further investments in the region.

The scheme floundered owing to the fact that divergent political interests could not be convinced of its viability. The OFS was not prepared in any way to relinquish its hard-won sovereignty and would not even send representatives to discuss the proposal. A deputation from the SAR did enter discussions, but only with great caution. Natalian politicians were most enthusiastic about confederation. Cape leaders, however, became suspicious of a plan that implied they would be footing the bill for an expensive new state that guaranteed little in return. Similar concerns were aired in parliamentary discussions in Britain.

By the late 1870s, the idea of confederation had been allowed to drop quietly. The closer economic links bonding the whole of southern Africa were not reflected in a political sense. Indeed, the idea had merely driven a wedge between various interest groups: the English- and Dutch-speaking white communities of southern Africa, as well as the Cape government and the colonial administration in London. Existing problems, meanwhile, between African communities and the settler states, continued to rumble on.

The Annexation of the Transvaal

While the OFS had developed into a viable state, in the 1870s the SAR was still struggling to establish itself. It remained politically weak and had little or no income. More problematic was the fact that it was home to a number of independently minded African polities. The Venda, to the north, were not prepared to relinquish land to settler encroachments and constantly engaged in raids upon Boer homesteads. Further eastwards, the Pedi, who had suffered much displacement due to the establishment of white communities on the veld, were searching for new pastures on which to settle. This resulted in simmering disputes with white farmers over land ownership.

In 1876, a SAR commando unit backed by a number of Swazi soldiers attempted to exclude the Pedi from lands around the settlement of Lydenburg in the northern Transvaal. Poor military organisation and tactics beset the campaign from the outset. The Pedi, well armed and effectively organised, were able to overcome an early reverse and inflict a defeat on the Boer commando. Forced back across the Oliphants River to Pretoria, the defeated army was forced to turn to the British for protection.

The longer-term viability of the SAR, in more debt than ever due to the campaign, was now brought into question. The British, with perhaps more than a little satisfaction, were happy to offer protection to the SAR and to this end, in 1877 it was temporarily annexed to Britain as the state of Transvaal.

The move, although far from popular, was welcomed by many Transvalers as a stopgap measure. A British military presence certainly offered the best guarantee of protection against both the Pedi and the Venda, as well as the re-emerging Zulu nation to the south. There were some suspicions concerning British motives, however. More militant Afrikaners suspected that the move was perhaps a means of introducing confederation through the back door. Certainly, the fact that the British seemed to be settling in for a long stay did nothing to discourage this point of view. When in 1879 British military forces defeated the Pedi (see below, p. 118) there were widespread calls for the British to withdraw as they had removed one of the biggest threats to the security of the Transvaal. However, the British were in no rush to leave. Ultimately they would have to be pushed out.

The Zulu War

Following defeat at the Battle of Blood River, the Zulu nation went through a period of consolidation under Mpande (1798–1872). Far more pragmatic than either of his half brothers Shaka and Dingane, Mpande as leader of the Zulus opted for a strategy of alliance and compromise with both the British and the *trekkers*. He understood correctly that this was the best means of keeping the kingdom he headed from obliteration. From the late 1840s, however, Mpande was able to set about reviving Zulu fortunes, centring his efforts on rebuilding the nation's military power. The memories of 1838 did not fade quickly, though, and a by now innate Zulu suspicion of Europeans remained strong.

Furthermore, despite Mpande's caution regarding neighbouring white communities, the Zulus never had an easy relationship with local settlers. In Natal, especially, conflict was never far from the surface. Natalian settlers were continuously frustrated in their efforts to obtain labour from Zulu tribes, and as we have seen, were forced to import indentured workers from India. There was also much antagonism over land rights. The Natal government did not recognise Zulu claims to land and was continually asserting the rights of settlers over the followers of Mpande. In 1872 a new Zulu chief, Cetshwayo (1826–84), came to the throne following his father Mpande's death. More docile than his predecessors and imbued with a dignity befitting his aristocratic status, Cetshwayo was a prudent and realistic ruler, determined to continue the work his father had started in consolidating the status of the Zulu kingdom. In 1873, he reacted with uncharacteristic anger against further settler incursions into Zulu territory, and decided to exact retribution by burning crops and seizing cattle and land.

There were further skirmishes between Zulu forces and Boer farmers along the Transvaal border. Again, the problems centred on land rights. Traditionally, the British had supported the Zulus against the settlers in this area. Following the annexation of the Transvaal, however, this situation altered. Wishing to secure the free passage of labourers from the north, the British immediately claimed the border region as their own, ignoring the claims of both the Boers and the Zulus. This move merely alienated the Zulus further from British authority and led them to be increasingly belligerent throughout Natal and the Transvaal.

Increasingly, the British saw the Zulu nation as representing a major obstacle to the further political assimilation of southern Africa. The Natal government protested vigorously against continual Zulu violations of its border. Patience was also running out in respect of the Transvaal border. The Governor of the Cape colony from 1877, Sir Henry Bartle Frere (1815–84) was an ardent advocate of the confederation plan. He believed that if he could score a victory over the Zulus in the Transvaal region, this would appease local Afrikaners and win them over to the idea of full assimilation within the British imperial system. He struck on the idea of disarming the Zulus, a move that would obviously remove any lingering threat to white settlers in the Transvaal.

This was easier said than done. A nation built entirely around its militia, the Zulus were never going to accept a proposal that would leave them unable to defend their interests. When, in late 1878, Frere issued an ultimatum that the Zulus disband their armed forces and accept a permanent British resident, Cetshwayo suspected a pretext for striking out against the Zulus. He therefore immediately started to assemble his regiments for battle.

In January 1879, a British colonial force incorporating units of Natalian Africans invaded Zululand. Perhaps underprepared and certainly over-confident, the British force got off to a disastrous start when they engaged Zulu forces at Isandlwana. Here, they were roundly defeated, with Zulu troops claiming some 1,200 casualties. This sent shock waves throughout the region, and especially panicked white settlers in Natal and the Transvaal. The British force, however, was resolved to exact revenge for the humiliation and set about re-grouping.

There was a further hold up at Rorke's Drift in the immediate aftermath of Isandlwana, although casualties among the Zulus were higher than among the colonial force. Thereafter, the British moved with caution, but acted firmly against an enemy that had proved its formidability. Over time, the superior firepower of the British was too much for the Zulus, who could not make their numerical advantage pay. Six months after victory at Isandlwana, the Zulus had been forced back and were defending their capital at Ulundi. It was here that the British took their revenge, burning the town to the ground. Cetshwayo was captured and sent into immediate exile in Cape Town.

The British exploited their superiority over the Zulus to the hilt. The nation was deliberately fragmented. Thirteen autonomous sub-chiefdoms, each reporting to a British resident, were created. These chiefs could wield little power based on tradition, but rather were expected to acquiesce in British hegemony. This was a recipe for disaster. Those chiefdoms who complied with British demands were widely resented by other chiefdoms who were less willing to give up either their land or independence. This caused great tensions within Zulu society and resulted in the unleashing of bitter rivalries and severe infighting. In a short time, there was all-out civil war among the Zulus. The British used this situation to carve up Zululand between the Transvaal and Natal. This merely fuelled the unrest and saw a spiralling of disorder. Shortly before his death in 1884, the British restored

Cetshwayo to his kingdom in an attempt to reduce the fissures within Zulu society, but the move was made too late to have much effect. Rivalries between the chiefdoms continued unabated and there were still attempts at overturning Natalian and Transvaler settler claims to Zulu land. Eventually, the British took direct control of the Zulu region, enforcing order via military rule and governing the Zulus through the Natalian government.

The Zulus continued to resist in places, but in so doing, merely left themselves open to further land confiscation and crop seizures. Ultimately the Zulus, as a means of meeting the heavy tax demands levied upon them by colonial administrations, were forced increasingly into the migrant labour system. There were a few instances of Zulu rebellion in the 1890s and first decade of the twentieth century, but these were easily extinguished by united settler–colonial forces.

THE FINAL DEFEAT OF THE PEDI AND SOTHO

Immediately after defeating the Zulus, the British turned their attentions to the Pedi of the north. A society that had battled long and hard for its independence, the Pedi had fought not only Boer settlers, but also Swazi and Zulu forces, in an attempt to maintain their autonomy. With the Zulus accounted for, the British seized the moment to bring this most troublesome of societies under control, for only then could they be sure of securing both the lands of the north and the potential labour forces who lived on it.

In the event, the subjugation of the Pedi was achieved with relative ease. The same could not be said of the Sotho. When the colonial administration attempted to disarm the Sotho in 1880, as a means of crushing resistance to local white authority, local communities resisted with a ferocity that was equally unexpected and difficult to break. It would take a whole six months before the Sotho could be brought to heel.

Afrikaner Nationalism

The final defeat and subjugation of troublesome African nations opened up another chapter of problems for the British in southern

Africa. Afrikaners began to assert themselves more forcefully across the region. In the Transvaal the call was made for the reversal of the annexation of the republic. This was a claim backed by Afrikaners resident in the OFS, Natal and the Cape, and coincided with a re-awakening of an Afrikaner national consciousness.

It was during the late 1870s that cultural Afrikaner nationalism first made an impact. The movement evolved among religious ministers and teachers in the south-western Cape. The leading light of this movement was Stephanus du Toit (d.1911), who believed that the Afrikaners were a chosen people, destined by God to rule all of southern Africa and civilise its black inhabitants. In 1877 he published a book entitled *Geskiedenis van Ons Land in die Taal van Ons Volk* (The History of Our Land in the Dialect of Our People), and the following year, started editing a magazine called *Die Afrikaanse Patriot*. Du Toit used the publication as a vehicle for spreading an Afrikaner world view, and for furthering an understanding of the Afrikaans language and Afrikaner history. The movement was also responsible for issuing school text books that peddled a slanted view of southern African history. How widespread the influence of this movement was is difficult to say. However, it coincided with a revival in Afrikaner religious observance, based on a strict adherence to fundamental Calvinistic doctrines.

In 1880, a political organisation called the Afrikaner Bond was formed in the Cape colony. This was a more broadly based body, focused on furthering the cultural, political and linguistic ties between the Afrikaner populations of the Cape, the Transvaal and the OFS. It also strove to encourage the formation of Afrikaner cultural groups as a way of enhancing a common community. In its earliest years the Bond attracted little support, possibly because its approach was largely moderate. Its leaders sympathised with the idea of confederation, in principle at least, and although the Bond favoured independent political status for southern Africa, it did not believe in severing all ties with the British empire. It was therefore not an exclusively Afrikaner organisation, and under the leadership of Jan Hofmeyr (1845–1909) in the 1890s, attracted the support of English-speaking Cape residents. After gaining a minority footing in the Cape parliament, Hofmeyr

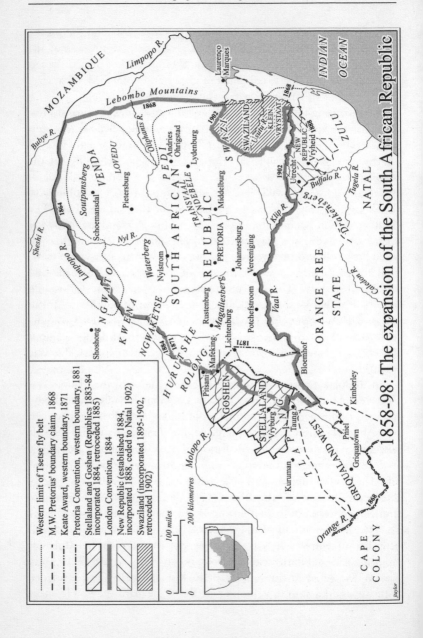

1858-98: The expansion of the South African Republic

Western limit of Tsetse fly belt
M.W. Pretorius' boundary claim, 1868
Keate Award, western boundary, 1871
Pretoria Convention, western boundary, 1881
Stellaland and Goshen (Republics 1883–84
incorporated 1884, retroceded 1885)
London Convention, 1884
New Republic (established 1884,
incorporated 1888, ceded to Natal 1902)
Swaziland (incorporated 1895–1902,
retroceded 1902)

200 kilometres
100 miles

formed a mutually beneficial political alliance with Cecil Rhodes, underlining the Bond's moderate stance. It continued, however, to promote Afrikaner culture wherever possible.

THE TRANSVAAL WAR OF INDEPENDENCE

The most obvious manifestation of this Afrikaner re-awakening was the preparedness of some Transvaal Afrikaners to assert themselves as a means of bringing to an end British domination of their state. In this, they were widely supported by their brethren in the rest of southern Africa.

Increasingly frustrated at the lingering British presence in the region, local commando detachments manned by volunteers were raised in 1880. They struck out at British forces, causing a great amount of civil unrest which brought into question the ability of the colonial forces to hold on to the region. British regiments, which were relatively few in number, found themselves cut off from one another and unable to defend themselves. Reinforcements arrived from the Cape but became held up at Laing's Nek. Hostilities, meanwhile, spread across the Transvaal. A British unit in occupation of a point known locally as Majuba Hill was surprised by an early morning attack launched by a small Boer commando. Although a relatively minor skirmish, it was nothing less than an outright defeat for the British, who suffered ninety-three fatalities against one Boer loss of life. The true significance of the reverse lay in the loss of British prestige this caused throughout the state, and indeed, the rest of southern Africa.

This was all too much for the newly elected British Liberal government. Already concerned at what they saw as an unnecessary and costly entanglement in a region known for its volatility, they decided to withdraw from the Transvaal and honour the earlier pledge to restore autonomy to the local Afrikaner community. This move was confirmed by a treaty signed in August 1881 at Pretoria, which gave to the Transvalers 'complete self-government', while reserving for the British 'control of external relations' and the right to conduct all 'diplomatic intercourse with foreign powers'. The *status quo ante* was fully restored and Afrikaner nationalism had claimed its first victory of note against the British.

British Controls Extended

Freed from responsibilities for the internal control of the Transvaal, the British in southern Africa turned their attentions to protecting, and wherever necessary furthering, their other regional interests. They also proceeded throughout the 1880s to act in a manner designed to sub-jugate the authority of African chiefs to their interests.

In 1884, the territory between the Natal border and the Kei River, inhabited by some Xhosa farmer communities and increasing numbers of settlers, was annexed to the Cape colony as Transkei, ostensibly to buffer existing British territorial interests. The following year, the region of Bechuanaland – modern day Botswana – was incorporated into the British empire. This move was made to pre-empt any expansion of German interests across the African interior from their newly established colony in south-western Africa. It was also done to ensure that the Transvaal republic was contained within its existing boundaries. Bechuanaland was a land of strategic importance, and also supplied increasing quantities of labourers for the Kimberley mines. Quite simply, the British could not afford to let the region fall under someone else's influence. Wherever it was felt necessary to annex, the British did so as a way of protecting their local interests and in order to contain potential rivals.

The British also exerted their influence to protect settler interests against Africans. Throughout southern Africa, but especially around the diamond industry, there were clashes over land, livestock and other resources such as timber and fuel. In most instances, it was Africans who lost all such battles. There were also conflicts arising from pressures for various chiefdoms to supply labour to work the mines and on white farms. Colonial state taxes also undermined the authority of the chiefs and caused much impoverishment and not a little discontent among indigenous societies. Not surprisingly there were instances of minor revolt, but these usually resulted in the further loss of land and the indenturing of labour.

By the 1890s, the British had established effective control over a number of African polities, and had either defeated or appeased the most powerful African nations. Ever more Africans now lived and worked within the settler or colonial political system, and therefore were dependent on cash labour as the only means of economic survival. This process, it should be noted, was furthered by a rinderpest epidemic, which swept the region and afflicted some 90 per cent of cattle. This notwithstanding, the advance of colonialism could only be resisted for so long. Impetus was given to this reality by the second Mineral Revolution in gold.

Gold

As with diamonds, the discovery of huge gold reserves was a catalyst for mass change within southern Africa. This most precious of commodities was uncovered in the hills of the southern Transvaal in 1886, in an area known as the Witwatersrand (literally White Water's Ridge), some thirty miles to the south of Pretoria. Found in apparently unlimited quantities, this was the world's largest gold field, with the main gold-bearing reef stretching over some forty miles. The highest concentration of deposits was centred on the site of the future development of Johannesburg. The richness of the finds was counterbalanced by the fact that the average gold content in every ton of rock was easily the lowest in the world. Indeed, a ton of mined rock would only yield about an ounce of gold.

The real significance of the discovery of gold lay in the fact that the ore was used as the basis for most of the world's fiscal systems; most industrialised nations used gold to underpin their monetary currencies. However, world output had been in decline since the 1870s, as supplies in California, Australia and Latin America had begun to run dry. The Transvaal discoveries, therefore, were both well timed and almost certainly guaranteed to be exceptionally profitable. British financiers and politicians were particularly interested in the finds.

As soon as the discovery was announced there was a rush of speculators to the Witwatersrand region (commonly referred to as the Rand). People from far and wide descended upon the Transvaal. Holding companies rushed to buy up land wherever they could. The Transvaal administration quickly claimed the gold fields as public property and started to sell off small plots of land to the highest bidder.

Initially, mining was carried out on a small scale by independent operators. Small bands of labourers would use picks and shovels to remove rocks and earth which would then be sifted to extract gold. The boom lasted for an unusually long period, and although expansion of the area being mined extended rapidly, it took some months for the shallowest deposits to become exhausted. Meanwhile, speculation in land continued, and larger operators backed by European capital investors started moving into the region.

Once the shallow deposits had been mined, digging to greater depths was started. In some instances, the richest deposits could only be reached by trawling to a depth of some forty metres beneath the earth's surface. This required serious capital investment in sophisticated, modern technology. Specialists needed to be imported from abroad to oversee deep-level mining. Furthermore, the quality of the deeper ores was not on a par with the shallow deposits; it rapidly became usual to work three tonnes of rock in order to extract an ounce of gold, so scales of production needed to be increased if profitability was to be maintained. In a short space of time, production costs started to soar.

As had been the case at Kimberley, smaller operators could rarely afford to meet either the challenges of larger scale production or the costs involved. Most small operators sold out to larger companies. Some miners tried to pool their resources in order to overcome these logistical problems, but only a few such concerns were able to succeed. As the old-style independent prospector became obsolete on the Rand, so powerful mining houses started to exert control over the industry. By the early 1890s, gold production on the Rand was controlled by eight such businesses, each of which owned a number of separate mines. The largest of these was Wernher Beit which, following a collapse in the speculative boom in 1890, ended up with a substantial share of the Rand market.

The large mining houses learned much from the experiences of Rhodes and other speculators at Kimberley. They spread the financial risks between them, and took care to regulate the industry properly so as to protect it from unnecessary collapse. Tight regulations governing the mines were introduced and strict controls applied to the labour force. The gold was also marketed with care. In this way were profit margins maintained and the industry allowed to develop. In the 1890s, productivity on the Rand tripled, and by the end of that decade, southern Africa accounted for some 27 per cent of the world's total gold output.

There were problems inherent to gold production, however. The price gold could fetch on the world market was fixed at a particular rate. While this meant that harmful slumps could nearly always be avoided, it also placed a ceiling on profit margins. Consequently, mine owners had to keep a close eye on all expenditure and cut costs wherever it was practicable to do so. The one area where savings could most easily be made was labour. While skilled labour could only be attracted to the Rand on the promise of high wages, unskilled labour could be recruited cheaply from within southern Africa. This brought the industry into conflict with local agricultural interests, however, and so could only be obtained with the backing of the Transvaal government.

At this time, the Transvaal President was Paul Kruger (1825–1904). A conservative Calvinist, Kruger was as obstinate as he was old fashioned – he is reported to have believed that the earth was flat – and as a boy, had participated in the Great Trek with his hitherto landless family. All his life, Kruger had opposed the British; as a boy for their abolition of slavery, and after he came to settle in the SAR, for their

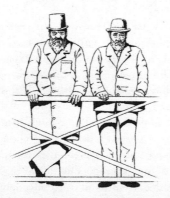

The President of the Transvaal, Paul Kruger, and Piet Cronje

annexation of his newly found homeland in 1877. As a military commander, he led a force against his adversaries during the Transvalers' war for independence in 1880–81, enjoying the kind of success that facilitated his attainment of the office of State President in 1883.

While his government was prepared to sell off lands to private speculators during the early gold rush and to legislate to allow for the creation of the large mining conglomerates, it was not prepared to allow the gold industrialists to accrue a monopoly over African labour, which would be to the detriment of local Boer farmers. This forced the mining houses to look further afield for labour, to Portuguese east Africa especially, but also to other southern African societies ravaged by conflict and hardship and no longer able to compete on the land with whites.

Initially, when competition for labour was high, wages paid to Africans were relatively good, but over time, these were deliberately depressed by the major mining houses. When labour supplies dropped, wages would increase but be lowered again once the requisite numbers had been recruited. The Kimberley model of housing African labour in compounds was closely followed, and pass controls were introduced to prevent both labour mobility and the possibility of desertion. These tactics worked in favour of the employers. By 1899, an estimated 97,000 Africans were working on the Rand.

TRANSFORMATION OF THE TRANSVAAL

As speculators flooded into the Transvaal, the region was transformed from a sleepy, pastoral state with virtually no income, into an urbanising society, marked out by its increasingly expanding and cosmopolitan population. Potentially, it was now placed to become the richest of the four white-controlled southern African states. However, the administration was wary lest its existing white population be overwhelmed by the newcomers. The conservatism of the Transvaal government meant it was never likely to become carried away by developments, but it also meant that for a long while its Boer citizens remained in a state of some considerable impoverishment.

The Rand evolved rapidly into an urban area, changing forever the local landscape and environment. The town of Johannesburg was built up on a scale larger than the development of Kimberley. From a series of digger tents in the mid-1880s, by the outbreak of the First World War Johannesburg was a complex urban area, home to some 250,000 people. Blocks of land, enveloped by a rectangular network of roads, were auctioned off to property developers, who rapidly started building upwards. The city's distinctively uniform character was thus formulated from the beginning.

In its earliest years, Johannesburg was home to an overwhelmingly male population. Like Kimberley before it, it was a dangerous, edgy place, where the rule of law was often in the hands of local strong men. Liquor, prostitution and organised crime rackets offered as much opportunity for material enrichment as the gold industry. It was not a safe place to be and wages were often frittered away on drink and women, or could be easily lost to bandits on the way home from work. The criminal, violent culture of the place was furthered by the open corruption of local officials and policemen, who turned a blind eye to the activities of gangsters in return for regular pay-offs. In this way a thriving illicit drinking trade and culture took root, which served Africans who were banned from buying alcohol on the Rand in 1896.

At the same time, there was another side to Johannesburg, a city of polite, middle-class culture, dominated by English-speaking immigrants who lived in sheltered suburban areas. Here they built their own schools and churches, and were served by black servants, the only Africans freely admitted into such areas. So overwhelming was the English population that one contemporary visitor compared Johannesburg to 'virtually [any] English city', while for the same reason, Kruger referred to the city as 'the devil's town'. This was another world entirely – the world of the elite mine owners and their managers, who enjoyed the finer things in life and brought with them to the city all the trappings of European bourgeois life. The divide was stark, but once established, unbridgeable. From the outset, Johannesburg was a place of haves and have-nots, with the latter category including an increasingly resentful poor white population.

Secondary and tertiary industries sprang up around the gold mines and Johannesburg. Many business people moved to the region and competed for contracts to feed, water, clothe and supply the new urban area. The Transvaal government was happy to encourage such companies, for they were able to provide for the rest of the state's population at the same time. The government also slowly started to encourage local Boer farmers to cater to the needs of the new market. Kruger's administration was more cunning in exploiting other opportunities presented to it as a means of generating income. Primarily, the government acted to extract as much money as it possibly could from the mining houses, a move that frustrated the latter and created longer-term grievances of considerable magnitude.

Mining profits were all subject to a state tax. The government also levied import duties on essential mining equipment and machinery, and imposed the law in such a way that it was impossible for the mine owners to avoid these levies. A high tariff on transport was maintained and used to subsidise the cheaper transportation of locally produced agricultural commodities. A state monopoly of dynamite importation and sales – essential for deep-level mining – was also introduced and rigorously enforced.

None of this went down well with the mine owners who resented their already tight margins being impinged upon in such a manner. They also had little success in getting the Kruger regime to legislate in their favour in terms of labour access; the mine owners were powerless to affect the political decision-making processes of the Transvaal. As foreigners, or *Uitlanders*, that is to say, non-Afrikaner whites, they were denied citizenship and, therefore, the right to vote or stand for political office. This rankled, especially since they were subject to a high rate of tax on any profits. Nevertheless, the *Uitlander's* lot was not a bad one, and they could in no way be described as a repressed minority (a claim later made on their behalf by the British Colonial Office).

The Transvaal gold industry continued to increase in value, until by 1914 it accounted for 40 per cent of the total world output. Long before this time, the economic centre of southern Africa had shifted from the Cape to the Transvaal. In general, the discovery of gold had turned the whole of the region into one of great economic and political significance, one which the British especially could not afford to ignore, as they found their premier world ranking under increasing threat from other industrialised and imperial nations. Southern Africa, meanwhile, had changed from an underdeveloped, pre-industrial region into a place with a highly capitalised economy and a rapidly industrialising society.

Political Conflict: The Transvaal and The British

After the victory of Majuba Hill and the reversal of the annexation of the Transvaal, across the whole of southern Africa there was a significant growth in Afrikaner nationalist feeling. This was channelled in two directions. Firstly, there was increased resentment against British influence wherever it prevailed, and in some cases, where it was merely perceived to prevail. This certainly led to growing agitation against British customs and laws across the interior. In the Transvaal, it gave credence to Kruger's policy in respect of the *Uitlanders*, the majority of whom were British citizens and all of whom used the English language when conducting business.

Secondly, there was a growth in anti–African sentiment. Most manifestly, this resulted in widespread calls for the extension of Boer controls over African societies wherever the two cultures came into contact. Bolstered by the new power that it could derive from gold revenues, the Transvaal state in the 1890s was able to assert control directly over a number of African societies living within, or close to, its borders. A series of limited wars were launched, effectively bringing under Boer control the northern Transvaal Venda, as well as the Ndebele tribes resident in Rhodesia. Meanwhile, Swaziland was opened up to Transvaal influence via a convention negotiated in London. This effectively weakened Swazi autonomy, as Boer commandos policed the area and demanded from Swazi chiefs annual tributes which, if not honoured, could be paid by sending labourers to the Transvaal instead. The Swazi king had also signed away to the Transvaal government the right to collect customs and excise revenues in return for a fixed annual income.

The Transvaal had been free to pursue such a policy in the 1890s as its independence had been bolstered the previous decade. In 1884, Kruger met representatives of the British government in London to sign a convention. Under the terms of this agreement, the British agreed to recognise the authority of the President of the South African Republic, as it was still known to the Krugerites, and the local British resident was withdrawn. The British also indicated that they were prepared to let formal controls over the Transvaal's foreign relations lapse, although the previous agreement governing these was not officially negated.

The convention made sense in the context of the time at which it was signed. It suited the British, in the aftermath of the collapse of plans for confederation, to leave the Transvaal to its own devices and concentrate on consolidating its colonies at the Cape and Natal as a means of ensuring its ascendancy throughout southern Africa. To this end, there was also a desire among British imperial strategists to see the emergence of a viable, independent state to the north of their colonies, able to deal with troublesome African polities while guaranteeing a steady supply of cheap labour.

What nobody legislated for was the discovery of gold. This immediately changed the parameters of the economic and political state of southern Africa. The emergence of this industry meant that British paramountcy over the region could no longer be maintained. Economically, the benefits of gold were accrued by the Transvaal government; politically, the British had already relinquished all control over that administration. Consequently, the British were unable to influence Kruger in any way, nor persuade him to support the interests of the mining houses on terms other than his own. Thus, Kruger's refusal to succumb to *Uitlander* demands for less taxation and some form of political representation could not be effectively opposed, either by the Cape or Natalian regimes, or by the British government. His protection of local farmer interests was a further irritant to important lobbies in the Cape and Natal, who found the lucrative Rand market flooded with cheap, Transvaal-grown produce.

This challenge to British power within southern Africa could not go unchecked for long, especially because the protection of British economic interests was at stake. Opposition to Kruger in the 1890s became centred on the exclusion of the *Uitlanders* from the political process, and was characterised by attacks on the Transvaal regime as being backward looking, prejudiced and unable to provide adequately for the needs of the gold industry.

There was some truth in all these allegations, but *Uitlander* grievances were undoubtedly manipulated by others and used as a convenient political stick with which to beat Kruger. The *Uitlanders* in the 1890s accounted for perhaps as much as a half of the Transvaal's total white population and were mostly clever, business-minded people who had an open outlook, but they were nevertheless driven by an instinctive desire to make money. Their concern for politics was limited to how far the decision-making process affected their ability to turn a profit. They were perturbed by the stringent controls and taxes imposed upon them by the Transvaal government, but not necessarily surprised by all such regulations, which were both expected and a commonplace in other parts of the world.

Many *Uitlanders* argued that they should be given a political voice, if only because they wanted some say in how their tax monies were spent. Many could also see that the Transvaal was not being developed at a sufficient pace to meet the growing needs of the mining industry. However, none of this threatened the viability of the industry; it merely put a cap on potential profit margins. There were other criticisms of the Transvaal government, such as its refusal to allow the use of English in the courts or schools, or to tackle the obvious judicial prejudice exercised against *Uitlanders*. Its failure to loosen labour controls also enraged many mine owners, as did the refusal to negotiate over transport tariffs.

Kruger, however, had no intention of diluting his state's independence, which had been a long time in coming. In all aspects of government, he was single minded and followed a determined policy of keeping the internal politics of the Transvaal free from outside interference, either from other powers or from the foreigners resident within his borders. The more vociferous his opponents became, the more Kruger dug in. In taking this stance he could be sure of the support of his loyal constituents, most of whom lived off the land and were granted favour by the regime.

He was also astute enough to understand that the Transvaal could not afford to stand completely still (as, indeed, his critics suggested was happening). Kruger therefore made some effort to modernise the state by overhauling its administration and investing in its infrastructure. He brought in Afrikaners from outside the Transvaal who had the skills required to oversee the development of the state. Among this number were men such as the Cape-born Jan Christiaan Smuts (1870–1950). A graduate of Stellenbosch University, and more recently Cambridge, Smuts was a highly intelligent and motivated individual, who Kruger appointed as the Transvaal's State Attorney. This was the beginning of an illustrious career that would see Smuts go on to dominate early twentieth-century South African politics and carve out for himself a role as an internationally respected statesman.

A programme of public works resulted in the creation of a modern communications network, crowned by a rail link to the Portuguese colony port of Lourenço Marques (the British responded to this development in 1895 by annexing Tongaland, thereby curtailing any further potential links between the Transvaal and the sea). Yet Kruger blatantly ignored any criticisms levelled against him. Internal political opposition centred on the more progressive Piet Joubert (1831–1900), who was an instrumental player in the Transvaal War of Independence and who four times challenged Kruger's presidency. While no supporter of the *Uitlander* cause, Joubert and his supporters attacked Kruger's mostly isolationist stance and campaigned against governmental corruption, which favoured a particular set of landowners at everybody else's expense and saw them claim for themselves a number of lucrative governmental concessions. However, this opposition could be readily ignored, as it had no popular backing and only an ineffective political programme.

More difficult to ignore were the increasingly stringent attacks from the British. Kruger's stance was an affront not only to their hegemony within southern Africa but also to vital business and capital interests within the region. These could not go unchallenged indefinitely. Throughout the early 1890s the Cape government, acting largely upon instruction from London, attempted to engineer some kind of compromise deal with the Transvaal government. It attempted to persuade Kruger to take the Transvaal into a customs union with the Cape. The overture was dismissed out of hand, re-negotiated, then rebuffed once more. Pressure was subsequently exerted on a number of fronts to force a relaxation of the Transvaal's franchise laws in favour of *Uitlander* participation in the political process. Again, Kruger refused to budge, much to the frustration of Cape representatives.

A conflict in some form or other was becoming ever more likely as the political temperature began to rise. The building of the rail link to Lourenço Marques concerned the British who, as we have seen, then acted to ensure that the Transvaal remained land-locked. Kruger, meanwhile, aware that the British were attempting to encircle the Transvaal, retaliated by attempting to divert trade towards Lourenço Marques and away from the Cape and Natalian ports by introducing prohibitive tariffs on the short rail link between Johannesburg and the Vaal River. Shippers attempted to get around this problem by using ox wagons to cover the distance but Kruger closed off this route to all trade. The British government reacted immediately with the threat of force. The Transvaal backed down, but a moral victory of sorts was claimed by Kruger.

There is little evidence to suggest that at this point the British wanted from Kruger anything other than a fair share of power over the gold industry as a means of ensuring that London's interests were protected. This meant him governing in a way acceptable to the mining magnates. However, Kruger was not amenable to any overtures and remained determined to protect the integrity of the Transvaal republic. As the dispute over rail tariffs illustrated, a conflict in defence of these respective positions was waiting to happen.

THE JAMESON RAID

Patience was wearing thin at the Cape and, further away, in London. In 1895, a number of leading mine representatives entered into discussions with Cecil Rhodes. Together they hatched a plot to engineer a rebellion, aimed at overthrowing the Kruger administration.

As ill-thought out as it was desperate, the plan was an unmitigated disaster. The idea revolved around an *Uitlander* uprising in Johannesburg, stirred up by agents of Rhodes and armed with guns smuggled in from the Cape. The rebellion would be backed up by a small force, led by Rhodes' close friend and ally Leander Starr Jameson (1853–1917), which would enter the Transvaal from Bechuanaland. To be pulled off speedily, the idea was to present the coup to the world as a *fait accompli* justified on humanitarian grounds, that is, as the liberation of the *Uit-landers* from lingering political repression.

In the event, the raid was easily thwarted. The uprising at Johannesburg failed to materialise. Furthermore, the Transvaal government was tipped off in advance of Jameson's raid, and so was able to meet the invading force head on. Jameson and his 500-odd troops were rounded up shortly after they stepped on to Transvaal territory.

The failure of the raid worked in Kruger's favour. It had been clearly illustrated that the threat posed by the British and their agents to the Transvaal was a very real one. In the eyes of many Afrikaners resident elsewhere across southern Africa, this came as something of a shock and resulted in a loss of respect for British rule and institutions. The OFS and the Transvaal immediately started to negotiate a defensive alliance against any future British intrigues, which was concluded with utmost haste. The British also lost most of the support they had previously enjoyed in the Cape from the Dutch-speaking community. Support for the Transvaal, then, was established as the focal point for heightened anti-British feeling in southern Africa.

Cecil Rhodes, whose hand could clearly be seen behind the plot, was forced to step down as Prime Minister of the Cape colony. A subsequent British parliamentary inquiry into events surrounding the raid was deemed a whitewash in Africa, as all major protagonists other than Jameson were exonerated from blame. Relations, meanwhile, between the British and the Transvaalers had been further soured. Over the next few years, tensions between the two would be heightened further as both sides intransigently defended their positions and refused to accede to any sort of compromise.

TOWARDS WAR

If there were lessons to be learned from the Jameson debacle they were not heeded by the British Colonial Office. Outwardly more hawkish in their general outlook, the British were now no longer in the mood for negotiated settlements. Instead, they wanted to re-establish their supremacy across southern Africa.

The Colonial Secretary, Joseph Chamberlain (1836–1914), who had been deeply implicated in the Jameson fiasco, decided to send Alfred Milner (1854–1925) to the region as Cape Governor and British High Commissioner to South Africa. A strong advocate of British imperial expansion, Milner was known as an uncompromising character and did not hide his dislike of Kruger. On arrival in Africa in 1897 he immediately instigated a forward policy against the Transvaal government, with the full backing of the Colonial Office.

Although Milner was quick to announce that 'We [i.e. the British] don't want the Transvaal any more than the Orange Free State, but only fair treatment for British industry and capital in the Transvaal', the fury of his earliest attacks on the Kruger regime suggested that he had in mind something altogether more decisive. He used every means available to him to belittle Kruger and undermine his government. A crude propaganda campaign, aimed at restoring credibility to the notion that the *Uitlanders* were a repressed minority, proceeded for over a year. More seriously, there was an influx of troops into the Cape and Natal, and these were strategically positioned throughout the two colonies for a possible attack upon the Transvaal.

At first, Kruger appeared to moderate his stance in the face of this onslaught. He suggested that perhaps he would consider modifying state laws to accommodate some *Uitlander* demands. However, when this overture was dismissed out of hand by Milner, Kruger renegotiated the defensive alliance with the OFS. He also sounded out both Portugal and Germany about a possible military alliance (there were, in fact, strong political links between Kruger and the Kaiser, as well as trading contacts, but the possible military alliance was superseded by an Anglo-German agreement reached in 1898).

Then, following his re-election in 1898 with an increased majority, Kruger reacted to the new military threat posed by the Cape and Natal by dramatically increasing state spending on the military, thereby rearming his standing forces with the latest weaponry imported from France and Germany. Strong fortifications to defend Pretoria and Johannesburg were also built.

This merely strengthened Milner's resolve to force a denouement. By early 1899 he was determined to bring Kruger tumbling down. The OFS premier, M.T. Steyn (1857–1916), attempted to bring the two factions together, and arranged for a conference to be held at Bloemfontein in May. However, neither Kruger or Milner, who came face to face for the first time, were much in the mood for compromise. Milner, in particular, was determined that negotiations should come to nothing and adopted a wholly confrontational stance. The conference ended both quickly and acrimoniously. The scene was now set for war.

Kruger returned to the Transvaal convinced that the British were determined to attack his state and given the chance, take it by force. He therefore offered the franchise to all *Uitlanders* after seven years of continual residence. This was rejected by Cape officials on behalf of the Uitlanders, who now demanded the franchise for all foreigners who had already lived in the Transvaal for five years or more. To this Kruger would not, indeed could not, accede.

In June, Milner and Chamberlain met to discuss the evolving situation. It is conceivable that at this point the Colonial Secretary might have acted to restrain Milner. In the event, he did no such thing. By August, the British were preparing to send military detachments to the Cape. Simultaneously, a last round of negotiations was allowed to founder on trifling sticking points.

Kruger's hand was eventually forced with the humiliating posting of British infantry along the length of the Cape–Natal borders. This was another affront to the integrity of the Transvaal, but it also highlighted the fact that Kruger was faced with the stark choice of war on the one hand, and on the other, the dismemberment of the Transvaal. By standing his ground he had nothing much to lose.

On 9 October 1899, the Transvaal government sent to the British agent in Pretoria an ultimatum demanding the withdrawal of troops from the Cape border and assurances that further military units would not be landed in southern Africa. The British were given forty-eight hours to reply to the ultimatum. The request was ignored. On 11 October the Transvaal, backed by the OFS, declared war on Britain.

The South African War

Once the decision had been made to go to war, the Afrikaner republics decided to move quickly, before British reinforcements arrived from

Europe. Both sides claimed to have right on their side. The Transvalers were at war as a means of defending their integrity. On the other hand, the British continued to announce that they were at war to defend the rights of *Uitlanders* in the Transvaal. Both parties claimed the moral high ground. In reality, few neutrals doubted that the battle was largely to do with economic determinants, that is to say ultimate control of the southern African gold industry. The mood in Britain was largely optimistic, although significant anti-war and pro-Boer movements rapidly started to voice opposition to the campaign.

The British military were also optimistic. There was a feeling that sheer weight of numbers was on their side. In total, the republicans could call to arms perhaps 85,000 men, including Free Staters, Cape Dutch and sympathetic foreigners from Ireland, France and elsewhere. The British, however, had the resources of the world's mightiest empire behind them. If needed, they could bolster their forces with troops from India, Canada, Australia and New Zealand, ultimately bringing the size of their force to some 400,000 men. Furthermore, the British infantry and artillery would be equipped with superior technology, in greater quantities than the Boers could ever imagine. The sense of self-belief in the ranks was thus enormous, and nobody in October doubted much that it would all be over by the end of the year.

Such optimism was to be short-lived. The republicans had moved quickly to seize the advantage from their opponents and they largely achieved their aim. They enjoyed numerous early successes, aided by the fact that British military planning was poor and organisation of the ranks pitiful. British units were acting under misguided instruction and were given little time to adjust to the climate in which they were active. Furthermore, they also found the terrain hostile and not conducive to the sort of fight they had been led to expect. Most surprisingly of all, the Boers were no pushovers, a belief deliberately spread through the British army prior to engagement.

The Boer army was, indeed, an ill-disciplined outfit in comparison to its professional opponents. Overseen by a central War Council, headed by Piet Joubert for the Transvaal and Piet Cronje (d.1912) for the OFS, the rank and file were organised into local commando units, comprising volunteers in the main. These commandos, which would be anything from a couple of hundred to a couple of thousand men strong, remained attached to the area in which they were raised. The officer corps of each unit would be elected from within the ranks, but these leaders had no effective power to enforce orders or make men fight. An individual had the right to opt out of an assignment. He might also, at short notice, grant himself leave and return to his home. It could therefore be a problem keeping commando units in the field, especially when faced with a tough or unpopular task. However, as one recent historian of the conflict has noted: 'The majority of them were tough, determined fighters who ... did not fall prey to what would appear to be a hopeless lack of discipline.' In fact, a great sense of kinship pervaded the Boer ranks and also they were imbued with a great sense of optimism. They were well equipped with German Mauser rifles and backed by French-made heavy field guns, the 'Long Toms', and believed that their local knowledge would be a decisive advantage in the field. A couple of reverses, akin to Majuba, it was thought, and the British would quit the war.

A WHITE MAN'S WAR?

This was no straightforward campaign between two white forces. Both sides could call upon local black men or cajole them into service. Blacks therefore played a notable role in the South African War, ensuring that this was no white man's battle.

Many African tribes took the opportunity presented by the outbreak of hostilities to reassert their claims to lost lands by taking advantage of the preoccupation of local white communities. For the most part, Africans tended to side with the British against the Boer, as they saw the latter as a traditionally more troublesome foe. Consequently, the Zulus assisted British forces across difficult terrain and used their local knowledge to help track down Boer guerrilla units. They were also employed as a defensive guard to watch over vital communications links, such as the Cape to Kimberley rail line.

The Zulus also used the war to try and claim back territory previously lost to Boer settlers. This was a tactic similarly pursued by the Pedi, Venda and Tswana tribes throughout the border regions of the Transvaal. Other African communities merely acted to defend what they had and protected their land against Boer guerrilla skirmishes as well as against British units seeking shelter. Both sides attempted to draft urban black workers into their ranks, either as combatants or, more commonly, as auxiliary workers (transport drivers, messengers or scouts).

The longer the war raged, the more destructive it became, and much suffering was inflicted equally on Africans and on whites. Many African communities became caught up in crossfire and other settlements were subjected later to the British scorched earth policy. Both Boers and Britons commandeered cattle and crops when the need arose.

Africans did manage in some instances successfully to reclaim lands previously lost to settlers. Across the OFS and Natal in particular, African families were quick to occupy homesteads and land deserted by fleeing Afrikaner communities. However, the extent of such gains was limited and in the aftermath of the war they were reversed in favour of white families.

THE FIRST PHASE OF COMBAT

British troops had massed on the Natalian approaches to the Transvaal. The plan was for this force to draw in the Boer commandos, leaving space behind into which could be sent British reinforcements from the Cape. It was a simple idea and perhaps a little too obvious, for the Boer armies were determined to block any British moves into the Transvaal. They also aimed to cut off communications to Kimberley, before launching an offensive deep into the Cape colony.

Initially outnumbered by something like two to one, British forces found themselves everywhere under immense pressure. By the end of October, Boer forces had laid siege to the three towns of Kimberley, Ladysmith and Mafeking. These had only limited strategic significance, but the Boers had nevertheless taken hostage thousands of British military and civilian personnel. The defence of these towns proceeded in earnest, and temporarily became the focal point of the war for the British.

The British offensive only got under way in November, once sufficient numbers of troops had been landed at the Cape. The immediate goal was to relieve the towns under siege but matters got off to a bad

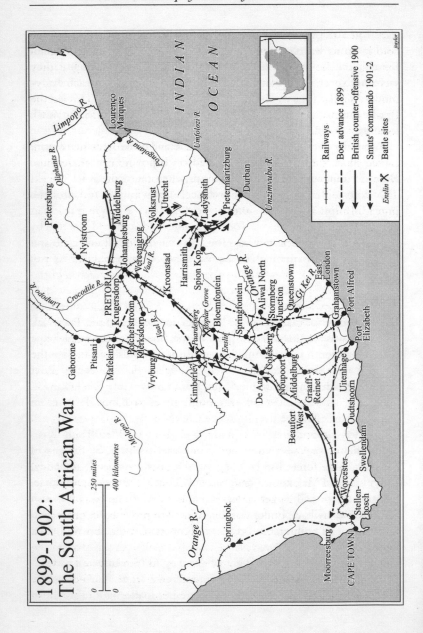

1899–1902:
The South African War

start when the army was defeated before it had even left the Cape colony on its way to Kimberley. First at Stormberg, then at Magersfontein, the Boers inflicted reverses that were as devastating as they were unexpected. In Natal, as the British attempted to reach Ladysmith, a similar rout was inflicted at the town of Colenso. This led the British commander-in-chief, General Sir Redvers Buller (1839–1908), to suggest that Ladysmith should capitulate.

The news of the defeats, which had all occurred in quick succession, caused shock throughout the British forces and at home, where there were solemn analyses of what was quickly christened the Black Week. The expected British walk-over of the Boers was now not possible. Instead, British forces had either been vanquished or were trapped in morale-sapping sieges.

Nonetheless, a decisive victory was still the expected outcome and the end to which strategists continued to work. Someone had to pay the price for Black Week, however. Buller, who no longer held the confidence of the British military or political authorities and was widely derided as a coward for his suggestion that Ladysmith should surrender, was relieved of his duties. In his place, Field Marshal Lord Frederick 'Bobs' Roberts (1832–1914), Britain's most famous soldier following a number of previously well-publicised campaigns in India during the time of the Mutiny, and later in Afghanistan and Ireland, was given overall command of the South African force. The change in regime did not translate into an immediate reversal of British fortunes. The tactical ineptness so far seen at command level continued for some weeks, until the nadir was reached in late January 1900 at the battle for Spion Kop.

Although removed from his post as commander-in-chief, Buller was not withdrawn from the fray, but sent by Roberts to oversee the Natal army. This was an odd situation, made odder by the fact that Roberts tended not to give Buller orders but merely to make tentative suggestions. For his part, Buller was determined to prove his critics wrong and wanted to push on to Ladysmith. Roberts advised that the Natal force should stay on a defensive footing, but Buller, as the man on the spot, overruled his commander and marched for the besieged town.

Initial infantry and cavalry attacks were limited in their effect against a well-positioned and equally well-prepared enemy. The British commanders were at something of a loss, as their local knowledge was limited and they could not find competent guides to steer them towards Ladysmith. The force approached the dominating hill position of Spion Kop. Unsure as to what to do – the army could have chosen to by-pass the point – Buller decided to take it, in the belief that it would give him some kind of strategic viewpoint to be exploited later.

A force of some 30,000 men was amassed on one side of the Kop. The Boers, minding the reverse approaches to the hill, did not challenge the infantry until they neared the summit of the point. This attack was seen off with relative ease and as a heavy fog was descending the leading column, who believed they had reached the top of the hill, decided to entrench.

This was the first of many dreadful errors. When the mist lifted, it became apparent that the force was not at the summit of the Kop, but had stopped far short of it at a lower crest. Even worse, the entrenched force was dangerously exposed. It found itself directly in the line of fire of a Boer artillery unit, and some 300 yards to the right, open to a commando infantry attack. Further, the British field of fire was severely restricted by the location of the trench.

The ensuing engagement was a confused affair, especially from the British point of view, characterised in equal measure by immense bravery on both sides. There was much fighting at close quarters, resulting in dreadful fatalities, but no way through for either side. As night fell, the British, who were short on supplies and in much need of reinforcement, decided that the position was untenable. The order to evacuate was announced.

Ironically, the Boer command had also reached the same decision. However, before the retreat was fully enacted, a watch reported that the British had left and the position was quickly re-occupied. A psychologically important victory had been achieved at the cost of some 300 dead. For the British, defeat was far more costly. Not only was Ladysmith still under siege, but the attempted relief had cost an estimated 1,700 lives. Humiliated and in charge of a broken army, Buller retreated across the Tugela River.

The rout was to have a terrible, lingering hold over the British army in South Africa. Joseph Chamberlain thought it 'a stunning fiasco', a view shared by a disbelieving population at home. The British government had heard enough, and reacted to Spion Kop by sending the country's best military mind to serve on Roberts' staff. General Lord H. Horatio Kitchener (1850–1916), the hero of Omdurman, was diverted from his new post as Governor-General of the Sudan, and appointed chief of staff, acting effectively as second in command to Roberts.

By February, the move appeared to be paying dividends. The appointment of Kitchener, in particular, had a positive effect on troop and staff morale, and he was able to oversee a limited, but effective reorganisation of the lines. On 15 February, the town of Kimberley was relieved, and at the end of the month Ladysmith was finally liberated. Thereafter, British forces launched an offensive operation that saw them rolling into the OFS. By the middle of March the capital, Bloemfontein, had been occupied. Everywhere, Boer commandos were being forced onto a defensive footing or into retreat. The OFS was fully occupied by May, and at the end of that month, annexed to the British empire. That same month, to scenes of unprecedented rejoicing across Britain, Mafeking was relieved. Now moving towards the Transvaal from three different sides, in the space of a week the British captured both Johannesburg and Pretoria. This was in early June. Within three months, the Transvaal had been annexed and Paul Kruger forced to seek refuge at Lourenço Marques, from where he sailed into exile in the Netherlands.

Such a turnaround in fortunes was remarkable not only for its swiftness, but for the number of important victories and gains that it encompassed. Less than a year after the declaration of war, the conflict seemed to have turned decisively. By the end of 1900, even Roberts was convinced that the job was done and the war over.

Such an assumption was not only premature but based on an unrealistic analysis of the situation across southern Africa. The British may have annexed both Boer republics, but they had effectively defeated neither. As Afrikaner forces were rolled back they simply became far more resilient and determined. They also started to employ a new tactical approach which would become increasingly difficult to counter.

For their part, British forces were still not performing to capacity and the successes merely papered over a number of cracks. In general, the army was badly organised. Supply lines were not properly protected, nor did vital stocks get through to the intended destination on time. Unit movements were at best erratic, and lines were often over-stretched and exposed to commando units. Swept away by the ease with which the cavalry and infantry had gained ground, these essential problems were not properly addressed by the army's hierarchy when the time was ripe for doing so.

This did not bode well. When the Boer commandos started to practise tactics of guerrilla warfare, employing their local knowledge to maximum effect, the British forces were not sufficiently prepared to counteract such an onslaught. Fighting in smaller units, with little or no baggage and using only rifles, the guerrilla commandos were extremely quick and very difficult to track down. They would strike out at any legitimate target, mostly rail and other communication links, before moving on at speed. The job for the British was then to track down the guerrillas, which was far from easy. The Boers could rely on a network of farms and homesteads across southern Africa in which to hide, where they would be offered food and shelter by sympathetic families. The pursuing British were hampered by their inability to move at speed and, more tellingly, the widespread non-co-operation of local Afrikaner communities.

THE SECOND PHASE OF COMBAT

In late November 1900, a few months after the annexation of the Transvaal, Lord Roberts declared a British victory and left for home. He left Kitchener in charge with a brief to 'mop up' and oversee the unconditional surrender of those Afrikaner forces still active. An amnesty offer was taken up by some Boers but not enough to weaken the emerging guerrilla campaign. Far from being over, the war was entering its deadliest phase.

It became increasingly clear to Kitchener in early 1901 that he was still faced with a formidable enemy. He was incensed by the targeting of rail links and frustrated by the inability of his army to track down the perpetrators of such sabotage. He maintained Roberts' earlier tactic of burning all farms within a ten-mile radius of a guerrilla operation. Rather than act as a deterrent, however, this seemed merely to spur the guerrillas on.

Kitchener decided, therefore, to step up the campaign against the remaining commandos. The essential problem for the British army was that, although in occupation of the veld, they had little control over the land or Boer army movements across it. Kitchener went back to the drawing board. He hatched a plan for dividing the interior into small plots, each to be fenced off with barbed wire and patrolled from a blockhouse. These areas would be swept of civilians and subsequently guarded by the cavalry. With movement thus restricted, Kitchener hoped to isolate the enemy and make it easier for them to be tracked down. Within a year there were 8,000 blockhouses and over 3,500 miles of fencing in place.

The second part of Kitchener's strategy was to extend the policy of homestead and farm burning (the aim of which, according to Milner, was 'to knock the bottom out of the great Afrikaner nation for ever and ever Amen'). It developed from being a merely reactive measure into a concerted programme of scorched earth. Boer settlements were, therefore, targeted indiscriminately and with no thought for human or material consequences. In all, many farms were razed in this way.

Combined, the blockhouse and scorched earth measures affected not only guerrilla units but civilians as well. There were many victims, including children and women, as thousands of refugees were left to wander the veld completely destitute. The problem grew to the extent that the British military authorities were forced to round up anyone they found and take them to a military camp. No more than open pens, with in many cases not even the most basic of provisions, conditions in the camps were appalling. Not surprisingly, outbreaks of typhoid, dysentery, measles and other diseases were endemic and accounted for thousands of lives.

By the late summer of 1901, there were fifty such camps, often described as the first concentration camps, housing over 70,000 Afrikaner women and children. Separate camps were set up to accommodate destitute African families. The number of camps was to rise steadily until the end of the war. However, by that point, their administration had been taken out of the hands of the military and efforts were made to improve sanitary arrangements, health care provision and the quality of rations provided to inmates. Nevertheless, the camps were terribly unhealthy places and the suffering in them was dreadful.

When news of the camps reached Britain it caused an angry backlash, led by the increasingly vociferous anti-war lobby. The Quaker Emily Hobhouse (1860–1926) was at the forefront of the movement to see conditions in the camps improve, and in this, she and others enjoyed some success. Nevertheless, the government was openly attacked on the morality of the way in which the campaign in Southern Africa was being conducted. The Liberal leader of the Opposition, Henry Campbell–Bannerman (1836–1908), posed the question: 'When is a war not a war? When it is carried on by methods of barbarism in South Africa.' It was a view shared by ever more people.

Yet such opinion could not affect the desire of the government and military authorities to prosecute the war to an outcome wholly favourable to the British. For the truth of the matter was that the 'methods of barbarism' were having the desired effect. The victimisation of non-combatant Afrikaners made it ever more difficult for the commandos to remain active. Furthermore, the blockhouse system and scorched earth policy were slowly rendering guerrilla tactics untenable. The active units, increasingly isolated and with ever less support, could not hold out indefinitely. They also believed that the longer the struggle went on, the worse conditions would become for the rest of the Afrikaner population. As the Boer general Jacobus de la Rey (1847–1914) noted at the time, 'everything has been sacrificed – cattle, goods, money, wife and child. Our men are going about naked and our women have nothing but clothes made of skin to wear. Is not this the bitter end?' The notion that the British were attempting systematically to exterminate the Afrikaner people slowly sapped the will to fight on.

The resilience of the Afrikaner people, and the determination of the remnants of the Boer army, were remarkable throughout the whole of 1901. Despite a ruthless onslaught across southern Africa, the British struggled to bring their adversaries finally to heel. It was not until the end of the year that Boer leaders, including future Prime Ministers of

South Africa, Louis Botha (1862–1919) and Jan Smuts, were persuaded into peace negotiations with the British. These were protracted discussions that took place against a backdrop of intermittent fighting, carried out by intransigent commando units and highly focused British forces.

By the middle of May 1902 the war was all but over and discussions were stepped up at Vereeniging. On 31 May, the Boer generals formally surrendered to the British, feeling that this was their only hope of salvaging a future for the Afrikaner people.

Peace

A war that was widely believed at its outbreak to be a trifling affair that would be over in a matter of months, if not weeks, lasted for nearly three years. It had been an amazingly destructive campaign, causing much misery, destruction and death. Figures pertaining to the South African War remain contentious, but it would be safe to say that the British suffered 22,000 losses (many from disease). The Boer army lost 7,000 men, and perhaps as many as 25,000 Afrikaner civilians also lost their lives in the military camps or as a result of fighting. African deaths in the camps alone have been calculated at 14,000, though this figure may be a conservative estimate. Furthermore, thousands of acres of farmland were destroyed and tens of thousands of homesteads destroyed. Entire communities were ruined, families broken up, friendships lost forever.

Against such a backdrop, the negotiation of a peace settlement was never going to be a straightforward process. The Afrikaner delegates to the discussions wanted strict safeguards put into place that not only would protect their culture, but also offer strong indication that the future prosperity of the Afrikaner people would be upheld in a British-dominated southern Africa. For its part, the London government was concerned to protect the gains made during the campaign.

Terms acceptable to both parties, which would form the basis for negotiation, were reached only slowly. It would be some weeks before the Treaty of Vereeniging could be agreed, but the eventual outcome was favourable to a majority on both sides, leading Kitchener to proclaim, 'We're good friends now.'

Under the terms of the treaty, the Afrikaners, who at first had tried to get protectorate status for the OFS and the Transvaal, agreed to forfeit their independence in return for the release and immediate repatriation of all prisoners of war. They also negotiated the right to bear arms, protection for the use of the Dutch language in schools and courts and limited economic safeguards. The British therefore agreed to recognise Boer property claims, to rebuild destroyed homes and honour Boer war debts up to £3 million (in the event, Milner would spend some £16 million restoring destroyed lands and property). Relief for war victims would continue until no longer deemed necessary. The way was also left open for future negotiations regarding a return of Afrikaner political autonomy within a self-governing colony. In the meantime, full political rights were bestowed upon all white males in each of the four colonies.

Most pertinently of all, the British gave assurance that they would not extend the Cape franchise to the defeated states *before* the introduction of self rule. In other words, blacks would not be enfranchised anywhere else in southern Africa until a democratic form of white government had been inaugurated. In this way were the Afrikaners given a decisive influence over the future political status of the majority African population.

Immediately, the OFS and the Transvaal were assimilated into the British empire and along with the Cape and Natal governed by Milner, the British High Commissioner to South Africa. This was the first time that all four colonies had come simultaneously under the same administration. The future state of South Africa was beginning to take shape.

ONE CONSEQUENCE OF THE WAR

Alfred Milner in 1902 was driven by a vision – a vision of a single southern African state, peopled by go-ahead Britons who would oversee an efficient, industrialised nation, floated on mineral wealth and resting on the best industrial base modern technology could provide. What he failed to take into account was that the Afrikaner people, although defeated, were hardly beaten. Their national aspirations were still intact. If anything, the war effort and the ruthlessness shown by the

British in winning the campaign had served merely to reinforce distinctions of the Afrikaner culture and ethnicity. It had also pushed to the forefront of Afrikaner politics a generation of men who were not only highly talented, but equal to the challenge of defending their cause under British hegemony. Milner, and those who followed in his footsteps, would not be able to have it all their own way.

Reconstruction

The moral consequences of the war were such that the victors agreed to underwrite the costs of rebuilding vast areas of southern Africa populated by Afrikaner communities. This was part of Milner's policy of reconstruction, which attached great importance to a speedy economic recovery as a prerequisite to political stability. Money was earmarked for spending on various projects such as the railways and agriculture as a means of getting the mines back to full productivity as quickly as possible. Plans for a customs union were announced and government loans made available to help people back on to their feet.

All claims for compensation were dealt with by a bureaucracy that was soon overwhelmed by its work load. In total, Afrikaners lodged over 60,000 claims for damage to property, livestock and land. Few of these were disputed and most were paid in full. Africans, who were also technically eligible for compensation, were not treated in the same equitable manner as whites. With a need to limit pay-outs, the decision was taken to reduce all African claims to one-sixth of their value. In consequence, the amount paid to Africans was derisory and many were left with nothing at all.

Milner was personally involved in the process of reconstruction. He worked hard at getting people back to work on the land, thus facilitating a full industrial and agricultural revival. His aim was to move white farmers away from subsistence production to commercial activities, and therefore he encouraged maize and wheat production as well as meat and milk ventures. In this he enjoyed much success, despite a prolonged drought from 1903 until 1908. However, this swing towards capital agricultural practices excluded African farmers who could apply for start-up loans which they were rarely granted.

Consequently, many African cultivators found themselves squeezed off the land. This suited Milner's design, for he wanted African labour to meet the needs of the re-emerging mining concerns. The flow of Africans to the mines and cities was further guaranteed when the administration undertook to import some 60,000 indentured labourers from China to work on the land. This force actively undercut African demands for a decent wage level and better working conditions.

In 1903, internal customs duties across southern Africa were abolished. A single economic union was introduced, which included not only the four colonies, but also the High Commission territories of Basutoland and Bechuanaland, linked by a single railway network and given a common currency. Swaziland was added later. This was an expensive undertaking, as the incorporation into the rail network of the former republics had to be started almost from scratch.

By 1905, southern Africa was well on the way to making a full recovery; Milner's programme of reconstruction was marked by success. This is not necessarily the way he felt about matters, however. For this there were two reasons. Primarily, Milner's vision was built on a mass wave of immigration from Britain, which he believed would ensure British cultural and political domination of the region. Over a million and a half acres of land were set aside for the immigrants. But they never arrived, the plan wrecked by a British parliament concerned about the repercussions of such a programme. The land was ultimately settled by Afrikaners.

Secondly, by 1905 it was clear that although British economic ascendancy across southern Africa had been achieved, the administration had failed to impose its political will. This was especially true with regard to the Afrikaner population. In the immediate post-war period, Afrikaner nationalist sentiment began to flourish. Common cultural bonds were emphasised, and although Afrikaner political leaders followed a conciliatory path in dealing with the British, the majority of the rest of the population formed into a focused movement that was determined to uphold its cultural distinctiveness. The former republics may have been subjugated to the broader needs of British imperialism, but this did not necessarily translate into political acquiescence.

The one area where there seemed to be great community of purpose between the British and Afrikaners was their attitude to the African population. Throughout the period of reconstruction, black rights were ignored and their status, political, social and economic, was eroded even further. In all spheres of life, African needs were subjugated to those of a white minority that was more and more openly prejudiced in its outlook and actions. This situation was becoming ever more pronounced and would get far worse over the coming decades.

CHAPTER SIX

Unification and Segregation: South Africa in the early twentieth century

Historical consensus has been reached over the fact that the process of colonial conquest in southern Africa, which started in the 1650s and involved the subjugation of both the land and the indigenous peoples of the region, was completed in the immediate aftermath of the South African War. Laws passed during this time, limiting African access to land and curtailing rights to participation in the political process, were given a legal basis in the 1909 Act of Union. Many Africans reacted to this assault on their liberties by attempting to stay out of the cash labour economy for as long as possible. However, it was ever more difficult to survive by traditional practices and through subsistence labour. Thousands upon thousands of Africans were forced to seek employment on white farms or in the urban industrial sector.

Racial discrimination was by this time a commonplace across the region and it caused increasing resistance within certain African communities. This was most marked in Natal. Here, there were widespread protests over loss of land to white settlers, and unrest at the way in which the colonial authorities were governing in the reserves. Matters came to a head in 1906, when the government attempted to impose a £1 poll tax on all African males not already paying the hut tax. Some communities simply delayed payment for as long as possible. Others decided on outright defiance. A minor Zulu chief, Bambatha (d.1906), led an open rebellion that attracted thousands of followers. The colonial authorities reacted by sending troops into the reserves, who looted houses and burned the fields of actual or suspected tax resisters. When two white policeman were killed south of Pietermaritzburg panic spread among the settler population causing the authorities to step up their campaign in the reserves. Systematically, the rebellion was crushed and Bambatha was hunted down and killed. A further 3,000 Africans, mainly Zulus, also lost their lives. This was the last major rebellion against white rule for some years to come.

The white communities were forced to unite in the face of such resistance. A political alliance between Afrikaans and English speakers was cemented when, in 1906, the British Liberal government restored internal autonomy to the OFS and the Transvaal. This act, agreed on in principle at the Peace of Vereeniging, was a deliberate attempt to conciliate Afrikaner politicians and paved the way for talks leading to political union. The policy worked. Local elections, held in 1907, returned Afrikaner majorities in both states. In the Transvaal, the clear winner was the *Het Volk* (The People) party, led by the influential ex-generals Louis Botha and Jan Smuts. This party, which campaigned on the promise of maintaining rural white hegemony at the expense of African producers and cultivators, worked towards reconciliation between English and Afrikaans speakers and quickly instigated an alliance with moderate Britons. This was beneficial to the region as a whole. Not only did it make the job of administration easier, it also created a sense of stability and fostered conditions that encouraged investment from abroad. Both factors were vital if the planned union was to become a reality.

The Union of South Africa

The common market instigated across southern Africa by Milner confirmed the economic unity of the region. The subsequent mutual conciliation of other Afrikaner and British interests meant a similar political arrangement was inevitable.

To this end, a National Convention met at Durban and Cape Town between October 1908 and February 1909. Consisting of fourteen Afrikaner and sixteen British delegates but with no African, coloured or Asian communities represented, the aim of the Convention was simply to reach agreement over a constitution for a new South African state. There was an immediate divergence of opinion over the eventual composition of the Union, between those who wished to see a federal state brought into being and those who desired a unitary nation. This was settled in favour of the unitary model. Thereafter, the Convention was characterised by compromise. A set of four principles was established and formed the basis for the subsequent constitutional agreement.

Firstly, it was agreed that the four colonies would be bound into a unitary political body under parliamentary sovereignty. This would be established along the lines of the British system, with an upper and a lower house. Secondly, it was confirmed that in each colony, existing franchise laws would be left unaltered. This meant that non-whites would be without the right to vote except in the Cape. Thirdly, parliamentary constituencies were to be weighted equally in terms of voter numbers, thereby ensuring an equitable share of power between urban and rural areas. Lastly, safeguards were to be put into place protecting the Dutch language, and English and Dutch were to be the joint official languages of the state. There was to be no Bill of Rights.

These principles, to varying degrees, entrenched in the constitution the supremacy of the white minority at the expense of the African majority. African political and traditional leaders were dismayed by the proposed constitution. There were no efforts to see the franchise extended to Africans at any point during the Convention. Nor did Cape representatives attempt to have their franchise laws, allowing limited black participation in the political process, extended elsewhere. Parliament was to be a preserved white interest. Insult was further added by new laws which excluded Africans from standing for election. Instead, a number of seats were to be set aside for special senators whose remit would include representing African opinion and interests.

A delegation of moderate men led by the teacher and Xhosa-language newspaper editor John Jabavu (1859–1921) was sent to London to protest against the draft constitution before it was ratified by the British parliament. Although given the time to express its opposition to the appropriate authorities, nothing the delegation said could convince the right people to act on its behalf. Simultaneously, an alternative African Convention was convened at Bloemfontein in March 1909 to demand an end to racist discrimination and the creation of a colour-blind franchise, open to all adult males. Although a formidable body, this

Convention had no means of asserting its call nor the necessary resources to mobilise a protest movement against the new constitution. In April, the elite African Political (later People's) Organisation (APO), a Cape pressure group that fought to distinguish coloured people from Africans, attacked the constitution as being 'un-British', and called for the existing Cape franchise laws to be extended throughout the Union. But again, nothing came of this action. In the future, organisations such as the APO would only be able to make themselves heard by working in concert with African and Indian pressure groups.

In the end, the South Africa Act of 1909, confirming the Union of South Africa, was passed easily through the British parliament. The new state, populated by four million Africans, half a million coloureds, 150 thousand South Asians and 1.275 million whites, came into being at the end of May 1910. Two assemblies, elected by white males, formed an administration headed by a Governor-General, who was the British king's representative in South Africa. Although heralded as the march of progress by many people in South Africa and Britain at the time, for the majority of the region's population, Union was unmistakably a step backwards.

A NEW STATE

The state created in 1910 is, in a geographical sense, little altered today. At the time of inception it was decided that the protectorates of Basutoland, Bechuanaland and Swaziland would remain outside the Union for a minimum of five years, until the British government could be convinced that the 'native policy' in these places was equal to its own, loosely defined standards. These High Commissioned territories – so-called because they were overseen by the South African Governor-General – were never incorporated into the South African state. Bechuanaland achieved independence in 1966 as Botswana. Swaziland and Basutoland (modern-day Lesotho), although heavily dependent on South Africa both politically and economically, were never assimilated into the Union.

Concessions to the regions, enacted at the time of Union as a means of off-setting the powers of central government, are also still in place. Administratively, South Africa is run from three different locations:

Cape Town is home to parliament, the executive is situated in Pretoria, the judiciary in Bloemfontein. This arrangement has endured although it is slightly impractical and a little clumsy.

EARLY POLITICAL ALIGNMENTS

After the period of reconstruction, the British administration in South Africa worked towards a political union as the safest and surest way of fostering economic growth and prosperity. This was achieved because a substantive and influential body of Afrikaner politicians saw in Union the means of furthering their own political ends. Increasingly, they also shared the same economic goals as the British. It was further believed that the best way of upholding white interests throughout the region was via a united settler front.

This is not to say that the moderates had it all their way. There were some Afrikaners who were not as readily prepared to accept the new political climate of conciliation, and who therefore actively sought to overturn the Union. Their main concern was that Afrikaner influence would be diminished in a shared government and that state resources would be lavished disproportionately on British people and business concerns. Although very much on the margins at the time of Union, this lobby would become increasingly powerful over the next decade.

Segregation

The Union of South Africa's first elections were held on 31 May 1910. An exclusive franchise, representing under a quarter of the Union's total population of 6 million, returned Louis Botha as Prime Minister. Although an Afrikaner, Botha, a successful general in the South African War, had earlier in his life been an outspoken critic of the policies of Paul Kruger. This single-mindedness now translated into a determination to unite white political interests and to this end, in 1911, he founded the South Africa Party (SAP), representing equally the interests of moderate English and Afrikaans speakers. In common with the majority of white politicians at this time, Botha believed that white and black interests were not and never could be one and the same thing. His administration acted upon this belief.

Over time, a concerted policy of segregation was imposed. With its roots lying in previous legislation such as the Shepstone reserve programme in Natal, segregation was a deliberate attempt to enforce separation between Africans and whites in every sphere of life: the political and administrative, as well as the economic and social. Where segregation already existed it was to become more pervasive; where it did not exist it was to be enacted. The end result was the permanent repression of the majority population of South Africa and its total elimination from the political process.

Segregation was never clearly defined and it emerged over a period of some thirty years. However, its implications were obvious, as was its end result: the subjugation of all black communities. Moreover, because it was never clearly defined the policy was never limited. In consequence, segregation could be applied across the board and in almost any circumstances. Legalities were the only constraint upon the enforcement of the policy and these could be changed if necessary.

The first phases of segregation emerged out of the findings of the South African Native Affairs Commission (SANAC), which was convened prior to the Act of Union and sat from 1903 to 1905. The brainchild of Milner, SANAC's aim was to formulate policies for South Africa's African population. A largely conservative body, the Commission's brief was to propose the means by which white power and authority could be maintained in a future united southern African state. Its final report was far-reaching, and although not wholly implemented, formed the basis for the so-called native policy of future administrations.

SANAC investigated existing practices within the four colonies, and where it felt these worked, proposed they be extended across the entire region. Thus, the Shepstone system of separate 'native' administration, and the demarcating of land between black 'reserves' and areas of white settlement, was a prime recommendation. The Commission proposed the creation of African 'locations' in urban areas while, at the same time, that pass laws be enacted to administer the flow of labourers into the towns. In terms of the franchise, SANAC was strongly opposed to the extension of the Cape laws to the rest of the country. It also decreed on matters such as education, wage levels and working conditions, generally deciding on schemes that would free the government of any expenditure on African welfare.

Because SANAC was constituted as a consultative body, established African, coloured and Indian political bodies and leaders were mostly happy to co-operate with the Commission. How much the views of such groups were taken into account when SANAC drew up its final report is reflected in the fact that all findings were wholly unsympathetic to the opinions they had expressed. When SANAC's report was published, those non-whites who had participated in the consultative process were largely dismayed. However, the uneven manner in which segregation was initially imposed led many of these men to believe that the report was an extreme document never to be substantially implemented. By the time they realised this was not true, it was too late.

SEGREGATION IMPLEMENTED

In the second decade of the twentieth century, segregation became a reality across South Africa, affecting the daily lives of all the country's black inhabitants. In a time of relative hardship, millions found life a constant battle for survival. The inequitability of this situation was compounded by the fact that the government was openly providing relief for poor and unemployed white folk who, as potential voters, were viewed as a constituency whose plight could not be ignored. Moreover, discrimination meant that Africans were everywhere losing out to whites in the job market, even in areas of employment such as domestic service where they had traditionally formed the bulk of the labour force.

This was the backdrop against which segregation was at first played out. Discrimination was, at times, extremely petty: in the Cape, for example, laws were passed restricting the sale of liquor to Africans. Basic liberties were everywhere impinged upon. Pass laws restricted an individual's freedom of movement. Urban segregation was introduced, limiting areas of black residence to specific localities. The right of Africans to own property came under attack and, ultimately, would be outlawed. An industrial colour bar that was given legal status by the Mines and Works Act of 1911, restricted Africans to unskilled, poorly paid jobs on the Rand. On the docks, it was increasingly common for

African workers to be housed in barracks, where they were effectively under the control of their employers.

In the rural areas of the country such discrimination had been common for some time but was now extended. Legislation exclusive to the eastern Cape, restricting each African family to a tiny plot of land, was in 1910 extended throughout the rest of that colony. This made it virtually impossible for an average sized family to sustain itself through agricultural practices alone. Matters were even worse in Natal, where Africans, and after Union, Indians, were prevented from owning land. Meanwhile, locally enacted legislation meant that across the country sharecroppers and tenant farmers, 'squatters' in the idiom of government, were being evicted by the thousand, with vacated plots being turned over to poor white farmers. This process was particularly marked throughout the OFS and the Transvaal where there was a tendency for the administration to respond to popular white notions that Africans were prospering at their expense.

AFRICAN RESPONSES TO SEGREGATION

Although a co-ordinated response to the onset of legislated discrimination was slow in coming, there was a tradition of resistance to the extension of white controls across southern Africa, and this was evident in the early 1900s. Disparate, localised movements could be effective for only so long. Nevertheless, many communities participated in campaigns against the extension of land controls and tax demands. Mostly, these activities were of a passive nature or might extend to a boycott of local white trading stores and other symbols of colonial rule. On occasion, however, instances of armed resistance broke out, most notoriously with the Bambatha rebellion of 1906.

The callous disregard for African rights in all spheres of life both leading up to and in the aftermath of the Act of Union ensured the emergence of some kind of formal, organised response from black communities. The African riposte came in the shape of the South African Native National Congress (NNC), which was formed in 1912 and was the forerunner of the African National Congress. Initially a collective headed by mostly missionary-educated, middle-class men, the NNC was a moderate, liberal body which aimed to bring together

Africans as a means of protecting such black rights as still existed while ensuring there was no further erosion of these. This was the beginning of African nationalism in South Africa.

Initially, the movement was a small one because it had little mass appeal and, further, no desire to attract any such following. There were a number of reasons for this. Primarily, when the NNC first met at Bloemfontein in 1912, its self-appointed leadership contained no men of radical persuasion. The delegates were drawn overwhelmingly from the westernised African elite, and were by profession mostly teachers or journalists or church ministers. They had been instructed in the 'British way' of democratic institutions and so, as a body, were steadfastly loyal to the British empire. In consequence, in the Congress there was no commonly held belief that white rule was necessarily a bad thing. As an example of this, the NNC's first President, the teacher, Congregationalist church leader and journalist John Langalibalele Dube (1871–1946), who had spent many years studying and working in the United States, supported the policy of segregation because he believed it empowered traditional African rural leaders. This opinion pervaded the ranks of an organisation that, far from trying to bring an end to colonial rule, merely wished to have some bearing on its course.

The NNC then was a cautious body, not dissimilar to the Indian National Congress in its earliest years. The Congress wished to

John Langalibalele Dube, President of the South African
Native National Congress

influence policy makers and so its approach was limited to petitioning in Cape Town and London and to forming delegations which would be sent to discuss (rather than argue) a particular point with the relevant authority. There were attempts at spreading opinions through newspapers and journals but this was very much an exercise in preaching to the converted. The NNC had no means of reaching out to the masses. Indeed, around the time of its inception, the Congress was at pains to distance itself from popular protest movements against the pass laws and other discriminatory legislation.

The NNC was a continuation of formal African political organisations prior to the Act of Union. One of the first such bodies, the Natal Native Congress, also headed by Dube, was formed in 1900 to further the aspirations of prosperous, westernised peasants in Natal. Other similar groups emerged around the same time in the OFS and the Transvaal, and like the Natal Native Congress, were moderate bodies that limited their campaigns to petitioning. The most radical call made by any of these bodies was for the extension of the Cape franchise throughout the rest of southern Africa.

However, when this legislation was *not* extended to the other three colonies at the time of Union, as had been widely predicted by African political leaders, there was some questioning of the failure to elicit a favourable response from the British government. This did not extend to examining the efficacy of moderation and petition, but rather, the effectiveness of having numerous small congresses all making the same point, not necessarily in the same way and almost certainly at different times. A need for unity was spotted, and Dube took the lead in drawing together like-minded men in a single political body.

Traditional rulers were deliberately courted by Dube, for he believed they had a crucial role to play within society. He therefore formed a NNC Council of Chiefs on which sat paramount chiefs from a number of tribes. This group was expected to speak on behalf of its peoples at NNC meetings as well as spread the Congress' ideals concerning the transformation of African polities 'from barbarism to civilisation'. It would not be until the emergence of a more progressive leadership, in the middle of the century, that this Council would be abolished. The patronising ideals of the early Congress did not last quite as long.

Because of its moderate approach, the NNC had no effective means of influencing local or British governmental policy. It therefore remained a largely ineffective body for several decades. As a forum for potential opposition to colonial rule its symbolic significance far outweighed its actual importance. Under such circumstances, it did not take long for an amount of disillusionment to set in among the followers of the NNC.

COLOURED RESPONSES

At the time of union, the APO had still not made contact with African political organisations. Under the leadership of Abdullah Abdurahman (1872–1940), who had been the first coloured pupil accepted to study at the South African College in Cape Town, the APO continued to argue for special recognition of South Africa's coloured population as distinct from the African majority. It lobbied against the extension of pass laws to coloureds and for their right to access to white educational institutions in the Cape. When an APO campaign to see the Cape franchise laws extended throughout the country failed, Abdurahman did not abandon his largely loyalist stance to the government, but rather, continued in the belief that his demands for coloured–white equality would ultimately be met. It would be some years before he was finally disabused of this notion.

INDIAN RESPONSES

The Indian population had risen in number from some 10,000 in 1875 to 100,000 by the end of the nineteenth century. Many South Asians had travelled to southern Africa of their own volition in order to set up in business. Many had established themselves as successful merchants and traders. The Indian population of South Africa, concentrated mostly in Natal, formed a significant and distinct cultural grouping within the country at the time of Union and was wide open to many forms of discrimination.

Indians had formed political pressure groups in Natal and the Transvaal from the 1890s. However, these were organisations representing the interests of the prosperous mercantilist classes. They campaigned against trading and franchise restrictions, but did little or nothing to address the plight of the thousands of Indian indentured labourers in southern Africa. Matters were to change from the early 1900s, when Indian political groups slowly became more radicalised.

This was mostly owing to the efforts of M.K. Gandhi (1869–1948). Gujerati born, Gandhi had been called to the bar in London in the early 1890s before returning home to practise his new profession. He was a shy, nervous character and as a result, failed miserably in his first case. Subsequently, in 1893, he took a brief to represent an Indian merchant company in South Africa. He would remain there for a further twenty-one years.

Gandhi, on arrival in southern Africa, was an ardent loyalist to the British empire with an almost unshakeable belief in the notion of British fair play and justice. However, in a matter of years, he had been disabused of any such ideals. The discrimination he personally received at the hands of the authorities, coupled with the indignities and injustices daily wrought upon the Indian population of Natal, convinced him that he needed to seek some form of redress. He still believed that he could appeal to a sense of British justice but became convinced that a different tactical approach was needed.

This approach was based on Gandhi's changing outlook. He began to turn his back on Western ways, embracing instead a more ascetic view of life that incorporated a range of different eastern religious influences. Attaching these to ideas he extracted from the works of Tolstoy, Ruskin and other European thinkers, Gandhi developed a philosophy known as *satyagraha* (literally meaning soul-force). Sometimes mistaken for simple passive resistance, *satyagraha* was to guide him in all his political and social campaigns, starting in 1907 in South Africa.

His first activity in Natal was an attempt to overturn discriminatory taxes levied on all indentured Indian labourers who wished to remain in South Africa once their term of employment was at an end. This movement enjoyed some popular support when it was broadened to encompass protests against franchise limitations and restrictions on Indian business activities and freedom of movement. However, passive protest could only go so far, and the authorities merely ignored Gandhi and his followers until the campaign fell apart.

Until the time of his next major campaign, Gandhi focused his attention on ameliorating conditions for Indians in South Africa while educating potential followers in the ways of *satyagraha*. He enjoyed only limited success on either front. However, when in 1912 the Botha government declared that all future immigrants from South Asia would be classified as undesirables, Gandhi was well placed to lead a protest movement. The tactic of protest was the deliberate flouting of unjust laws as a means of highlighting the discrimination inherent in the system. Other issues were also incorporated into the protests, including the right of Indians to own property, a ban on men entering South Africa with more than one wife, and restrictions on Indian movements into the Cape and OFS. The movement began with the deliberate breaking of a law which forbade Indians to enter the Transvaal from Natal. Other protests followed, such as pass burnings and the non-payment of some taxes. Momentarily, the Indian movement linked up with a simultaneous strike wave among rural workers. Splits quickly emerged, however, when the authorities reacted with characteristic ruthlessness.

Gandhi was one of thousands of Indians imprisoned. Strong protests by the Government of India, concerning the brutal treatment meted out to unarmed protestors, forced the South African authorities into a compromise. The ban on polygamous families entering South Africa was lifted, as was the tax on indentured labourers. The victory was, however, not absolute. Restrictions on Indian freedom of movement, and their right to own property, remained in place. Gandhi nonetheless could claim a slight moral victory and left for India. He had had a radicalising effect upon Indian politics in South Africa, but he could not bridge the material gulf that existed between the commercial Indian elite and the majority of impoverished labourers. Indeed, the former were largely pleased when Gandhi decided to leave Africa.

Native Land Act, 1913

The Native Land Act of 1913 was the first piece of far-reaching seg-regative legislation passed in South Africa, and was a cornerstone of that policy. The implications of the Act were clear, limiting as it did African ownership of land to specially created reserved locations. This shook some politicised Africans out of their moderate state. The NNC, however, reacted in the expected manner by sending a feeble delegation of protest to London.

Simply put, the Act outlawed the renting or purchase of land by Africans anywhere outside areas designated as reserves. The reserves covered a mere 7 per cent of the land total of South Africa, that is 22 million acres, and were both removed from areas of white land ownership and deliberately placed away from the most desirable areas of agricultural commerce. Land was demarcated either as 'white' or 'native' and there could be no change between the two categories. So, in effect, African cultivators were banned from some 93 per cent of the land of the Union (or, viewed another way, 67 per cent of the population were restricted to 7 per cent of the country's land mass). Furthermore, sharecropping was forbidden in the OFS, and while tenant farming was allowed to continue, the tenant was now required to give a minimum of 90 days' labour a year to the landlord.

This did not bode well for the future. Where reserves already existed in Natal they had been plagued by disease affecting livestock and problems relating to over-grazing. Drought and famine were also huge obstacles to prosperity in these areas. This forced Africans to seek work as wage labourers on white farms or at the mines. In future, ever more people would be forced to sustain themselves from a limited area of land, suggesting that unless the reserves were properly managed and invested in, the same problems, in exaggerated form, would emerge to catastrophic effect. The government was aware of this possibility and earmarked more land for further classification as reserved territory at a later date. (In 1936, the area reserved for Africans was doubled.)

While the government's strategy was to force ever more Africans into the reserves, it simultaneously planned to give as much help as it could to white farmers in establishing themselves on vacated plots. Legislation passed in 1912 divided into sizeable plots land previously owned by the state or large land-holding concerns. These were made available for purchase by white farmers at concessionary rates. Furthermore, capital loans (at fixed rates of low interest) were easily obtainable to allow for investment in machinery, livestock and homestead improvements. The government also undertook to invest in infrastructural developments to enable white farmers to move their produce to markets. Special low rates were introduced on the railroads to encourage profitability.

The terms of the Act not only gave whites unrestricted access to the best land but also gave them increased powers over African tenant farmers, from whom they could demand labour hours. This further aided the spread of commercial farming activities, for it guaranteed a cheap supply of regular labour. Many sharecroppers in the OFS were similarly forced into a tenant labour relationship with landowners.

The implementation of the Act caused much dislocation among rural African communities and no small amount of suffering. The one area of exception was the Cape, where the Act could not be immediately enforced due to prevailing franchise laws. In practice, sharecropping also continued in many areas of the Free State, simply because it was more economic for white farmers to continue with this type of arrangement. Sharecropping promised a guaranteed yield that did not have to be worked for and bypassed the need to pay African farmers and their families a cash wage. The Act, then, was not implemented in a uniform manner and many of the practices technically forbidden under its terms continued on the quiet.

EARLY RESISTANCE IN THE RESERVES

The forms of protest characteristic within rural African societies in the period after colonisation quickly emerged in the new reserves. In general, there was a marked resistance to the authorities, with individuals refusing to honour tax demands, failing to register for passes and declining to register their land. The reserve chiefs, now government employees, were also attacked as being mere collaborators with the state. Overall, such protests were limited in their effect and the harsh realities of life in the reserves soon superseded any notion that the *status quo* could be radically altered.

Instead, communities channelled their energies in other directions in the hope that renewal could be had by other means. There was a perceptible growth in independent churches, most of which had strong African-Christian roots. These organisations gave thousands new hope in the face of their plight at the hands of the government, and often

fulfilled not only a social need but also a political one. Many of the so-
called 'Ethiopian' churches adopted a counter-segregationist stance,
rejecting any idea of African assimilation into white society and calling
instead for a return of Africa to African people. The notion appealed to
increasingly more Africans in the early decades of the twentieth century
and separatist religious sects, some with a millenarian outlook, proliferated from a recorded 96 in 1918 to over 800 by the end of the
Second World War.

AFRICAN LABOUR ON THE RAND

Within a short time of the passing of the Native Land Act it was clear
that the new areas of African settlement were not going to be able to
sustain a growing population. Most lands remained underproductive
and suffered from over-grazing and serious erosion. This was symp-
tomatic of the fact that, in order to reach subsistence levels, families
were forced to work the land throughout the year and could not afford
to leave it fallow for even a short period of time. The only way around
this problem was to send young men, or a family head, to work at the
mines, as a means of easing pressure on the land and raising a cash wage
to make up harvest shortfalls.

There was then, in the early years of the Union, increased immigration of Africans to urban areas, especially to the Rand. Here, Africans were subjected to strict pass law controls and they faced protests
from white miners who resisted all attempts at their being replaced
by cheap migrant labour. There were protests against the pass controls in 1913, and that same year, black industrial action against
unfair treatment at the mines. Both movements were dealt with
ruthlessly. Pass offenders were imprisoned, while the right to strike
was limited to whites. A general strike of white workers the following year centred on calls for protection against competition from
Africans. Both the mine owners and government made vague
promises to appease the strikers, a move that did nothing to guarantee the safety of black workers. Physical attacks on Africans became
an everyday reality in the mines and on the streets of the cities. Their
lives were as much a daily struggle to survive there as they were in
the reserves.

The First World War

As a dominion state of the empire, Britain's war was equally South Africa's war. When in early August 1914 George V (1865–1936) declared war on Germany, he did so on behalf of countries such as South Africa, who were then constitutionally obliged to fight that cause. For the ruling SAP this presented no moral problems whatsoever. The government, Afrikaners and Britons alike, backed the metropolitan country and supported the Prime Minister, Louis Botha, as he rapidly prepared the South African military for active service.

However, there were substantial lobbies who opposed the country's entry into the war, and others who argued vehemently that South Africa was fighting on the wrong side. There were those who believed a neutral stand could and should be made on a war that had its origins in European *realpolitik* and had nothing to do with Africa. There were other hard-line Afrikaners who objected to fighting on behalf of Britain and against Germany, a country seen as a natural ally of the Afrikaner people. This latter group caused some internal security problems for the administration. There was an uprising in the western Transvaal, and one army general defected with a small band of troops to German South West Africa. However, the rebellion was contained and in 1915, German South West Africa was conquered, to be administered thereafter by the Union government.

All formal and most informal African protests against the Native Land Act came to an end once war was declared. For its part, the NNC approached the government with an offer to raise African troops for combat. Similar offers were received from a number of chiefdoms, acting independently of the NNC. The Congress acted in the certain belief that in the longer run such a gesture of loyalty would elicit a favourable response from the authorities in Britain to their demand for greater political representation. The South African government, however, was not keen to take up the offer and responded that, 'the present war is one which has its origins among the white people of Europe and the Government are anxious to avoid the employment of its native citizens in warfare against whites'. Under the exigencies of the war this stance was modified only slightly.

Immediately war was declared, colonial and German forces clashed along the South African borders with the neighbouring German colony. German South West Africa was easily occupied once the British navy cut off its coastal supplies in July 1915. Thereafter, a South African force led by General Smuts was deployed in a successful campaign in German East Africa from February 1916. In both instances, Cape coloureds were to be found in service. In eastern Africa, a few African soldiers saw action, but were mostly employed as servants.

South African forces joined the allied ranks in Europe and fought on the Western Front. Performing heroically at the Battle of Delville Wood in 1916, the force was severely depleted in the Belgian campaign of 1917 and throughout the final phases of the war the following year. In total, South African fatalities during the First World War in Africa and Europe were a combined 7,304 (715 of whom were African).

African regiments were also formed for service in Europe, mostly as auxiliary workers. These units would unload ships, carry stretchers, or fetch fuel. They lived under strict segregation and were not permitted to fraternise with European troops or civilians. Conditions in these compounds were especially harsh as supplies were rationed and liquor prohibited so, unsurprisingly, there were instances of unrest when discipline broke down. During their working hours, however, Africans did manage to spend time with troops from other countries (mostly Britain and France) who were usually welcoming and supportive of protests against the unnecessary privations of African life at the front.

At home, South Africa was greatly affected by the First World War. With European trade interrupted and import routes cut off, the manufacturing sector was given a huge boost and underwent a period of rapid expansion. The value of goods produced within South Africa almost tripled in the four years of the war and export orders soared. In order to meet the needs of the manufacturing sector African migration was encouraged by the suspension of petty pass restrictions. However, the average worker, black or white, was not the recipient of the material rewards of this boom. The cost of living rose as cheap imports dried up and inflation began to take a hold of the economy. In order to maintain costs, meanwhile, many employers sought to cut wage levels.

The new land legislation ensured that white farmers who were established could make a decent living during the war. The same was not true for the rural black population. Left to fend for themselves in the reserves, increasing numbers of Africans were left facing destitution, which fed unrest in the urban areas where more Africans had hoped, but failed to find refuge. The mood in black urban ghettos and in the mining compounds turned militant, and trade unions began to protest against living conditions and high prices in mine stores. The demand for higher wages was also made. A series of strikes started in the mines in 1915 and quickly spread to Johannesburg, where municipal workers joined in with calls for better housing and an end to pass restrictions. This period of militancy lasted until 1917, when prices and the cost of living began to drop. They would both start to rise, however, in the immediate aftermath of the war.

The Post-War Era

South Africa suffered in the same way as other nations that had been directly involved in, or stood on the peripheries of, the war: its economy had been distorted, the social equilibrium altered, and as a consequence, there was a certain amount of political fallout. However, in South Africa each of these factors had a unique, racial twist. The economy had in fact undergone a period of industrialisation, but this had led to the increased urbanisation and radicalisation of the African population who were paid an average wage that could not cover an inflated cost of living. The white population, financially better off and governed by a different set of laws, resented the presence of black workers in the mines and cities of South Africa, and demanded the extension of safeguards to protect them from all such 'competition'. In this call they were backed by an agitated, ever more vociferous Afrikaner nationalist lobby that wished to adopt a tougher line against Africans while severing all ties with Britain.

Botha died in 1919 and was replaced at the head of government by Smuts, who had represented South Africa at the Versailles peace conference, which had confirmed his reputation as an international statesman. Although he was able to win a general election held in

Two segregationists: Louis Botha and Jan Smuts

1920, he had to fend off stiff competition from the recently formed National Party (NP). Headed by another ex-Boer general, JBM Hertzog (1866–1942), who had been trained in Holland as a lawyer and subsequently sat as a judge in the OFS, the NP came into existence as a consequence of Hertzog's opposition to South African participation in the war. Its guiding rationale was to defend Afrikaner interests. To this end it lobbied for South Africa to opt out of the British empire. It was also contemptuous of the majority African population, a stance that attracted to the NP a formidable support base throughout the country.

This was a challenge to the NNC and other black political organisations. For its part, the NNC leadership was split between its traditionally moderate leaders and a new generation of men who had cut their political teeth agitating in the urban areas of the Transvaal and the docks of Natal, and who identified more strongly with the militant tendencies prevalent in these places. There was a debate of sorts as to which way the NNC should go, but ultimately, the moderates were happy to leave the radical work for the African trade unions, who in the immediate aftermath of the war were involved in a number of industrial disputes.

THE EMERGENCE OF THE ICU

There were sporadic strikes of municipal workers across South Africa in 1918. The following year, African dockers at Cape Town, on strike for better pay and working conditions, had started their dispute by refusing to load fruit for export when tens of thousands of South African workers were near to starvation. A similar protest by dockers in Port Elizabeth resulted in the police shooting dead nineteen strikers. This caused a backlash across South Africa that was only slowly contained by the authorities.

African mine worker agitation culminated in an all-out strike in 1920. The strike included a variety of issues: pay (which was running at about one-fifteenth that of white miners); the high rate of injuries and deaths among African miners (four in every thousand were killed on average each year by accidents understood to be largely avoidable); and generally poor living conditions. The police were aided by white miners in breaking the strike. However, despite its repression, the mine owners took heed of the dispute and relaxed the colour bar for a while, but there was no improvement in the conditions under which African miners lived and worked.

An organisation called the Industrial and Commercial Union (ICU) had a hand in guiding all of these strike actions. Formed in Cape Town by docker representatives in 1918, the leadership of the ICU was assumed by the Nyasaland-born Clements Kadalie (1896–1951), a charismatic figure who proved himself to be a most able political organiser. Over the next few months, Kadalie set about assimilating other locally based labour organisations into the ICU. In this way was a network of support built up, representing and championing alike the interests of rural and urban labour.

By the mid-1920s the ICU was claiming a membership list of some hundred thousand. Certainly, it had far more members than the NNC and a genuinely popular base of support. Its influence was widespread throughout the country, and although the ICU probably never fulfilled its claim to represent all South Africa's black workers, it was undoubtedly the only serious African political organisation in the region at the time. It could claim support among not only the black urban working class but also among the small, lower-middle class who found life incredibly difficult in a segregated society. This caused a certain amount of disquiet among employers and officials who had never had to deal with a popular protest movement before.

The success of the ICU lay in the fact that it was an umbrella organisation able to attach itself to any sort of legitimate grievance. Consequently, it was active across the countryside as well as in the towns, where it supported campaigns against land losses, low wages and increased rent demands for tenanted land. It was also able to lend credence to localised issues and link these in with wider, sometimes national agitations against colonial rule.

However, in its very success lay the roots of the ICU's downfall. As the union became bigger, the more it posed a threat to the forces of law and order and commerce. Inevitably, the ICU aroused the disapproval of the state, the police, large business and landowners everywhere. Meetings and rallies were increasingly difficult to hold and would often be broken up by unruly opponents of the movement. The police harassed ICU volunteers and union members were forced out of their jobs. Meanwhile, although it won a few victories for farm workers in the courts, the judiciary for the most part tended to side with land and mine owners.

In the long run, the ICU found it more difficult to achieve benefits favourable to its members. Its radical stance became less easy to maintain, and was gradually diminished. Before its collapse at the end of the 1920s, the ICU had briefly united large numbers of Africans across the country in a common cause. Furthermore, it had been sufficiently strong to fight issues on a national platform and through a dedicated, internationally respected leader (Kadalie had forged strong links with the international trade union movement). Its victories might all have been short-lived but an example for future generations had been set.

THE RAND REVOLT

After the war the division of industrial labour along racial lines was cemented. The truth of the matter was that any concessions made to African labourers caused a reaction among white labourers who feared their position was in some way threatened. The same was also true in reverse, although of course employers were more likely to act in favour of white demands, or go some way towards meeting them.

This situation was illustrated in 1921 when white trade unions started agitating against a slight reduction in white miners' wages and attempts to replace white workers with cheaper African migrants. The mine owners, who were merely attempting to reduce their overheads, were acting in contravention of the 1918 Status Quo Agreement, which reserved specific tasks for whites. Despite this, the owners refused to negotiate, which led to confrontation on a large scale.

In early 1922 a general strike was called in defence of white jobs and amidst calls that the white standard of living be maintained. Orchestrated partly by the newly formed Communist Party of South Africa, and certainly influenced by the wave of worker militancy seen across Europe in the aftermath of the Great War, the so-called Rand Revolt quickly evolved into an insurrection. Afrikaans and English speakers united and marched on Johannesburg, capturing the city hall and hoisting a red standard over it. Armed commando units were formed by militants, who protected workers marching under the slogan: 'Workers of the world unite and fight for a white South Africa.'

The movement was wholly racist in tone and outlook. Opposition was most militant when it was directed at African workers and although strike breakers were attacked regardless of colour, it was blacks who were singled out for the most brutal beatings. For a number of days, the police lost control of the situation. Every time they attempted to intervene they were beaten back by the striker commandos.

Eventually the government interceded on behalf of the mine owners and acted with a ruthless determination to crush the revolt. The army was sent in under a state of martial law. The air force was used to bomb crowds while artillery guns were employed against the commandos. For a week a state of open warfare existed between the army and the commandos, with the latter only brought to heel after a particularly vicious episode of artillery fire. At the end of the strike, some 700 had been injured and over 150 white strikers were dead. A further four men would subsequently be hanged after trial. Thirty Africans were also murdered during the course of the revolt by crowds of white vigilantes.

Peace was quickly re-established, although the longer-term political implication of the revolt was a hardening of white attitudes and a loss of popular support for the SAP. More immediately, white wages were not restored to their previous level. However, proposals to place Africans in jobs delineated for whites were dropped by the mine owners, who now came to realise that compromise with white workers, at the expense of African labour, was preferable to any sort of serious disruption to the industry. In this respect, the Rand Revolt achieved its fundamental aim of safeguarding the supremacy of white workers in the mining industry.

THE NATIVE (URBAN AREAS) ACT, 1923

The trend of the war years, which saw ever more Africans migrating to urban areas to meet the demands of the manufacturing sector, continued into the early 1920s. Predominantly young and male, the migrants lived in crowded and insanitary accommodation, sending back home the bulk of their income. In this way, earnings made on the Rand were used to further the development of agriculture in the reserves.

The influx of Africans, although subject to legislation, was increasingly difficult for local authorities to control. The pass laws were easily evaded, although the fact that in most major towns Africans could only afford to live in run-down suburbs meant they were largely contained within certain districts, usually on the outskirts of a city. Nevertheless, white communities objected to this presence and, as we have seen, workers were wary of the threat posed by cheaper migrant labour. Local traders were similarly concerned about being undercut by new arrivals. There also spread spurious but damaging rumours that plague and other diseases emanated from the African areas.

The government only had loose controls over Africans in urban areas and relied on an advisory council for dealing with complaints or any other issues that might arise from concerned white residents. Pressure was exerted for controls to be formalised, resulting in the appointment of the Stallard Commission. This group suggested tighter influx controls, the permanent segregation of Africans in separate urban areas, as well as stringent curbs on black rights to own property. All of these points were adopted in the 1923 Urban Areas Act. Not only did this allow for forced segregation and forbade the granting of freeholds to Africans, it went so far as to state that Africans 'should only be permitted within municipal areas in so far and for so long as their presence is demanded by the wants of the white ̦population'. Urban 'locations' to match rural 'reserves' therefore came into being, the costs of administering and policing these to be met through rent charges and government monopolies on beer halls. As with the earlier land legislation, the Urban Areas Act could not be imposed in a uniform and steadfast fashion, but it was nonetheless a landmark piece of legislation in the era of segregation.

RURAL HARDSHIP

The inflow of African migrants into the towns was further boosted by a world-wide depression in agriculture which hit South Africa in the mid-1920s and continued into the next decade. Quite simply, the bottom fell out of agricultural markets. White farm owners across South Africa, faced with produce that could not reach a decent price, attempted to offset their losses by cutting the wages of tenant farmers or increasing rent demands. In some cases, tenant farmers found themselves unable to meet their existing rent commitments and so were evicted. Others, offered perhaps as little as a third of their expected wage, simply could not afford to live off the land and so were forced from it. The reserves, meanwhile, had reached crisis point. Few were productive enough to allow for subsistence farming, most were overcrowded, and all were ill-served in terms of infrastructure. They were, in short, economic and social backwaters.

The Pact Government

In 1924, Jan Smuts ('whose footsteps', quipped Hertzog, 'dripped with the blood of his own people') paid the price for his ruthless suppression of the Rand Revolt when he lost that year's general election. He was defeated by the combined forces of Hertzog's NP and Frederick Cresswell's (1866–1948) Labour Party, who had come together to represent the interests of commerce, manufacturing and white urban labour. They campaigned on a platform that had widespread appeal among the enfranchised white population, promising to maintain living standards for 'civilised' (i.e. white) labour where they already existed, and where they did not, raising them to an appropriate level. Keying into the resentment that still lingered after the confrontations of 1922, the Smuts regime was caricatured as the stooge of big business. Smuts was also personally attacked for his supposed favouritism towards English speakers and British interests in South Africa.

The so-called Pact government, led by Hertzog, immediately acted in line with the general tenor of its election programme and as a means of demonstrating its willingness to live up to its promises. Symbolically, a new national flag was unfurled in place of the Union Jack. In 1925, Dutch was replaced by a newly formulated Afrikaans as the joint official language of the country. No move was made to sever the imperial bond with Britain, however, as it was recognised that such a proposal would be politically explosive. Furthermore, trade between the two countries remained good and diplomatic relations cordial. However, as a dominion state of the empire, South Africa at this time was enjoying increasing independent status. This was underlined in 1927 when a separate foreign ministry was created, and South Africa started to appoint its own foreign ambassadors. That same year, the roles of British Governor-General and High Commissioner were divided, and thereafter the British monarch's representative in South Africa would no longer also be the diplomatic envoy. The 1931 Statute of Westminster confirmed the dominions as 'autonomous communities within the British Empire ... united by a common allegiance to the Crown', giving legal expression to South Africa's newfound standing.

At home, the Pact administration persevered with the segregation policy, extending it wherever possible by rolling back any remaining political or social concessions to Africans. It also furthered the bureaucratisation of the state, a move that affected the daily lives of the African and coloured and Asian populations.

The new government's promises to 'civilise' labour resulted in a concerted programme of job creation. This was facilitated by removing blacks, coloureds and Indians from government jobs and wherever possible, on the railways and in the administration, blacks were removed from their posts and replaced by whites. Private industry was brought into line with this effort through the 1926 Mines and Workers Amendment Act. This legislation resulted in specific skilled and semi-skilled jobs being preserved for whites only and was an extension of the colour bar that already existed in the mining industry. Again, this created a new plethora of jobs for whites while consigning Africans to unskilled and menial work.

Wage rates were also fixed along racial lines. Even in unskilled or agricultural jobs, white workers were to be paid a rate suitable to 'persons whose standard of living conforms to the standard of living generally recognised as tolerable from the usual European standpoint'. Africans, meanwhile, 'whose aim is restricted to the barer requirements of the necessities of life as understood among barbarous and underdeveloped people', would be paid commensurately to those 'requirements'.

The Pact acted in a similarly protectionist manner to aid white farmers. Their monopoly over land was upheld, and the reserves would continue to supply labour on the cheap. Import tariffs on agricultural produce were increased, while simultaneously the government undertook to buy surpluses for export at a guaranteed price. The system of loans for poor white landowners was also extended.

This wave of legislation was more overtly racist in tone than anything that had preceded it. It was backed up by new laws allowing for greater police controls in the reserves and over urban black locations, extensions of pass controls, and further restrictions on black and Asian ownership of property (in this case, among the Indian population). Partly a response to heightened rural and urban unrest and resistance and the emergence of the ICU, the new battery of laws also created a black labour surplus to be used by white farmers and businesses. The overall effect was to cast in stone the policy of segregation that had been building for a number of years.

All of this appealed to the majority of the electorate, whose fears were deliberately whipped up in the face of a supposed 'black peril' and the 'degeneration' of white society as a result of an African onslaught. The NP played upon such pernicious ideas time and again, and wherever the opportunity arose, reiterated the fallacy that the 'barbarous' African could not be civilised.

NATIVE ADMINISTRATION ACT

Official thinking held that although Africans could not be 'civilised', this did not mean they did not need to be controlled. It was therefore decided that every administrative step should be taken to ensure the stricter management of the reserves. The Native Administration Act extended the Natal system of tribal law and order to the OFS and the Transvaal, applying at the same time a codified 'Native Law', to be implemented by government-appointed chiefs, who would be responsible for those Africans living under them and collect any taxes due. The Governor-General, as 'supreme chief' of South Africa, was ultimately responsible for all chiefs. He had the right to remove appointees and had the power of veto in courts that were meant to sit in accordance with traditional African laws.

At a stroke, Africans in the reserves were removed from the remit of the government courts and administrative system. This was defended, even by the most liberal-minded of people, as a necessarily positive move and on the grounds that traditional African society could only be protected from outside influence if it was fully segregated from any such influences. Of course, defining these 'traditions' was not an easy task. Not only were they dependent on differences of region, language and culture, but they were neither static nor monolithic. As a result, much African 'tradition' had to be simplified or, in some cases, invented by white administrators and academics in the early 1900s.

The NP also used this piece of legislation to attack the growth of African militancy and the increasing radicalism of the ICU and affiliated organisations. It outlawed speeches or actions likely or intended 'to promote any feelings of hostility between Natives and Europeans'. Ambiguous in the extreme, this clause armed the authorities with an excuse for arresting suspected activists and for breaking up lawfully constituted rallies and meetings.

RURAL PROTEST

Years of drought and harvest failures exacerbated an already volatile situation among the rural African communities of South Africa, who by the late 1920s were under government-sponsored tribal control in the reserves, or living under growing pressure as tenants on white land during a time of economic slump. Under the circumstances there was a radicalisation of the rural black population. Thousands more each year were putting their faith in millenarian movements, awaiting the arrival of salvation and the New Jerusalem. Others took direct action, organising consumer boycotts or resisting colonial controls on a local basis, and to some effect. In the OFS and the Transvaal, the ICU encouraged farm labourers to take on oppressive landlords in the local courts. A few victories were recorded but these were no more than symbolic triumphs.

The Great Depression

The modern economy of South Africa, with a few blips, had enjoyed a steady period of growth in the first decade and a half of the Union. This was helped to no small degree by the willingness of the government to spend heavily on public building and infrastructure schemes and to lend money to small businesses at a low rate of interest. The agricultural depression that set in during the 1920s brought this period of expansion to an end, although South Africa could still rely on its mineral exports to keep the economy on a relatively even keel.

The Great Depression, which started in 1929 with the Wall Street crash, had an adverse effect on South Africa. Demand for its staple products declined sharply, the value price of gold dropped, and foreign investors began to withdraw their capital. Commercial agriculture was especially hard hit as demand fell and prices rose. Local industries were similarly affected and forced to operate with skeleton staffs. Export levels were not sustainable as long as the South African government remained on the fixed gold exchange.

However, gold was to be the country's saving grace. Once the American government acted in 1933 to save the value of the dollar by devaluing it, the British acted similarly in respect of sterling. This led to a rapid increase in the price of gold and gold production. The South African government's revenue therefore escalated and secondary and tertiary industrial growth was stimulated. The value of gold exports rose from £47 million in 1932, to peak eight years later at £118 million. With this money filtering through, the economy went into a period of boom, manufacturing picked up and foreign investors returned to the region.

The rural economy was slower to recover, however, as the export market remained sluggish and cheaper imports became widely available. The government reacted quickly by imposing tariffs to protect industries such as sugar production and more generally extended state subsidies to farmers. Nevertheless, acute poverty afflicted much of the rural population; Africans were left more or less to fend for themselves or to rely on missionary charities. Poor whites were helped by the government which, spurred on by influential organisations such as the Dutch Reformed Church, instigated relief schemes and set about creating jobs.

Two major developments, the setting up of a state-owned iron and steel corporation (Iscor) and an electricity supply commission (Escom), were both constituted to favour employment of a white labour force at the expense of unfettered profitability. As both bodies were state monopolies, they expanded at a rapid rate. Iscor and Escom both acted as a stimulus to secondary industries such as engineering and metal working, and the state backed schemes to develop the nascent chemical industry. White workers were also fitted into the expanding ranks of the army and navy and into the national and local police forces. Industrial colleges were also established to train poor white children in skills that could be employed in the industrial and manufacturing sector.

The boom in industry, coupled with the agricultural depression, resulted in a shift of the white population towards the towns, where they went to seek better wages. Once again, the government intervened to protect the rural white population, by acting to keep parity of wages in the agricultural sector. The 1937 Marketing Act extended the co-operative system instigated by Cape wine producers to all agricultural products. Producers would pool their harvests, which would be sold at a fixed rate to a government control board, who would then grade stock. The commodity would be exported at a subsidised rate but sold internally at a fixed and necessarily higher price. The system favoured large-scale producers and major landowners, but squeezed out poorer white producers and all black tenant farmers, who found it increasingly difficult to market their wares. The Act also pushed up the cost of living in South Africa to a level higher than the world average.

THE RESERVES EXPANDED

Brewing crises in the reserves centred on long-standing problems: overcrowding, food scarcity and starvation, chronic and endemic diseases, high infant mortality rates, and ruination of the land, which in places translated into near desert conditions. This became a political issue in the early 1930s, although few politicians or consultative bodies were prepared to grapple with the crux of the matter, which was that the reserves were entirely unsuited for their designated purpose. Instead, in 1936, the area set aside for Africans was doubled to less than 14 per cent of the total land area of South Africa. This was not enough, however, to ease population pressure or to tackle disease and child mortality.

Another effect of the new land Act was to add to the pressure on tenant farmers outside the reserves. New taxes were imposed that could only be bypassed by working for a landlord for anything between three and six months out of each year. Meanwhile, there was a new drive finally to outlaw sharecropping practices throughout the Free State. Ever more Africans were forced to migrate to the reserves, or to work full time for white farmers, or to try their luck at the mines. The net was being closed around the African population of the country.

Afrikaner Nationalism Resurgent

The Great Depression ended the Pact government, resulting in the rehabilitation of Smuts as a leading figure in the Fusion administration, formed in 1934 by an alliance between Hertzog's NP and the SAP (the two amalgamating for a time into the United Party). A clear rejection of any form of Afrikaner separatism, the United Party (UP) represented an alliance of mainstream white politics in favour of major capitalist interests.

Despite all that was being done to further the cause of the Afrikaner people, the formation of the UP caused an ultra Afrikaner nationalist backlash. Daniel François Malan (1874–1959), a Dutch Reformed Church minister, one-time editor of the nationalist mouthpiece *Die Burger*, and former Pact government cabinet member, reacted by leaving the NP and forming the 'Purified' National Party (HNP). Thereafter, the HNP became the focus for ardent Afrikaner nationalist sentiment, and campaigned strongly for an ending of the British connection and an extension of controls over the non-white population of the country. Malan was an earnest individual, described as 'a man who saw Afrikaner nationalism as ordained by God' and he aimed to mobilise this sentiment and capture political power by drawing into a common unit all Afrikaners, regardless of class, occupation or place of birth.

In this aim he was aided by a secret society known as the Afrikaner Broederbond, which strove to forge a stronger sense of identity and fraternity among the Afrikaans people. Originally set up after the First World War as a vehicle for encouraging the formation of alternative Afrikaner cultural organisations and to stimulate Afrikaner education, the Broederbond grew in influence as it attracted a wide-ranging membership that included members of the clergy, businessmen and politicians. It was crucial in mobilising support for Malan's party, and thereafter shared in the HNP's future successes. It was also integral in encouraging Afrikaner economic independence, supporting business ventures and setting up saving schemes that were channelled through Afrikaner banking houses.

THE CAPE FRANCHISE REVOKED

The influence of the minuscule African vote in the Cape was effectively curtailed in 1930 when the government extended the vote to all adult white women (a mere two years after the vote was extended to all women over the age of twenty-one in Britain). It was finally ended by the 1936 Representation of Natives Act, passed in the face of stiff opposition from a number of non-white political groups (but none from within parliament). This was the last major segregationist act, completing a process that had started some three decades previously. African, coloured and Indian political interests were thereafter exclusively represented in parliament by three especially assigned representatives. An advisory Natives Representative Council was set up but did not ask for or ever try to involve coloured and Indian politicians. However, the government rarely, if ever, took any notice of its suggestions.

No body of opposition had been able to affect the outcome of this legislation. The ICU was a shadow of its former self. The African National Congress (ANC), the new name for the NNC, was an avowedly moderate body which was barely active during the early to mid-1930s. Indeed, the leadership of the ANC was largely out of touch with the masses and spurned popular or direct action. Rather, it contented itself with furthering the social and educational status of the majority of the South African population. Its marginalisation at this time is perhaps best reflected by the fact that it did not always hold annual meetings.

In 1935, the ANC's President, the Oxford-educated, Johannesburg-based lawyer Pixley Seme (1880–1951) attended the All Africa Convention at Bloemfontein, which was called as a means of co-ordinating opposition to the continuing segregationist policies of the government and the proposed withdrawal of the Cape franchise. Seme was one of 400 delegates, among whom could be found representatives of the Communist Party, the APO and the South African Indian Congress. Primarily moderate, professional men, the delegates at the Convention discussed the prevailing political climate at length, then agreed to petition the government. This protest was dismissed out of hand and the Convention melted away.

The Townships

Segregation was still sometimes avoided in the towns and cities where rural migrants continued to swell African numbers during the 1930s (the urban black population at this time doubled in a little over ten years). In response, pass law legislation was stepped up in 1937 to reinforce this inflow and moves were made to fence off the segregated locations.

But the locations could not accommodate the demands of the population. Housing became a major problem, with people crowding into slum areas and setting up home wherever they could, often in someone else's back yard. Squatter camps started to spring up, with illegal shanty towns emerging adjacent to overflowing locations. Served by not even the most basic of amenities, these were squalid places ravaged by poverty and increasingly, crime, where hope did not run high. It was in such circumstances that townships like Soweto started on the outskirts of Johannesburg.

By the late 1930s, most South African conurbations had acquired a unique set of characteristics. The historian Leonard Thompson has described them thus:

> The largest and most conspicuous part was a spacious modern town, consisting of a business sector where people of all races worked during the day and suburbs of detached houses, ranging from opulent to mediocre, owned by white families and served by black domestics. Separated from the modern town was a black location, where mud, clapboard, or corrugated iron buildings, with earth latrines, stood on tiny plots of land and were served by water from infrequent taps along the unpaved paths and roads. With various anomalies, the same principle applied in a hundred or more country villages.

The residents of the locations and shanties reacted to their plight in various ways. African–Christian worship flourished, and other forms of self-help groups came into being, such as voluntary associations and resource pools. Collectivism characterised the approach of many of these communities in the early days of their existence. There also emerged out of the locations a distinct cultural response. Popular music influenced by American ragtime jazz and traditional styles evolved in a distinctive manner, and would be played at shebeens (illegal beer halls) and carnivals. Sport was also important in the locations, and pursuits such as boxing acted as crucial diversions for bored young men.

However, many did not face up to their plight and the harshness of their surroundings in a wholly positive manner. Many took solace in strong liquor, others in marijuana use. There were also places where the police did not dare go, so violent were they. Gangs of organised criminals who were prepared to exploit a need for drugs, or were willing to offer 'protection' to local businesses for a fee, had an increasing hold in the locations and townships. These were dangerous places, where the discontented and disillusioned survived by any means they could.

This is not to say that all hope or sense of community evaporated overnight. In the late 1930s and early 1940s, a number of political actions emanated from urban African areas across South Africa, such as rent boycotts against poor housing conditions and stayaways in protest at low wage levels and high rents. After 1940, a series of bus boycotts in the Alexandra township on the outskirts of Johannesburg succeeded in getting fares to and from the city lowered. Equally as impressive, some squatter communities enacted their own systems of administration where the local authorities were unwilling to do so.

The Second World War

South Africa's entry into the Second World War was not as straight-forward as had been the case in 1914. As a dominion state, South Africa had the right to choose whether or not to fight. The decision was never going to be an unanimous one.

Smuts immediately voiced his support for Britain and argued for entry into the conflict on the side of the allies. Hertzog supported taking a stance of benevolent neutrality. Malan led the Afrikaner opposition to any sort of participation in the war. When the decision was put to a vote in parliament, it was decided by a slender majority of 80 to 67 that South Africa should fight alongside Britain and against Germany. The white population was once again openly divided by this outcome. Hertzog resigned his post, thereby splitting the Fusion administration and leaving the way open for Malan to appropriate control of the NP. Smuts, meanwhile, assumed the role of Prime Minister, much to the chagrin of his opponents.

Some 335,000 South African troops saw active service, with about a third of this number being African or coloured conscripts who were generally employed as non-combatants. This force was deployed in northern Africa and later Italy, and played a crucial role in the 1942 campaign for Madagascar. Total losses amounted to 5,500, a quarter of whom were black.

The material impact of the war on South Africa was enormous. The economy in general, and agricultural production in particular, was given a great boost by the conflict. As imports dropped off, the manufacturing sector of the economy was stimulated to the point where all pass laws had to be suspended for a period of time. The government also invested heavily in the war effort and spent some £650 million, most of which was invested in South African goods and manufactured items. The demand for gold throughout the war remained high and foreign capital was invested in the South African armaments and ammunition industries. (It is estimated that South Africa produced as much as a half of all rifles and pistols used by the allies during the war.) The strategic importance of the Cape was also recognised during the war and local shipyards and docks were used to repair shipping.

The social and political consequences of the war were, however, more ambiguous and a notable anti-war movement developed. There were other groups throughout the country who expressed sympathy for Nazi Germany and some of these were prepared openly to demonstrate their fascistic tendencies, although they were mainly concerned with building Afrikaner power. One such group was the *Ossewabrandwag* (Ox-Wagon Sentinels or OB, a reference to the Battle of Blood River) which, at its height, claimed a membership of 30,000. Originally formed in 1938 as an organisation to celebrate the centenary of the Great Trek, it rapidly developed into a paramilitary group with its own uniform.

In late 1941, the OB began a campaign of sabotage against the government and its supporters, bombing electricity connections and the country's communication infrastructure. One scheme, to sink a ship across the entrance of Durban harbour thereby restricting access to allied shipping, was foiled. The government moved forcefully against the OB. In early 1942, hundreds of members of the OB including 300 policemen were detained under emergency war legislation. Of those arrested, only a fraction were tried for treason, with a few being found guilty. None were handed the ultimate penalty, however, of the death sentence. Among those jailed as an OB conspirator was Balthazar Johannes (John) Vorster (1915–83), a future Prime Minister of the South African Republic.

Other opponents of the war chose to adopt a less extreme approach. Headed by the lawyer Oswald Pirow (1890–1959), who would also feature prominently during the apartheid era, the New Order Party contested the 1942 election on an openly anti-African and anti-Jewish platform (there had been a small migration of European Jewish refugees to South Africa in the 1930s). Sixteen New Order members were elected to parliament in 1942, although all lost their seats the following year and the party disappeared entirely.

In the circumstances, Daniel Malan appeared tempered in his opposition to the government. He continued to argue for the right of South Africa to stay out of the war, and in the longer term, to leave the British empire and be able to appoint its own head of state. It was a stance that attracted ever more support, and it was this movement that, to great effect, would turn on Smuts and his allies after the war.

The Radicalisation of Black Political Groups

Moderate African forms of protest had completely failed by the late 1930s, following the implementation of the final, most far-reaching phases of segregation. The continuing neglect of black, coloured and Indian needs and aspirations, coupled with the rise of extreme white political factions, led to a sharp radicalisation of each of these communities during the early war years.

The first manifestations of this process were seen through the Non-European Unity Movement (NEUM) which represented a broad spectrum of interest groups. Nominally left wing in leaning, the NEUM believed that a concerted programme of boycott and non-co-operation could be used to good effect during wartime conditions. In 1943 it published a ten-point programme, calling for a united stand against segregation and the establishment of democratic rule. 'of the people, by the people, for the people'. However, the NEUM struggled to translate its fighting talk into practical opposition. The Communist Party, which reformed itself after 1936 and adopted a more encompassing racial outlook, was more active in organising black mine and industrial workers during the war, but was unable effectively to establish a broader following.

The ANC, under the presidency of the London-trained doctor Alfred Xuma (1893–1962), also enjoyed a revival in its fortunes. Xuma, who had virulently opposed the removal of blacks and Asians from the electoral roll in 1936, undertook a campaign to recruit new members into the ANC, thereby breathing some life into a hitherto moribund organisation. He stood against mass protests and other forms of affirmative action, however, keeping faith in moderate petition. During the war, he was to be over-ruled in this respect by a radical new generation of activists who questioned the efficacy of petitioning and the inability of the ANC to link up with rural and urban protest movements. While he resisted a lot of proposals for change, Xuma nonetheless acted to modernise the Congress, abolishing the Council of Chiefs and setting up a working committee to oversee the day-to-day running of the ANC.

The young men continued to push for greater change. In 1943 a Congress Youth League was set up, and included in its ranks Oliver Tambo (1917–93), Nelson Mandela (1918–), Anton Lembede (1914–47) and Walter Sisulu (1912–). Mandela has written that the League was formed because he and his colleagues felt the ANC had 'become the preserve of a tired, unmilitant, privileged African elite more concerned with protecting their own rights than those of the masses'. The Youth Leaguers were a new breed of thoughtful, well-educated men; Mandela, a man related to the Thembu royal family, and Tambo, would go on to run a successful law firm in Johannesburg in the 1950s, as would Lembede, while Sisulu had cut his political teeth in the mines. They argued vehemently that the ANC needed to align itself with the struggle of the masses. They also saw that only direct action such as boycotts and strikes could elicit a response from the authorities, and also argued that such strategies would empower individuals. Lembede in particular was keen to stress the need for Africans to assert themselves against those who oppressed them.

Black trade unions emerged more strongly during the war years. The African Mine Workers Union had a membership of some 25,000 in 1944, a mere three years after its formation. In 1946 it was to lead tens of thousands of miners on a strike for better wages and conditions that could only be suppressed using emergency wartime measures, and as a result of which twelve striking miners were shot dead.

THE AFTERMATH OF THE WAR

The Second World War had radically altered the climate of global opinion. The systematic attempts in Europe to exterminate people on

the grounds of their religion, and the horrors attendant on this holo-
caust and other atrocities around the globe, changed the world. There
had also been seismic ideological shifts, as laid down in the Atlantic
Charter and later the United Nations, and a swing in the world balance
of power, which suggested that the old colonial order was about to be
swept away. The notion that people everywhere would enjoy the right
to self-determination gained currency, if only fleetingly.

South Africa remained strangely isolated from all such sentiment.
There white, mostly Afrikaner politicians worked to ensure that the
supremacy of *their* people would be upheld. From the end of the war
until the general election of 1948, the NP became ever more stringent
in its attacks on Africans, Asians and immigrant communities who had
entered South Africa either during or after the war. In the campaign
prior to the election, the NP spoke once again of the dangers inherent
in the 'black peril' and rallied under the slogan: 'the kaffir in his place
and the coolie out of the country'.

This hit a chord with a substantial number of voters in the country –
exactly how many nobody could predict – who feared for their economic prosperity and were concerned over any future social change. So
while around the world ideologies based on race or discrimination
were on the wane, in South Africa they were truly coming into their
own. Attacks on black workers and boycotts of Indian traders were
commonplace during 1946 and 1947 and went largely unchecked.
Meanwhile, political support for the NP grew as it promised to rekindle
and extend in harsher form the policies of the segregationist era. The
talk now was of *apartheid*, a word literally meaning 'separateness', but
which in actuality meant much, much more.

CHAPTER SEVEN

The Rise of Apartheid,
1948 to c. 1970

In his autobiography, Nelson Mandela wrote that apartheid:

> ...represented the codification in one oppressive system of all the laws and regulations that had kept Africans in an inferior position to whites for centuries... The often haphazard segregation of the past three hundred years was to be consolidated into a monolithic system that was diabolical in its detail, inescapable in its reach and overwhelming in its power.

As this quote illustrates, the system of apartheid was not invented from scratch. It had been building for decades if not centuries, and had origins that were as deep-seated as they were complex.

As we have seen in previous chapters, there had always been a strong racial overtone in all European dealings with the black populations of southern Africa. This was exacerbated by the dependence of white farmers, and later industrialists, on cheap African labour. The process of the conquest of the land had also been at the expense of the indigenous peoples of the region. From the nineteenth century all of this was given a legal basis as white supremacy was systematised. By the outbreak of the Second World War, South African society had been moulded into an entirely discriminatory state.

Now this was to be taken one stage further. The stated intention of the NP in 1948 was to reinforce constitutionally the segregation of the black populations of South Africa from the white minority as a means of upholding the political, economic and social supremacy of the latter. Increasingly, this policy would unfurl in the face of international disapproval and mark out South Africa as a pariah state.

The 1948 Election

The NP played on the fears of the white electorate prior to the 1948 election. Malan campaigned on a ticket that promised to stem the breakdown of segregation, curb African migration to urban areas via the stringent imposition of pass controls, and attack the rising tide of black militancy and trade union activity. Malan also pledged the 'consolidation' of the reserves and the abolition of nominal black representation in parliament. All of this had been outlined in the 1946 Sauer Report, which had been commissioned by the NP and was the basis for that party's 'native policy'.

Although a close-run election, there was surprise when the NP beat the 79-year-old Smuts' UP in 1948, claiming five seats more than its closest rival with 41.5 per cent of the overall vote. The NP vote was mostly rural, and as these constituencies were less populated than the UP urban strongholds, it presented Malan with a victory through the back door. However, there was a significant swing of the Afrikaner working-class vote towards the NP on the Rand which ultimately proved decisive. In victory, Malan was less than gracious, claiming: 'In the past, we felt like strangers in our own country, but today South Africa belongs to us once more. For the first time since Union, South Africa is our own.' The Afrikaner population at this time represented a mere 12 per cent of the country.

The new government immediately set about implementing apartheid. It also acted to ensure that it could not be easily shifted from power, either constitutionally or via other means.

THE ANC REACTS

The war had briefly spread new democratic ideals among politicised Africans and a faith that equality would soon be achieved. Spurred on by the principles upon which the Second World War was being fought, in 1943 the ANC Youth League published a pamphlet called *African Claims in South Africa*. In this, the League set out its proposals for a future democratic South Africa in which full rights would be extended to all peoples, regardless of race, class or gender, and discrimination would be ended. The hopes outlined in this document were, at a stroke, dashed by the 1948 election result.

The victory of the NP elicited a further response from the Youth League in 1949 when its *Programme for Action* was published. More hard-line in its approach, this manifesto demanded 'national freedom' and political independence for the African population from minority rule. It rejected all forms of segregation, and advocated the use of industrial action, boycotts and civil disobedience as a means of bringing about liberation.

This document was important on a number of levels. It linked the struggle against discrimination with the plight of the masses and suggested that the only means of effecting change was through popular protest and struggle. The old tactics of moderation and petition were therefore consigned to the past, reflecting the fact that the Youth Leaguers not only had increasing control of the organisation but best understood how to mobilise a new generation of discontented members.

PROBLEMS IN DEFINING APARTHEID

The NP had spoken of apartheid in the run up to its election victory but had been careful not to define it too closely either as a cohesive policy or discernible philosophy. There was a basis of understanding that, whatever it meant, apartheid would translate into the separation and further subjugation of specific, racially classified groups of people. However, while no NP supporter would disagree with this essential tenet, there was some divergence of opinion as to how apartheid should be implemented practically.

There were those ardent racists who believed that the white and black populations of South African society should exist *entirely* in isolation from one another. This meant not only the political and social separation of the two communities but economic exclusion of all Africans from white society. This would necessarily result in the total reversal of industrial dependence on African labour. It was argued that in the longer run this would make white South Africa stronger and more independent. This was a high ideal, completely impractical, yet something which a substantial body of opinion was prepared to investigate.

More realistically, there were those who recognised and understood the dependence of white South African society upon black labour. These people, who were mostly businessmen and farmers, had voted for the NP on the understanding that apartheid would guarantee a cheap and disciplined labour force. They merely wanted tighter controls over black communities, which would include absolute social exclusion from white areas and the further political subjugation of the majority of the country's population.

The NP did not see why both points of view could not be accommodated and so made vague promises to both groups. The immediate aim was to extend social separateness across the country while attending to the needs of white business. How far this was taken in the future would depend on the economic success of the state, but there was talk of increased mechanisation that, in the long run, would obviate any need for African labour.

Early Apartheid Legislation

The regime acted quickly to implement apartheid and in its first few years in power passed a plethora of legislation which extended discrimination as far as was possible into every area of life. The effect was such that, in 1952, apartheid's so-called 'grand architect', the Minister for Native Affairs and future Prime Minister, Hendrik Verwoerd (1901–66), could claim that 'the various Acts, Bills and also public statements which I have made all fit into a pattern, and together form a single constructive plan'.

The basis of all such legislation was the calculated legal division of the people of South Africa into a hierarchy of race. Four categories were created (and enforced) under the 1950 Popular Registration Act for identifying people as either White, Coloured, Asiatic or Native. These divisions dictated exactly what individuals could and could not do, where they lived, and which laws were applied to their lives. Over the years, the categories would be extended into every corner of human activity. They allowed for no ambiguity, causing any amount of problems as, for example, many coloured people did not see themselves as such, but rather as belonging to the Native or, more likely, the White category.

Marriages between different categories were forbidden. The 1950 Immorality Act outlawed sexual relations between whites and all African, coloured and Indian South Africans, extending an already existing ban on sex between whites and Africans. These two acts caused a great deal of suffering, as families were broken up or rendered illegal. Many couples were forced to apply to the courts for the racial reclassification of one or other partner.

In the political sphere, the government quickly gave itself greater powers for controlling society and political organisations. Powers of censorship, which were at the same time petty and draconian, were used to silence speeches and writings. The 1950 Suppression of Communism Act was wide-reaching, allowing the Minister of Justice the powers to outlaw 'any person or organisation' viewed as Communist. Communism was defined only loosely and was extended to include any form of opposition to the apartheid regime. Once subjected to a banning order under this act, an individual would effectively have all civil liberties curtailed. They would not be allowed to attend meetings of a political or non-political nature, join an organisation, or travel to another part of the country. If required, the Minister could apply this legislation retroactively and without giving a stated reason. Furthermore, someone subjected to this legislation had no legal redress or means of challenging the charge. Using this statute, by 1955 the state was able to eliminate eleven members of the ANC's executive committee from active politics, although people such as Mandela continued to elude the authorities, at least for the time being.

The Criminal Law Amendment Act was a further attack on dissident political groups. This specifically forbade any form of civil disobedience, which again was loosely defined, and gave to the courts the power to impose on offenders the heaviest of penalties. In reality, this made not only political activity but also industrial action by Africans, coloureds and Indians illegal offences.

Simultaneously, the separation of the African population proceeded apace. The 1953 Reservation of Separate Amenities Act was a key piece of apartheid legislation, as it segregated the use of all public amenities and buildings, such as hospitals, restaurants, sports facilities and government offices. This was also extended to public transport systems. Consequently, buses had areas for whites and areas for blacks, and post offices had separate entrances for the white population and everyone else. Even park benches were categorised in this manner. To the outside world, this quickly became the most visible and shocking illustration of the inequities of life in South Africa under apartheid.

The Group Areas Act, which was described by Malan as 'the very essence of apartheid', made compulsory the segregated residence of all non-whites in especially reserved areas. This led to families being excluded from rural villages and lands, and in urban areas, to the forced removal of communities to out of town locations, often under the pretext of slum clearances. In this way the predominantly coloured area of District Six in Cape Town was cleared, while in Johannesburg the suburb of Sophiatown was re-classified as a white area, cleared of its African population and provocatively re-named Triomf (Triumph). This process entailed a great amount of upheaval and dislocation simply because of the numbers of people involved. To illustrate the point, over half of the 920,000 residents of Johannesburg were African. In Cape Town, half the population of 630,000 were coloured and about a tenth were black. Only half of Pretoria's 285,000 inhabitants were white, while in Durban, the half a million population was spilt almost evenly between Asians, Africans and whites. The Act could not be implemented either easily or cheaply and it created mass dissension among those forced to move home. The government, however, passed further laws to enable it to override local municipalities and forcibly remove Africans to new township locations. Such operations, which left thousands homeless, were carried out with great precision and ruthlessness by the security forces. Compensation claims were rarely acknowledged.

Despite ideological differences over the control of African labour, the government's Native Affairs Department set up labour exchanges for recruiting African labour in the early 1950s. These offices would then deploy labour in the cities but only in strict accordance with the needs of employers and the demands of the market. In this way, it was decided that migrants would only be allowed into towns when there was a job for them to go to and these would only become available once the existing supply of labour was in full employment. To ensure this was the case, squatting became an offence punishable through the courts. Any labour deemed 'surplus' could be immediately removed to an emergency camp or expelled to a reserve.

The pass laws were extended as a means of curtailing freedom of movement into urban localities, and these were administered for the first time through a centralised bureaucracy. Before long, hundreds of thousands of Africans were being prosecuted on an annual basis for infringement of the pass laws. The law now required every African to carry a reference book at all times, and it had to be signed each month by a recognised employer. This gave to an individual the temporary right to be in a particular place. An employer's signature or a special permit had to be in the book if they were in urban areas. Above all else, this was a heavy symbol of subjugation. However, the system was imperfect in as much as it required a lot of resources and was only policed with great difficulty. In order to allow for more rigid controls, the law was modified to exclude anyone not born in the town where they lived unless they had been in continuous employment for ten years. Anyone who did not meet these criteria would need a temporary visitor's permit, which had to be renewed after three days.

In general, the government had to steer a pragmatic line in terms of labour controls. While there existed a huge ideological need to enforce stringent controls over movement and areas of residence, this had to be balanced against the fundamental requirements of business and industry, which relied upon and expected a steady supply of labour. This was perhaps the major contradiction at the heart of apartheid in its formative phase.

EDUCATION

Prior to the advent of apartheid, African education had been the almost exclusive concern of the missionaries. It was they alone who ran schools that would teach Africans basic numeracy and literacy, and perhaps to a few skills that would equip them for life in the industrial sector. The mission schools and colleges were run entirely by volunteers and relied for funding upon charitable donations. In consequence, black education was underfunded and schools were overcrowded and run down. Over the years, fewer and fewer pupils were catered for in these institutions.

One of the first acts of the Native Affairs Department was to take African education out of the hands of the missionary societies and place it within its own remit. A Bantu Education Act gave the government overall control of African educational policy and ensured the extension of apartheid into the school system. However, this did not mean that primary education was made either free or compulsory for black children, although numbers did rise dramatically. There was no rise in educational standards, though; figures show that of 200,000 African children who entered the schooling system in 1950, only two in every thousand passed the matriculation test for university entrance twelve years later.

This was, in large part, the aim of the Act; as Verwoerd stated at the time, 'Education must train and teach people in accordance with their opportunities in life'. The government primarily wanted control of 'Bantu' education as a means of ensuring that a pliant manual labour force, free of the burden of a decent education, was delivered for exploitation in the industrial sector. To this end, limited skills of use only in industry and agriculture were taught in place of a more rounded, liberal curriculum. With time, the ploy became more obvious and a point of considerable political tension.

DISCRIMINATION IN PRACTICE

In the cities and townships of South Africa, assaults on black communities by the security forces became an everyday reality of life, allowed for under the terms of the myriad new laws. Attacks on individuals by police became more regular and would take many forms. Physical violence and harassment became pervasive, but subtler forms of torment, affecting an individual's ability to make a living, were also practised.

African business people everywhere came under increasing attack and were subject to boycott or, more straightforwardly, were forced out of city centres and predominantly white areas. Traders would have their licences revoked and street hawkers were suppressed. Black-owned taxi or bus services would be driven out of business as a means of eliminating competition with white firms. In the townships, shebeens, the undoubted centres of adult social life, were subject to regular police raids and owners would be prosecuted under stringent laws regulating the sale of liquor to Africans. Intended in part as an attack on the cultural life of the townships, a closed shebeen would usually reopen its doors in a matter of days. Defiantly, musicians and choirs would use such locations to voice their protests against apartheid.

THE POLITICAL BACKLASH

There was a mass upsurge of popular protest against apartheid laws and the effects these had on people's lives. However, the powers vested in the state meant that such protests were both hampered and thwarted at every turn by the security forces. Each new piece of legislation would, nonetheless, act as a stimulus to disquiet once its implications became apparent. The most popular forms of protest of the early 1950s, such as boycotts, stayaways from work and more general civil disobedience, were championed by the ANC's Youth League and encouraged, after 1952, by a new President and the future Nobel Peace Prize winner, Albert Luthuli (1898–1967).

The first formalised resistance movement, which attempted to draw together disparate yet similar protests, was the Defiance Campaign of 1952. Led jointly by the ANC and the Communist Party – the leaders of the former having to overcome an inherent distrust of the latter – this was intended as a passive protest against what the organisers termed

Albert Luthuli, President of the ANC and winner of
the Nobel Peace Prize in 1961

'unjust laws'. Influenced by Gandhian-ideas of self-sacrifice, a select few, which included Nelson Mandela who had been central to the planning of the campaign, were to lead a more widespread defiance of petty apartheid legislation such as amenities segregation, pass controls and curfews. The aim was not to eradicate such laws but merely to draw attention to them.

The deliberate flouting of such edicts enjoyed some success in highlighting the unjustness of the apartheid regime. Initially, the movement was peaceful and characterised by mass marches through cities, the public burning of passes, and the occupation of areas reserved for whites. Protests were seen in most areas of the country and were most evident in those places where the government's apartheid policies had had the biggest impact. However, over time, the peaceful nature of the movement was lost. Police provocation often resulted in rioting, looting and the wilful destruction of private property and public buildings.

Between June 1952 and January 1953 some 8,000 activists were imprisoned because of their involvement in the Defiance Campaign (arrest had been encouraged by the organisers of the campaign as a means of crowding out the prisons and courts, thereby placing a great strain on the machinery of government). Ultimately, the movement was crushed. Its leaders were arrested under the Suppression of Communism Act and would later be sentenced to nine months' prison with hard labour, suspended for two years; the police were ruthless in dealing with any shows of militancy. However, a vital point had been made. The campaign received much publicity in the world's press, and at the United Nations questions were asked about the legitimacy of the apartheid system, and an inquiry was launched into its workings and the condition of life in South Africa for the majority of the country's citizens. The ANC also gained from the protests. By keying into widespread disquiet and providing a recognisable outlet for all such frustrations, it attracted many new members. By 1953, it had an estimated 100,000 followers, a ten-fold increase in a little under two years.

THE REGIME BENEFITS

The government's hard-line approach to the Defiance Campaign lost it few friends among the white electorate. The decisive manner in which the protests had been dealt with was exactly what the regime's supporters wanted, and they applauded the actions of the state. Its credibility thus bolstered, the NP was returned to power in 1953 with an increased majority, although it did benefit from constituency changes that favoured voting patterns beneficial to the party. Nevertheless, the policy of apartheid would now continue unabated.

This increased majority was immediately used to isolate the coloured vote from the white vote. In order to facilitate this move, the government was forced to pack the Senate, giving it the two-thirds majority it needed there to change the electoral laws. In 1956 a separate electoral roll for coloured voters was established which had the right to elect four white representatives to parliament. Meanwhile, the Bantu Authorities Act curtailed African political representation at both the local and municipality level. Through these two acts, the political sphere was confirmed as an exclusively white domain.

The Freedom Charter

The different elements of the anti-apartheid movement within South Africa, representing black, Indian, coloured and dissident white groups, came together for the first time in June 1955, at Kliptown near Johannesburg. This was the Congress of the People. Nearly 3,000 delegates representing the ANC, the South African Indian Congress, the Coloured People's Organisation, and people sympathetic to the banned Communist Party and the South African Congress of Trade Unions met as a means of voicing their joint opposition to the regime, and also to answer white critics who had suggested that people of different ethnicity in South Africa could not co-exist.

Prior to the convening of the Congress at Kliptown, each of these organisations had gone to their constituents and asked for a list of demands and grievances. This was then submitted to a central committee, who formalised a Charter for discussion. The Congress was surrounded by state security forces, and although intimidated and harassed, the meeting was allowed for two days before finally being broken up. In that time, the Congress unanimously adopted the

Freedom Charter, a document that was to form the basis for opposition to apartheid over the course of the next thirty-five years.

The Charter stated:

> That South Africa belongs to all who live in it, black and white, and that no government can justly claim authority unless it is based on the will of the people. That our people have been robbed of their birthright to land, liberty and peace by a form of government founded on injustice and inequality. That our country will never be prosperous or free until all our people live in brotherhood, enjoying equal rights and opportunities. That only a democratic state, based on the will of the people, can secure to all their birthright without distinction of colour, race, sex or belief...

In detail, the Charter called for the repeal of all apartheid legislation and the institution of the 'democratic organs of self-government'. It also demanded that the 'natural wealth of our country ... be restored to the people', and that in the fields of education, health care and the judiciary equal rights for all be established. The document ended with the promise: 'The People Shall Govern.'

Although the Charterists were in no position immediately to enact all or any of their demands, the very existence of such a document was of the utmost importance. The government obviously thought so, for the following year it arrested 156 Congress leaders, including Sisulu and Mandela, and charged them with high treason. This charge was based upon the notion that the Charter, the work of Communists according to the prosecution, was a document intended to incite violence as a means of overthrowing the state. The right-wing lawyer Oswald Pirow was brought out of retirement to lead the state's case, but he was unable to build a credible prosecution. Although the trial was to last for five years, the defence was too wily for Pirow and the witnesses he called, and was able to exploit large inconsistencies in their testimonies. In the end, the trial collapsed and the defendants were cleared of any charges.

OPPOSITION TO THE CHARTER

Although the Charter was the work of many minds and interest groups, it did not enjoy the total support of all anti-apartheid activists in South Africa. Controversy revolved around two points: its alleged lack of political radicalism and its accommodation in one movement of African and non-African dissidents.

Militant trade unionists were dismayed that the Charter made no reference to the right to strike, which was outlawed at the time in South Africa. They were also upset that it did not go far enough in specifically defending workers' rights or guaranteeing the nationalisation of industry and redistribution of land. Others with radical political views felt similarly betrayed. There was, it was believed, a far from clear-cut commitment to socialist ideals, and so, the document was not far-reaching enough to placate many left-wingers.

More controversially, Africanists decried the involvement of non-African groups as amounting to no more than a 'political bluff'. There was a tendency within some politicised African circles to believe that liberation, first and foremost, needed to be psychological (this notion had been expressed by the ANC's Youth League in the late 1940s). Moreover, those who held this view were largely distrustful of white involvement in the Charter. Although only a minority view in 1955, this standpoint was to attract ever more adherents and, in 1958, led to a split from the ANC.

This faction formed the Pan Africanist Congress (PAC) in 1959 as a means of consolidating the strength of black African nationalism. Its ultimate aim was to reclaim 'Africa for the Africans'. The PAC was an essentially young organisation, inspired by other anti-colonial movements evident across Africa at the time. It rejected wholesale the structured party basis of the ANC and adopted a looser organisational approach as a means of allowing it to react spontaneously to emerging conflict and the frustrations emanating from within the African community. It did, however, sponsor sustained campaigns against pass controls and organised more militant boycotts and industrial actions. The PAC quickly captured a loyal following in the Vaal townships south of Johannesburg, and in other areas of the country where support for the ANC was weak.

MOUNTING PROTESTS

In the late 1950s, African protests against apartheid were stepped up across South Africa. Only some of these were directed or organised by groups such as the ANC or PAC, but both were quick to attach themselves to any movement that gained some momentum. In urban areas there were campaigns against pass controls, rising prices and poor living conditions (which often took the form of boycotts), the lack of job opportunities and police harassment. In 1957–58, the ANC led an industrial campaign for better working conditions for Africans and the introduction of a minimum wage of £1 a day. Although relatively successful in getting people to stay away from work, the movement ultimately collapsed under the weight of economic necessity and official harassment. Similar PAC campaigns were also suppressed by the state.

Meanwhile, conflict in rural areas, and especially in the reserves, showed no signs of abating at this time. The by now usual problems concerning over-cultivation and cattle disease meant a subsistence level of farming was rarely achieved in any reserve. This problem was compounded by a steadily growing population on reserved land. In general, the economies of the reserves were only kept buoyant by the wages of urban migrant workers. During the 1950s the government, aware of all these problems but reluctant to invest the necessary funds to turn the situation around, tinkered with the administration of the reserves and took small measures, which were largely resented, to make African agricultural production more efficient. But this was no more than paying lip service to the plight of millions. The condition of the reserves suited white governmental and capital interests for it was the best way of guaranteeing a pool of pliable and cheap African labour.

Protest in the reserves took a number of characteristic forms. There was resistance to tax collection and government agents risked their safety in many instances trying to extract dues from impoverished communities. There were also attacks on state-appointed chiefs, the nominal rulers of the reserves, who were resented as being no more than stooges of an oppressive regime. Under the influence of the ANC and the PAC, some links were forged between protests in the reserves and protests in the townships and cities. However, for the most part, rural disquiet tended to remain localised and so only had a limited impact.

At this time, all anti-state protests suffered from poor co-ordination and often lamentable communication. As a result, many campaigns floundered in their earliest phases or degenerated into directionless mob rioting. This made it easier for the police to intervene and quash dissent. The overall effect was that few, if any, campaigns realised their full potential.

The Regime Goes From Strength to Strength

In 1958, following the death of Malan's successor J.G. (Johannes) Strijdom (1893–1958), the leadership of the NP was assumed by Hendrik Verwoerd, erstwhile Minister for Native Affairs. Verwoerd, a child migrant to southern Africa from the Netherlands, had been a founder member of the HNP in 1934, and was seen by many white people in South Africa as the guiding hand and mastermind of apart-heid. He was consequently a popular choice for the premiership. This, in no small part, was one of the reasons for the NP's success at the 1958 general election when it won twice as many seats as all the other parties combined. The result was also a reflection that the electorate, who were enjoying a time of economic prosperity and feeling socially secure, not only supported the regime but had a firm belief in the principles it advocated and the policies it propagated.

Verwoerd was clear on a number of issues of vital importance to the electorate. Economically, he promised to maintain the protectionist stance that benefited both the agricultural and manufacturing sectors. He pledged to step up state action against all forms of restrictions and spoke of further limiting African freedom of movement. He was also in favour of loosening the constitutional and political ties with Britain, a country in the process of decolonising the remnants of its African empire.

This hard-line approach was rapidly adopted by the new adminis-tration. Verwoerd, who was shot through the head by a deranged white farmer in 1960 but remarkably survived the attack unscathed, confirmed his grasp on the NP by marginalising his internal opponents. He then set about ruthlessly eliminating any opposition to the regime at home, while simultaneously acting to preserve the 'moral purity' of his constituents by banishing 'infectious', that is to say, socialist or liberal, ideas from abroad.

The attempt to isolate South Africa culturally from the rest of the world was facilitated by the government imposing strict laws of censorship. The state therefore assumed a great influence over all forms of media and had the powers to suppress any statements, writings or works of art deemed dangerous or controversial. In this way, a uniform vision of society, and view of the world, was imposed upon white South African society from the early 1960s. This pervaded the education system, the bureaucracy of state, the police force and nearly all other walks of life. The influential Afrikaner Broederbond, which infiltrated every corner of government, was the 'invisible hand' behind this vision. Its members headed the South African Broadcasting Corporation, edited most national and local newspapers and controlled the Censorship Board.

SOUTH AFRICA LEAVES THE COMMONWEALTH.

Following stinging criticism of apartheid by other leading member states, and a white referendum in favour of withdrawal, South Africa left the Commonwealth in 1961. Although this extended South Africa's growing international isolation, the move became inevitable following the famous 'Wind of Change' speech made by the British Prime Minister, Harold Macmillan (1894–1986), in Cape Town in 1960. This was a frank iteration of the reality that everywhere nationalist movements were making formal colonial rule untenable and, by extension, making unsustainable the subjugation of peoples to the interests of settler societies. Macmillan stated that it was his government's belief that societies everywhere should be based on 'individual merit, and individual merit alone' regardless of skin colour 'for man's advancement whether political or economic'. Such sentiments were incompatible with the ideologies of the apartheid regime (a point Macmillan acknowledged in the speech) and provoked fury within NP circles, not least because they had been delivered in its own back yard.

South Africa, then, became a republic. A new, largely ceremonial office of State President was created to combine the constitutional roles previously filled by the Queen (as head of state) and Governor-General. To Afrikaner nationalists, this was a highly symbolic event, the end of a struggle for absolute autonomy that had started over 200 years previously with the Great Trek.

The Sharpeville Massacre

The government, imbued with a new sense of purpose and determination, and the anti-apartheid movements, which were increasingly militant in outlook, were set on course for some kind of showdown. This came on 21 March 1960 at the township of Sharpeville, near Vereeniging. That day, a large crowd of some 5,000 people were taking part in a wider demonstration against the pass laws, which was inspired, if not wholly orchestrated, by the PAC. The plan was for the protestors publicly to burn their passes after a rally. The security forces were determined to prevent this from happening. Elsewhere, demonstrators were intimidated by low flying military aircraft and dispersed by police baton charges. Such tactics did not work at Sharpeville. The police reacted to this defiance by firing into the crowd. In total, sixty-nine demonstrators were shot dead (of whom eight were women and ten were children) and another 180 wounded. The crowd had been relatively peaceful and completely unarmed. Thereafter a State of Emergency was declared across much of the country, under the terms of which civil rights were suspended, political meetings forbidden and the

The Sharpeville Massacre

security forces given wide-reaching powers to detain suspects. The ANC and the PAC were officially outlawed and their leaders were, wherever possible, detained.

There were serious and instantaneous repercussions after Sharpeville. Among the country's African population there was much shock at the shootings, an emotion that quickly gave way to resentment. Spontaneous, popular protests in the form of short strikes and stayaways were evident for some months and mostly dealt with ruthlessly by the state. Politically speaking, many African political activists came to the conclusion that non-violent forms of protest were now effectively redundant and they started to formulate new methods for opposing the regime. The white electorate, meanwhile, showed no signs of losing faith in the government.

Around the world there was immediate outright condemnation of the massacre at Sharpeville. Opinion was outraged and thousands of people, in many countries, joined the emerging international anti-apartheid movement. Many world leaders spoke out in opposition to the South African government for the first time. There were attempts made at the United Nations to have serious economic sanctions imposed against South Africa, a move that faltered after an American and British veto (both countries had high levels of investment in South Africa and moved to protect these). Nevertheless, there was a significant withdrawal of foreign capital from South Africa as many companies decided that they could no longer justify, or risk, investing in the region. The government was forced to impose currency controls to stem this flow.

Some historians suggest that Sharpeville was an event of such importance that it was, in all reality, a decisive turning point in the history of twentieth-century South Africa. If this was the case, it was not necessarily apparent throughout the country at the time. The government, and Verwoerd in particular, ignored all international criticisms of the massacre, including those concerns expressed at the UN. Indeed, foreign condemnation of the incident seemed only to strengthen the resolve of the NP in its policies and determination to stamp out all forms of protest and opposition. It responded to world opinion with a blank refusal to accept any blame for the atrocity and argued instead that it was the protestors themselves, the dead and injured included, who were to blame for the shootings. Although morally indefensible, such a stance paid dividends. Once the threat of sanctions had been lifted, normality returned to the economic life of the country; foreign investors returned and South African exports to Europe, the United States and, most notably, Asia increased at a rapid rate in the early 1960s.

AMENDMENTS TO THE LAW

The government stepped up the offensive against its opponents at home in the immediate aftermath of Sharpeville. New security legislation imbued the Minister of Justice with enormous new powers for dealing with political activists. The 1963 General Law Amendment Act gave to the police a whole host of powers that could be invoked arbitrarily and tended to bypass the judicial process. Under this law, a suspect could be detained without charge and kept in solitary confinement for a maximum ninety days (extended in 1965 to one hundred and eighty days). There was no right to a lawyer. In the first year of its existence, 200 people were detained in this manner, rising the following year to 850. It was quite common for a detainee to be released and then immediately re-arrested under the same legislation and forced to serve another period of arbitrary detention.

Towards the end of the decade, the security forces were enlarged and united into the Bureau of State Security (Boss). This was an organisation as sinister as it was notorious. Composed mostly of handpicked Afrikaners, the Boss was shielded from any form of public scrutiny and allowed an almost unfettered budget from the public purse in order to pursue its 'defence of the Republic'. Its remit encompassed internal and external security, espionage, and operations against actual or suspected anti-apartheid movements and activists. Those detained by the Boss could expect to be subjected to brutal and humiliating methods of investigation, or worse, be murdered (such incidents might be euphemistically recorded as 'fell from a window' or 'slipped on soap in shower'). Before it was superseded by the Department of National Security in the early 1970s, the Boss had been key in the transformation of South Africa into something of a police state. The Bureau had also taken a large chunk of the country's defence budget, which rose from 38.5 million rand in the early 1960s to 1,350 million rand in 1970.

New Tactics of Resistance

The banning in 1960 of the ANC, the PAC and other movements of opposition to the government did not mean that these organisations were totally suppressed or that they ceased campaigning against the regime. Indeed, in the aftermath of the Sharpeville atrocities, African nationalists in particular chose to employ alternative, more direct tactics for pursuing their goal of liberation. In the case of the ANC, this was to result in the formation of a military wing that was to be at the vanguard of an armed struggle aimed at undermining the very foundations of the apartheid state. The main advocates of this new strategy were ex-Youth Leaguers such as Nelson Mandela and Walter Sisulu. In his manifesto to launch Umkhonto We Sizwe ('Spear of the Nation' or MK), Mandela wrote, 'The time comes in the life of any nation where there remain only two choices: submit or fight. That time has now come to South Africa. We shall not submit and we have no choice but to hit back by all means within our power in defence of our people, our future and our freedom...'

MK was formed in late 1961 and operated as a clandestine guerrilla army. Over the next three years it carried out a concerted campaign of sabotage, targeting power stations, communications points, post offices and government buildings. Initially, such tactics worked well and caused no small amount of panic in government circles and among the white communities of South Africa.

Other groups adopted a similar approach. The radical white National Committee of Liberation planted a series of bombs in Johannesburg and Cape Town city centres and also sabotaged government-owned installations. The PAC formed its own underground movement Poqo (meaning 'pure' in Xhosa). Poqo's stated aim was to provoke a general uprising of the black population by eliciting a military backlash from the security forces. To this end, it indiscriminately murdered policemen, government agents and suspected police informers. This certainly did elicit the planned response from government forces. The concurrent uprising, however, failed to materialise.

The security forces, the strength and determination of which Poqo and MK had certainly underestimated, responded fiercely to guerrilla tactics and launched an unrelenting counter-offensive against the underground movements. Although initially hampered in this by the very nature of their opponent, with time the police were able to infiltrate many key underground cells and build a formidable network of spies and informers. Ultimately, the guerrillas were unable to maintain the integrity of their operations under such circumstances. By 1964 a sweep against the underground movement's leadership had succeeded in forcing many of them into exile abroad. Those who could not escape, including Nelson Mandela, after living clandestinely for more than a year were arrested under the General Law Amendment Act and imprisoned.

Consequently, many leaders of the underground movement were tried during the Rivonia Trial of 1963–4, so-called after the name of the farm outside Johannesburg which had acted as the secret head-quarters of MK and where the movement's high command were arrested by the security forces. Mandela, who along with nine co-defendants was charged with sabotage, submitted to the court an articulate and heartfelt defence in which he surmised that, 'we had either to accept inferiority or fight against it by violence'. He also added that, 'I was made, by the law, a criminal, not because of what I had done, but because of what I stood for, because of what I thought, because of my conscience.' These men, who were handed down life sentences, would spend years in incarceration and become symbolic of the iniquities of the apartheid system. Mandela especially, who served twenty-seven years in prison, would become the focus point for the worldwide anti-apartheid movement in the 1970s and 1980s.

Abroad, the ANC top formed an organisation in exile to keep its campaign going. Oliver Tambo presided over a party that had head-quarters in London, Dar-es-Salaam in Tanzania, and Lusaka in Zambia. In its earliest years, the ANC in exile had difficulty in functioning effectively, for it could not easily keep abreast of events in South Africa and had trouble courting foreign governments, who were wary of an organisation that openly advocated the tactics of armed struggle. This situation would change only as popular opinion around the world became less tolerant of the South African government. Nevertheless, the external mission failed to keep up the momentum of the underground struggle in South Africa. Consequently, the ANC's influence across the country declined sharply during the 1960s. The same was true of the PAC, which was further undermined by internal ideological rifts resulting from the adoption of Maoism by the exiled leadership towards the end of the decade.

The Regime Assured

The elimination of the ANC and the PAC from South Africa was a huge victory for the government, which once again had proved its willingness to confront and defeat all forms of opposition. For the time being, organised political resistance had been crushed. While this did not lead to a mass acceptance of apartheid by the majority of the country's population, it did remove any forum for expressing discontent and dissatisfaction. With no formidable political opposition, the government was therefore able to concentrate on consolidating its political power.

For the rest of the next decade the regime was secure at home. Its position was bolstered by an economic upturn that saw an increase in foreign trade, a steady inflow of foreign capital investment, and a notable increase in industrial growth. South Africa's economy grew year on year from the late 1940s to 1975, its GDP rising on average at a rate of 4.75 per cent annually. The obvious beneficiaries of this increase were the white minority, who appeared happy to continue to support a regime that guaranteed material comfort and security. Large capital-based firms such as the mining conglomerate Anglo American also did well under such circumstances.

However, South Africa was under increasing pressure during this period from the world community. Apartheid was condemned ever more vociferously on moral grounds. Little was yet done, though, to bring the system of rule to an end. South Africa had important allies in the shape of the United States of America and Britain, who each had important trading links with the country, and deliberately cultivated South Africa as an ally in the global Cold War. It would be some time before the moral imperative overrode in significance the economic and strategic significance of South Africa's friendship with these countries.

The Bantustans or Homelands

The increase in urban African protest and political activism in the early 1960s resulted in the administration placing greater controls upon non-white freedom of movement. Pass controls, limiting migration to towns and cities, were more stringently applied. Attempts entirely to remove black rights to residency in urban locations foundered when influential business groups, fearing the loss of a regular and cheap supply of labour, complained and forced the government to back down. Nevertheless, segregation was more strictly enforced and African rights to residency curtailed. As an example, an African – or Bantu, in the parlance of the state – could no longer legally seek work in a town, or be employed by a business, if that person had not first registered at a state bureau of employment located in a homeland. These bureaux did little to smooth the way to finding a job. Further legislation disqualifying Africans from buying freehold properties in townships forced Africans into tenant relationships with local municipalities and prevented individuals or families from putting down permanent roots in a particular locality. Wages also remained desperately low, further widening disparities of wealth along racial lines.

With black urban access effectively restricted and opportunities limited, there was strong, but not overwhelming pressure on Africans to locate in the reserves. The first to be moved out were those deemed to be 'non-productive', that is to say, single women with dependant children, the old and the unfit. Thereafter, the reserves were gradually made into self-administering homeland units, based loosely on ethnic lines. Laws passed in the late 1950s re-cast the reserves as Bantustans (or homelands), run wholly by a local African elite who had effective political and economic control over their populations. This process, described by one historian as 'the Balkanisation of the country', was an attempt to separate entirely the white minority population from the

African majority, with the latter being forced into economically autonomous locations away from the urban centres of South Africa. It was further believed that, in this way, African political aspirations could be either fulfilled or negated, as loyalties were directed towards the tribal leaders who controlled the homelands. The regime also hoped that the plan would undermine its critics, both at home and abroad, as nominal self-determination would be given to the African population.

The homelands scheme was based on the findings of the 1956 Tomlinson Commission, which had been asked to formulate a strategy for developing 'Native' areas that would be socially and economically viable in their own right. The Commission inquired into the provision of general welfare and education and decided that the only means of creating durable homelands was through a programme of mass government spending. The Commission's report was lengthy and partly suppressed by the government, who were not prepared to accept much of its findings. Nevertheless, it was used as the starting point for turning reserves into homelands.

In 1959, eight Bantustan homelands came into being (two more would later be created) each imbued with a high degree of self-autonomy. Under the scheme, local chiefs, appointed by the South African government, were invested with all powers of administration. Africans were allocated to a homeland along ethnic lines, with each location forming a distinct 'nation' based upon principles derived from a particularly narrow reading of pre and early colonial history. Tribal divisions were deliberately exaggerated to give credence to the notion that the homelands were the rightful, historical home of a particular ethnic group.

At a stroke, around 80 per cent of the land area of South Africa became the preserve of the white population, a reality enforced by constitutional methods. Africans, whether resident in a homeland or a designated white area, were effectively stripped of their rights to South African citizenship. They were now members of nominally independent tribal nations, their new nationalities imposed at the behest of the apartheid regime.

From the outset, the homelands could neither accommodate nor sustain their populations. Each 'nation' was designed to rely on

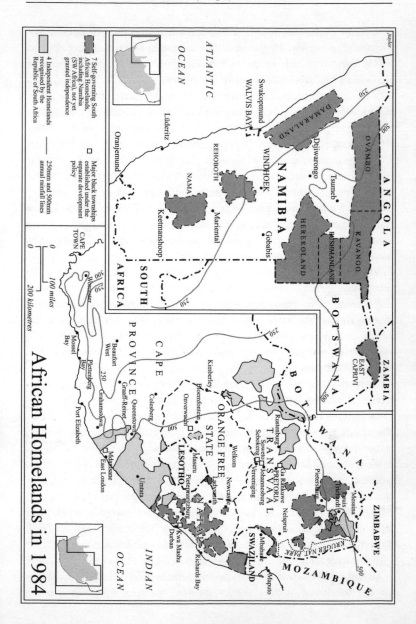

African Homelands in 1984

Legend:

7 Self-governing South African Homelands, including Namibia (SW Africa), not yet granted independence

4 Independent Homelands recognised by the Republic of South Africa

□ Major black townships established under the separate development policy

— 250mm and 500mm annual rainfall lines

Scale: 0 — 100 miles / 0 — 200 kilometres

Map labels:

ATLANTIC OCEAN

Swakopmund, WALVIS BAY, Lüderitz, Oranjemund

NAMIBIA — DAMARALAND, OVAMBO, KAVANGO, EAST CAPRIVI, HEREROLAND, BUSHMANLAND, NAMA, REHOBOTH, WINDHOEK, Otjiwarongo, Tsumeb, Mariental, Gobabis, Keetmanshoop

ANGOLA, ZAMBIA, BOTSWANA, ZIMBABWE, MOZAMBIQUE

SOUTH AFRICA

CAPE PROVINCE — CAPE TOWN, Worcester, Mossel Bay, Beaufort West, Pletenberg Bay, Port Elizabeth, East London, Kimberley, Graaff-Reinet, Queenstown, Colesberg, Grahamstown, Umtata, Mdantsane

ORANGE FREE STATE — Bloemfontein, Welkom, Onverwacht

TRANSVAAL — PRETORIA, Johannesburg, Soweto, Vereeniging, Rustenburg, Ga-Rankuwe, Sebokeng, Nelspruit, Pietersburg, Louis Trichardt, Messina

LESOTHO, SWAZILAND

NATAL — Pietermaritzburg, Ladysmith, Newcastle, Durban, Kwa Mashu, Richards Bay, Mbabane, Maputo

Maseru

KRUGER NAT. PARK

INDIAN OCEAN

250, 500

agricultural industries which, it was hoped, would provide subsistence for the community. However, the government was not prepared to invest sufficient funds in any of the homelands nor to follow many of the other proposals laid out in the Tomlinson report. There was, then, a lack of infrastructural development and few basic amenities to support the local populations. Nor was sufficient land made available to render the scheme plausible. Nonetheless, the forced relocation of the urban African population proceeded on a massive scale. Between 1960 and 1963, some three and a half million people were dispossessed of their homes and removed from 'white' South Africa. Over the course of the decade, the combined populations of the homelands rose by over 70 per cent. Most of those who were relocated found themselves living on barren, isolated land, with few adequate resources at their disposal and little opportunity of finding alternative employment. The townships, meanwhile, were emptied at a startling rate.

The first legislative homeland assembly came into being in the Transkei in 1963. Other homelands, in Bophuthatswana, Venda and the Ciskei, were granted self-government (and thus, independence) during the 1970s. Each had an elected local assembly and the paraphernalia attached to a real state – anthems, flags and the like – but failed to have their status officially recognised by any country other than South Africa.

In truth, each of the homelands was totally dependent upon South Africa. It was the latter that provided the homeland governments with their budgets and upheld their internal and external security. Further, the chiefs were in all reality official employees of the South African state, and took direction from that government. This placed the chiefs, who had considerable patronage and much wealth, in a precarious position, as their legitimacy as independent rulers was always open to question and they often struggled to gain the respect of their subjects. Many were branded as collaborators with an oppressive system and had little influence or control over those they were supposed to lead. Others were openly corrupt and authoritarian in demeanour.

Moreover, economic autonomy could not be attained in any of the homelands. The South African government would not allow industries to be developed within the homelands for fear that a politicised proletariat might emerge. Instead, businesses and industries were encouraged to establish themselves on the borders of the homelands, where they would still have access to a cheap labour force. This merely revealed the fact that an underlying motive of the homeland project was political, *not* economic, African independence. In so many ways, the apartheid administration wanted the best of both worlds.

Some homeland governments only toed the line in respect of the South African regime when it suited them to do so. Others were prepared to force the issue of independence and assert their right to govern as they pleased. The most striking example of this was the opening of Sun City by the Bophuthatswana government. Operating under similar circumstances to casinos on Native American reserves, Sun City was a pleasure haven for white South Africans, offering gambling, entertainment and inter-racial sex at a location less than a hundred miles from Pretoria. This was an affront to conservative and puritanical white South Africans, but as the law stood, there was nothing that could be done about the complex.

Ultimately, the homelands failed for the same reasons that the earlier reserves had failed. There was insufficient investment to stimulate local economies that suffered from over-population and a desperate shortage of good, available lands. In almost all instances, homeland populations were producing far less than they needed to consume, and this situation was compounded as land quality deteriorated and erosion set in. Previously cultivable locations, in the Ciskei for example, were turned into treeless scrub during the 1960s.

New Forms of Opposition Emerge

The battery of new legislation passed in the early 1960s, coupled with the outlawing of organised African political groups and new measures of censorship, ensured that resistance to, and protests against, apartheid remained muted within South Africa for the best part of a decade. The forced removal of populations to the homelands further disrupted the potential for urban resistance to the government. The economic growth prevalent at this time also meant that the majority of Africans, although never well paid, were kept in employment. This also helped to decrease political tensions across the country.

There was some rural resistance to the Bantustan programme from the late 1950s but this was easily contained as the homelands were geographically dispersed and often composed of disparate pockets of land scattered over a wide area. Nevertheless, there was a degree of ferment in most of the homelands and few chiefs managed to avoid personal attack. The South African government was quick to blame all such unrest on ANC 'agitators', although the truth of the matter was that the ANC had not yet overcome its suppression to any notable degree.

The vacuum left by the ANC and the PAC was only slowly filled by other groups. The most significant of these was to emerge in the late 1960s on the university campuses of South Africa. The Black Consciousness movement was more of an ideological than a party political movement. Its adherents rejected wholesale multi-racialism and argued that black South Africans were too dependent upon white liberalism and paternalism, tendencies that held them in a state of psychological subjugation. They therefore advocated complete black separatism instead, arguing that this was the only way black people could acquire a pride in themselves and their people.

As a movement, Black Consciousness was hampered by the fact it had only vaguely defined ideas in terms of political and economic matters. It also suffered greatly from internal rifts and dissension. It was a mostly intellectual movement, led in South Africa by idealists such as Steve Biko (1942–77). Biko had been expelled from college as a teenager for his brother's alleged links with Poqo. However, he went on to study medicine at Durban, where he became politically active. Increasingly critical of his university's predominantly white students' union, in 1969 he formed the breakaway South African Students' Organisation, which strongly advocated black separatist ideals. In the early 1970s, Biko extended his activities beyond student circles, undertaking a series of projects in and around Durban that aimed to educate local black youths, and improve the social conditions in which they lived. Such activity caught the attention of the authorities, and in 1973, Biko had his liberties curtailed by the state.

Nevertheless, he continued his struggle, gaining recognition as a leading black rights campaigner both across South Africa and internationally.

Under Biko, the Black Consciousness movement in South Africa never gained a wholly popular or committed following, although its ideals appealed to disaffected youths in the townships. In part, it suffered from the fact that Biko was hampered in enacting a comprehensible programme for political action and unable to confront the forces of the government in a direct way. Nonetheless, the Black Consciousness movement had by the mid-1970s created a big enough impression to give impetus to a new wave of township protests. Simultaneously, however, it continued to rely on individual actions as the most effective means of achieving black salvation.

THE ASSASSINATION OF VERWOERD

In 1966 a second attempt was made on the life of Verwoerd when he was stabbed in parliament by a white messenger. As before, no clear motive for the attack could be discerned. This time, however, Verwoerd was not so lucky and he died of his wounds. He was succeeded by John Vorster, the man jailed during the Second World War for his fascist sympathies. Although Vorster was pragmatic enough to realise that some of the pettier aspects of apartheid needed reforming and he began to repeal the strict segregation of public amenities, for example, his time in office saw an intensification of repression across the country. Increasingly, the Vorster administration depended on the Boss to maintain order and security at home.

Vorster also allowed the Boss a wider remit abroad as a means of staving off potential revolutionary threats from neighbouring states which, it was believed, threatened to undermine the longer-term security of the South African state. Consequently, the South African army became embroiled in the defence of Ian Smith's minority government in Rhodesia. South African forces were also deployed in Angola, and later Mozambique, as a means of undermining the forces of revolution in those states. These were costly campaigns and sometimes, as in the case of Angola, characterised by humiliating defeat.

The Sporting Ban

During the time of Vorster's rule, the international severing of sporting links with South Africa in response to apartheid rule began to bite ever harder and was perhaps the one sanction that rankled with a majority of the white population. South Africa had always had a strong tradition of sporting activity and achievement, and games such as rugby were followed especially closely by Afrikaner men. The ending of international rugby matches (with South Africa unable to either host matches or freely play abroad) has been described as 'a heavy psychological blow to Afrikaners, who were accustomed to demonstrating their superiority through their sporting prowess'. South Africa was excluded from the 1960 Rome Olympics and then expelled from the IOC in 1968. This was a further humiliation that brought genuine pressure on the government to rethink its extension of complete segregation to every level of sporting activity at home.

The total sporting ban, which was imposed piecemeal, became inevitable following a controversial Springbok rugby tour to Britain in 1969–70. A Stop the Tour Committee followed the team wherever it went, guaranteeing a heavy police presence. Violence often ensued, deflecting attention from matters on the field, but ensuring maximum publicity for the anti-apartheid movement. Thereafter, tour organisers became reluctant to extend invitations to the South African national team of any sport for fear of inciting similarly controversial scenes. Nevertheless, the Springboks continued to tour occasionally, but never could escape the glare of publicity, or avoid being burdened with the blame for the South African government's domestic policies.

Huge cash enticements were offered to international sporting teams to make the opposite journey and tour South Africa. Equally as controversial, the West Indian, Sri Lankan and Australian cricket teams all visited during the 1980s. More commonly, renegade teams would make 'unofficial' visits, playing to large and predominantly white crowds in exchange for huge cash wages. Many famous individual sportsmen were also tempted to ply their trade in whites-only sporting leagues in South Africa. Other sporting governing bodies imposed sanctions only slowly. In boxing, which was increasingly driven by lucre in the 1970s, the WBC imposed the boycott only when it had no suitable South African contenders coming through the ranks. The WBA ignored the sanctions issue entirely, and at one point, had a white South African judge for its President.

South African Critics of Apartheid

There also existed a formidable body of white South African writers who did little to disguise their disdain for apartheid during the 1970s. A constant irritant to the government, which try as it might, could never fully suppress such critics, these men and women did much to extend the cause of the world-wide anti-apartheid movement and were able to provide a biting commentary on life under the system. The Afrikaner poet Breyten Breytenbach (1939–) returned from exile in the 1960s to be jailed in the 1970s. Upon his release, he immediately returned to Europe to continue his campaigns against apartheid. Alan Paton's (1903–88) *Cry, the Beloved Country* (published in 1948) was a damning critique of apartheid that received a wide readership around the world. Others, such as the playwright Athol Fugard (1932–), and the novelists André Brink (1935–) and Nadine Gordimer (1923–), reacted strongly against censorship in South Africa and made every effort to embarrass the government abroad. Meanwhile, Joseph Lelyveld's account of

The great novelist, Nadine Gordimer who won
the Nobel Prize for Literature in 1991

apartheid rule, *Move Your Shadow*, won the acclaimed Pulitzer Prize for Literature in 1985 when he was the South Africa correspondent for *The New York Times*.

This body of intellectuals was throughout the 1970s joined by prominent South African lawyers, economists, historians and social scientists, who all used their specialised fields to highlight the hypocrisies, contradictions and general inequalities inherent in the apartheid system. The clergy, apart from those of the Dutch Reformed Church, joined the chorus of protest, stating in the late 1960s that apartheid ran contrary to the fundamental and underlying tenets of Christianity. Student groups and women's organisations, notably the white, middle-class Black Sash, also campaigned against the state. In parliament, from 1961, Helen Suzman (1917–) ran a one-woman movement against human rights and other state abuses in South Africa. Over time, such criticisms became more difficult for the government to ignore or dismiss, and the part of these activists in the downfall of apartheid cannot be underestimated.

CHAPTER EIGHT

The Demise of Apartheid,
the 1970s and 1980s

The economic miracle that had bolstered the position of successive South African administrations since the Second World War came to an end in 1973. A world depression, caused by a rapid increase in oil prices, resulted in a drop in the value of gold. This led to spiralling inflation and an economic downturn that could not be arrested for three years. Within South Africa, the hardest hit were African workers. This fact was to lead directly to a period of great labour conflict and an upsurge in militant black political protest and trade union activity.

A wave of strikes broke out across the Rand and throughout Natal during early 1973 when an estimated 60,000 people refused to work. For the most part, these protests were a response to specific grievances relating to the cutting back of wage levels and the imposition of redundancies. In many ways, the strikes marked the ending of the break in widespread political activism that had followed the banning of the ANC and other opposition groups in the early 1960s. Once again, the regime had a fight on its hands.

But this was not the government's only problem. South Africa found itself poorly positioned to deal with the recession. The majority of the country's labour force was unskilled or semi-skilled – a deliberate ploy, it should be remembered, of apartheid strategists – and so, in terms of productivity, was unable to compete with other industrialised or fast-industrialising labour forces in Asia and elsewhere. Simply put, South African industry was no longer run efficiently and it could not compete on level terms with other nations. There was a general sense of stagnation throughout the industrial sector, and decades of state intervention meant there were few enough entrepreneurs in a position to offer a way out of the crisis. Even where such people did exist, they were hampered by legislation that prevented them from employing the right work force at the right price. In 1977 for the first time, a net rise was recorded in emigration of industrialists, business people and professionals.

Protests Revived

By 1976, ferment in the townships and homelands had reached crisis point. The frustrations of the past fifteen years of continued subjugation and brutalisation were coming to a head. Moreover, entire communities had reached the stage where they could no longer be expected to live in economic straits and social deprivation. Something had to give. The touch-paper was lit in the township of Soweto, on the outskirts of Johannesburg.

Conditions in Soweto were especially harsh. It was a bleak settlement, over-populated, with typically seventeen to twenty people living in a four-bedroom house, and underfunded, with as Rian Malan described, 'no cinemas, no bars, no hotels, no modern shopping centres, few recreational facilities, and no electricity. The place was a giant labor barracks, grimly utilitarian, and intentionally so.' There was a high level of unemployment, a complete lack of opportunities for advancement, and only a most elementary system of education in place to provide for the township's young people. There was a severe shortage of qualified African teachers, and schools commonly ran on a teacher–pupil ratio of one to every forty. Moreover, government funding amounted to very little for township schools. An African pupil would receive less than a tenth of the amount of funding spent on educating a white child. It was little surprise, then, that a crisis should arise out of the teeming schools of the township.

Conflict was sparked by controversial government proposals to force the use of Afrikaans in schools. This was a preposterous suggestion. Not only was it a politically insensitive move at a time when tensions were once more running high, it was also a highly impractical one. As matters stood, educational and teaching standards in places like Soweto were low in any case, but they were never likely to improve if instruction was given in a language that few teachers could speak and which the vast majority of pupils could not understand. The community would not let the plan pass unopposed. In June, 15,000 students commenced a protest march through the streets of Soweto.

THE SOWETO UPRISING

The police response to this march was to open fire on the crowd killing two students. The first of these, twelve-year-old Hector Petersen, was pictured being carried through the streets of Soweto, dying from shot wounds. The image was transmitted around the world, instantly becoming symbolic of the brutalities of apartheid. Global opinion was shocked and sharp criticism of the government quickly followed.

The shootings were a catalyst that released a furious response from the people of Soweto. Mobs went on the rampage, attacking the police, government buildings and other symbols of the state such as municipal-run beer halls. Schools in the township were subject to arson attacks and those that remained standing were boycotted. As the unrest spread, a number of whites became caught up in the riots. Many people were injured, two were killed. This provoked a ruthless and prolonged police response, resulting in an escalation of the troubles, hundreds of arrests and a number of deaths.

As part of this offensive, in August 1977, the Black Consciousness leader Steve Biko became the focus of a security forces hunt, after he was reported to have defied the restraining order previously placed on him for helping to distribute 'inflammatory pamphlets'. When the police finally caught up with him at a roadblock near Grahamstown, he was taken into custody for a period of eighteen days, during which time he was severely beaten. In early September, manacled in leg irons and handcuffed, he was transferred naked to a different location, where he was 'interrogated' for a further five days. Biko was in such a state at the end of this time that, after examination by a number of surgeons he was transferred to a prison hospital and kept overnight for observation. The next day, still unclothed, he was driven some 700 miles in the back of a truck to Pretoria. He died shortly after arrival of brain damage, undoubtedly the result of the beatings he had received while in

The Black Consciousness leader Steve Biko

custody. Such was the outrage that his death caused among opponents of the regime that some 20,000 people ignored police orders to stay away from his funeral.

From Soweto, the protests spread during the rest of 1976 and early 1977 to affect every township on the Rand, and eventually, most areas of the country. School children everywhere were joined by workers who instigated a series of effective stayaway strikes. In human terms the cost was great: thousands were wounded, hundreds lost their lives. However, the uprisings suffered from a lack of co-ordination and leadership. With time, individual pockets of resistance lost whatever impetus they had and burnt out, allowing the police to regain control of the situation.

An official investigation, which did not address directly any grievances expressed by the Soweto population during the course of the initial unrest, laid all blame for the uprising on unidentified 'agitators'. The number of dead was estimated at 176, although one independent investigation suggested it could have been as high as 575. The international community's response was one of outright condemnation, although the government reacted in the same way it had done after the Sharpeville massacre some sixteen years previously, and ignored all such criticisms. Indeed, the repressive nature of the regime was to become more pronounced over the next few years.

THE AFTERMATH OF SOWETO

Although not many politicians and administrators could see it at the time, and even if they had would have been loath to admit it, apartheid was becoming less tenable with the passing of every year. In the aftermath of the Soweto uprising, it was on the brink of failing entirely. For this there were a number of reasons. On one level, governmental claims that normality had been restored after 1976–77 were a palpable untruth. Law and order may have been reimposed but the period of unrest had severely threatened the *status quo*, and as much as this situation had shaken many white people, it had given new hope and belief to African communities everywhere. As one commentator was to note later, the country's 'psychic landscape had been transformed' forever.

Equally significant was the fact that Soweto marked the ending of a period of relative political quiescence. The concerns and demands that had resulted in the uprising still needed answering. Until the government moved substantially closer to fulfilling the political aspirations of the majority population, it could expect to face many more such revolts. This is indeed what happened over the next decade and a half, as sporadic unrest – in varying forms – manifested itself throughout the whole of South Africa.

Perhaps as significant was the fact that apartheid, as constructed by Verwoerd in the 1960s, was beginning to crack up in the late 1970s under the weight of numerous political, social and economic contradictions. Politically, apartheid relied on the imposition and maintenance of repression, up to and including the exclusion of the non-white populations from the formal political process. However, this meant merely that the regime had no formal means of, or channels for, communicating with African, coloured or Indian political leaders. It was therefore in a position whereby it could only respond to unrest by sending in the security forces, a tactic guaranteed to lead to the spiralling of any given situation. In the social sphere, it was clear that complete separation of the black and white populations could neither be properly imposed due to the sheer logistics and costs this would involve, nor made to work without substantial, near prohibitive investment. Social separation was also clearly a major source of discontent as it guaranteed the poverty of millions. In economic terms, the deliberate subjugation of the black work force meant South African businesses struggled to compete on the world market. Nevertheless, the requirements of industry and the reliance on cheap labour did not fit with some of the apparatus of the apartheid state. In consequence, the government was forced to loosen movement controls, and although the pass laws were kept, the strict prosecution of infringements was dropped in the early 1970s; thereafter fewer Africans were 'endorsed out' of the cities to the homelands.

Total Strategy

By the late 1970s the state of the South African nation was being transformed under the combined force of external and internal pressures. Increasing international disapproval of apartheid meant the possibility of sanctions loomed ever larger, threatening to destabilise further the security of the government. A UN-sponsored embargo on the sale of arms to South Africa from 1977 was especially effective and forced the regime into closer relations with other pariah states. The South African government also became more deeply involved in the internal politics of neighbouring states for fear that potentially revolutionary movements in such places would undermine the *status quo* at home. This was a massive, and in the event unsustainable, drain on material and human resources alike.

As we have seen, the economic stability of South Africa was no longer assured. This had implications in terms of the electorate. The government's open favouritism towards big business concerns caused a widening split in the previously solid Afrikaner vote, as working and lower-middle class people became increasingly frustrated by the government's unwillingness to legislate along lines favourable to their interests. There were also concerns over the growing African protest movements. Many whites questioned whether the regime still had the means for effectively suppressing its internal political opponents. Conversely, there was also a feeling that the Soweto uprising proved the fact that repression alone was not enough, and that the African majority could no longer be dismissed as a political irrelevance.

Under a new leadership the government attempted to seize the initiative for itself via the implementation of some domestic political and social reforms designed to uphold internal security. This was one side of a policy known as 'Total Strategy'. The other side involved the close co-ordination of foreign policy and all military activities. Both aspects were intrinsically linked in one overarching philosophy that was intended to give the South African government a better public image and allow for strategies that would maintain the regime's integrity in the longer term.

The man who masterminded the Total Strategy was P.W. Botha (1916–), a NP stalwart and parliamentarian who became Prime Minister in 1978, after Vorster was forced to resign following a scandal concerning financial abuses at the highest level of government in which he was directly implicated. Known for his arrogance and fiery temperament, which earned him the nickname of 'The Great Crocodile', Botha was both domineering and single-minded in his pursuit of Total Strategy. At the same time, he was dedicated to notions based only partly on a realistic analysis of the domestic and international political situations. As a result the chances of the Total Strategy succeeding were limited from the outset.

One of the main aims of the strategy was to step up security measures to protect South Africa from what Botha termed 'the full onslaught of Marxism'. He was not alone in believing that a concerted programme had been put into place that was designed to remove the NP from power by revolutionary means. It was therefore decided that defence spending should be stepped up and the security forces strengthened as a means of keeping any internal opposition in its place and protecting South Africa from foreign-sponsored intrigues. This was never intended to be a passive move. Throughout the 1980s, South African agents actively worked to undermine the governments of Lesotho, Mozambique, Namibia, Zimbabwe, Zambia and Angola, with the army becoming involved in a full-blown war in the latter country. After 1980, South African forces also made incursions into the newly independent state of Zimbabwe in an effort to destabilise the new majority government there, which was technically allied to the ANC.

In each case, with perhaps the notable exceptions of Angola and

Namibia, South African forces worked in almost complete secrecy and, it has been suggested, were only under the nominal control of their political paymasters. Certainly, there is no doubt that the security forces were involved in a programme of dissident assassination and sponsored private militia forces who acted to undermine the political opponents of the South African regime. Such tactics and the brutality that accompanied them spilled over into South Africa, where political killings and disappearances became more commonplace during the 1980s.

At home, Botha was determined to stamp out all African political opposition. However, this was tempered by a desire to reform society in such a way that the main grievances of the majority population would be eradicated, thereby removing the conditions believed to foster so-called revolutionary tendencies. This aim fitted neatly with a stated desire to govern more wholly in the interests of industrial and business requirements. Under Total Strategy, Botha believed he could secure white South Africa's political domination while at the same time solving the government's security and economic problems. It was an ambitious plan that would need more than a little luck if it was to be realised.

In 1979 Botha met with business leaders who demanded far-reaching social and political reforms. He later conceded that apartheid was 'a recipe for permanent conflict' and resolved to support 'free enterprise and orderly reform'. More tangibly, Botha enacted two important changes, the implications of which neither he nor his government could fully control. First, he legalised black trade union membership. This move was designed to formalise the growing, technically illegal labour movement and to prevent debilitating strikes and stayaways. It would also create the appropriate forum for industrial negotiations when these were required. This was a massive sop to major business concerns in South Africa. It also resulted in a strengthening of black trade unions throughout the country which, in the absence of a legal political opposition, throughout the 1980s took to organising and campaigning on a broad range of political issues. In essence, trade unions were for a few crucial years able to lead protests against the state and union membership became intrinsically linked to political causes.

Black workers, without a vote or any form of officially recognised political representation, used their union officials in the same way workers in other countries might use their locally elected political representative.

Secondly, the government undertook social legislation that dismantled the pettier, more restrictive aspects of apartheid that were in all reality either wholly or partially unworkable. The Immorality and Mixed Marriages Acts were abolished and, where it still existed, the segregation of amenities brought to an end. Although migratory controls remained in statute, these were now enforced only patchily and with hardly any consistency at all. Simultaneously, the industrial colour bar, which preserved specific jobs for white folk, was ended. Africans could now be offered apprenticeships in trade, and as a means of encouraging enough future candidates for such roles, education was made compulsory at primary level for all students. Better provision was also made for technical secondary education and training.

The Return of Guerrilla Warfare

These reforms were too little, too late for African political leaders abroad or at home in prison. The programme smacked of self-interest and few were convinced that it was intended to do anything other than appease big business interests and uphold the NP's grip on the reins of power. Without the extension of political rights to the black majority, there could be no let-up in the anti-apartheid movement.

The channels for formal or informal political negotiations still did not exist, however. Alternative tactics were therefore employed. The ANC's military wing MK re-engaged in the late 1970s. Working from bases and training camps in Angola and Mozambique, and peopled by young men who had fled South Africa in the aftermath of the Soweto uprising, MK was well placed to sustain a guerrilla campaign within South Africa. Deliberately targeting urban areas, in 1983 MK carried out a series of car bomb attacks. Thereafter, it successfully hit the military headquarters in Pretoria and plotted further attacks on the security and intelligence forces (some of which came off, many of which were foiled). It also targeted electricity installations and power stations. By the mid-1980s, however, the campaign faltered in the face of the number of civilians killed by guerrilla bombs.

By this time the MK had been eclipsed by the emergence of an alternative forum of opposition which adopted a markedly different approach in its attempts to bring down apartheid. This was the United Democratic Front (UDF), a multi-racial umbrella organisation of trades union, church and community leaders that dedicated itself to representing the banned ANC and stood for the principles laid down in the Freedom Charter. It completely rejected apartheid and called for its absolute repeal. It advocated non-violent resistance to all apartheid strictures via the boycott of government-run institutions. At first a largely middle-class concern, within a few years of its existence the UDF had a popular following and could claim over two million members.

The government could not so readily dismiss the UDF, an increasingly influential body that espoused democratic principles and unified people into one front 'regardless of race, religion or colour'. Neither could the old tactics of repression be easily used against such a body, or justified on grounds of internal security: a bishop or a lawyer, after all, were not likely to plant bombs or deliberately whip up dissension in the townships. Furthermore, the UDF clearly keyed into opinions held by millions of people across the rest of the world. The hostility shown towards the South African government, and practically, the economic sanctions imposed against it, were beginning to have some effect. The international movement, coupled with the actions of the UDF and other more covert forms of protest within South Africa, began slowly to have an effect upon the apartheid regime during the course of the 1980s.

The Tricameral Constitution

In 1984, a further round of reforms was introduced. It was hoped that these would give credence to the sincerity of the government's reforming zeal and acceptance for the social reforms that had already taken place. Realising that it had to grasp the nettle of political representation sooner rather than later, the administration attempted to win for itself a new bevy of allies while, at the same time, splitting into factions the increasingly united forces of opposition. It was a cynical move, remarkable only in the extent to which it failed.

A new constitution was announced that elevated the status of the office of President through the concentration of more political powers in the President's Council, and extended limited political representation and participation in government to Asian and coloured peoples. Africans were to remain entirely excluded from the parliamentary process. Under the scheme, separate parliamentary assemblies would exist for each of the three enfranchised racial constituencies. Each body would have control over the provision of education, health care and community administration for its people. The President would have overall executive control of each assembly, as well as responsibility for 'the control and administration' of African affairs, and an Indian and a coloured representative would each sit in Cabinet in positions without portfolios.

A white referendum supported the introduction of the new constitution by a majority of two to one. However, the UDF was strongly critical of the move, understanding clearly that it was a largely cosmetic reform designed to uphold the white monopoly of power. Some Indian and coloured politicians refused to become involved in the election process, and a majority of newly enfranchised voters deliberately snubbed the 1984 election. The African community, meanwhile, although not necessarily surprised by the failure to secure political rights (such a move would, after all, spell the beginning of the end of the NP's tenure in power) took to the streets in protest. The subsequent breakdown in public order led to the declaration of a State of Emergency in some parts of the country in 1985.

The government defended its decision to exclude Africans from the new constitution by arguing that Africans were properly represented in the homelands. This was true only in as far as the structures of political representation existed in each Bantustan. In reality, the homeland administrations could wield no political sway over the South African government. Their power rested entirely on their ability to administer their constituents and raise the taxes necessary to do this. Homeland governments were given more extensive powers in 1982, but this served merely to underline the fact that the African majority would continue to be excluded from the mainstream politics of South Africa. It was obvious that Botha's intention was not so much the reformation of the apartheid state, but rather, its restructuring in line with the prevailing patterns of power.

LULL BEFORE THE STORM

Around the time of the referendum concerning the tricameral constitution, the government relaxed its previously stringent powers of censorship and there was a short lull in the tactics of repression. Artists and academics temporarily found themselves at liberty to speak their minds, and in the media there was open criticism of government policy and the workings of the police and security forces. The *Cape Times* even disclosed accounts of condition in prisons, which had been an offence since 1959, and quoted leaders of the ANC in exile, such as Oliver Tambo. This era of new-found liberalisation was short-lived and ended as quickly and unexpectedly as it had begun.

The Failure of Total Strategy

If such a thing were possible, the new constitution alienated further the majority of the South African population from the powers of state. From 1984 and throughout much of the following year unrest and resistance from African communities reached new heights and was evident equally in the townships and rural homelands.

The UDF launched a campaign to collect a million signatures on a petition of opposition to the new constitution. It also organised a series of stayaways and boycotts across the country, and orchestrated a non-payment of rent campaign in the townships. This led to revolt in many areas of the country to which the security forces reacted with characteristic violence. A state of virtual civil war existed in the Vaal triangle and other urban areas. The police relied on violence and the detention of people without charge, illustrating the point that in the final analysis, despite all its reforms, the government was still dependent on repression and military moves to secure itself in power.

It was also an inadvertent advertisement for the collapse of the Total

Strategy. Designed to bring social and political stability to South Africa, it had achieved the reverse of these aims. Nor had the reforms altered the economic position of either the country or its population. Inflation and unemployment ran at a high rate throughout the period of reform, and a balance of payments crisis, brought on by the low price of gold on the world market, forced South Africa to apply to the International Monetary Fund for a series of large loans.

So rather than find resolution for the poverty that afflicted a majority of the African population, at this time the problem was merely exacerbated. In 1983, the average disposable income of Africans living in towns was a mere 22 per cent of that of whites. An estimated two-thirds of the African population lived below the minimum cost-of-living threshold. In the homelands, where some 1.4 million people were destitute, this percentage rose to four-fifths. With a birth rate that was rising steadily year on year, these problems were only ever going to become worse unless drastic action was taken. Some government ministers had made the connection between mass poverty and political dissidence, but there were not nearly enough of them. The two problems needed to be addressed at one and the same time.

THE BEGINNING OF THE END

In 1985 Botha attempted to engineer a way out of political deadlock on terms favourable to the government. He offered to release all political prisoners in exchange for the unconditional rejection of violence 'as a political instrument'. The move was rejected by men such as Nelson Mandela, who believed that 'Botha wanted the onus of violence to rest on my shoulders'. Instead, Mandela 'wanted to reaffirm to the world that we were only responding to the violence done to us'. Nevertheless, Botha decided that the time was right for making clandestine overtures to the ANC leadership and people like Mandela in particular. The offer was reiterated in private, but negotiations foundered on the sticking point of the use of violence as a legitimate tool of protest.

Across the country the political situation was spiralling out of control. In the Vaal triangle resistance continued against rent demands and high charges for electricity and water. In the townships there were regular attacks on symbols of authority and councillors were open to attack and the charge of collaboration. The UDF campaign was, meanwhile, showing no signs of losing momentum, and indeed, had spread to cover much of the OFS, Natal and the eastern Cape. Industrial protests were also gaining momentum.

Everywhere protests elicited a severe response from the security forces and violence became endemic. The state had no alternative tactic to repression. This was a vicious circle, and the situation was made worse by mob violence and indiscipline in the ranks of the police force. Repression inspired resistance and vice versa.

A State of Emergency was declared following riots that erupted after the police fired upon a procession called to commemorate the Sharpeville atrocities, killing twenty people. The army was deployed in townships and homelands across the country and censorship of the press was tightened. Thousands of people were detained and many more killed in the general mêlée. International condemnation of the government's tactics reached unprecedented heights.

The longer the situation continued unchecked, the more out of control it became. Locally based protests in the form of consumer and rent boycotts, and agitation and political mobilisation in support of the UDF quickly gave way to lawlessness in many areas of the country. By 1986, the police, whose actions by this time were often of a criminal nature, had lost the ability to assert themselves in townships that were increasingly ungovernable. In the townships around Johannesburg and Cape Town civil law collapsed entirely. This was replaced by unofficial regimes of the people, who took the law into their own hands, attacking actual and suspected informers, punishing alleged 'traitors' through 'people's courts', and in some cases, executing collaborators through 'necklacing' (that is, by placing a burning tyre around their neck). Such vigilantes were mostly young men who very often were supported in their actions by the community at large. Intimidation, of course, was rife.

In the meantime, the government's hand was forced by contacts made by independent interest groups with the ANC in exile. Throughout 1985–86, delegates of South African business representatives, trade union officials and churchmen visited the ANC leaders in Lusaka. More significantly, the ANC's President Oliver Tambo was officially received by the United States government in 1987. This indicated clearly that the USA saw the ANC as a critical part of any solution to the crisis in South Africa. It also bestowed upon the ANC the mantle of government-in-waiting, bolstering considerably its prestige and popularity at home. Botha continued to smear the ANC as a communist-inspired terrorist organisation, but few people seemed to be listening any more.

The Net Closes in on the Regime

Comprehensive anti-apartheid legislation, which forbade new investment in South Africa, ended air links between the two countries and curtailed American imports of South African goods, was passed in the United States in 1986 despite a veto from President Reagan. Previous allies of the regime, such as Israel and Malaysia, also curbed their trade with South Africa. The withdrawal of foreign investments and a decline in the import of capital goods hit the country particularly hard as sanctions seriously impeded the economy's ability to grow. In an attempt to deflect international criticism and reverse sanctioning, but also in response to the need to cut government expenditure, pass law legislation was revoked in 1986. This increased African migration to urban areas but had no beneficial effects for the government.

As foreign loans were called in and investment dried up, the economy spiralled into a state of crisis. The representatives of South African business now stepped up calls for a relaxation of the strictures of apartheid. The country's currency collapsed, forcing the temporary closure of the Johannesburg Stock Exchange. International links continued to be severed and only the Conservative government in Britain, led by Margaret Thatcher, was prepared to stick by the Botha regime.

The government refused to bow to international pressure, however, and continued to reject all calls for the introduction of majority rule. This stance was based on the fact that, although increasingly unpopular abroad and not in control of large areas of the country, there was not as yet any serious threat to the power of the central government. Nothing had yet happened to suggest that apartheid could not be maintained for the foreseeable future. So, rather than carrying its reform programme any further, the government abandoned any plans for the introduction of further political and social changes, and instead, reacted to any and all challenges to its power with a greater sense of determination.

ESCALATION OF VIOLENCE

In July 1986 the State of Emergency was extended to cover the whole of the country. The police were given wide powers of arrest and detention. The army was deployed alongside the police in townships the length and breadth of the country. Thereafter, the clandestine security forces were given greater freedom of manoeuvre as formal controls over their actions were relaxed. African communities responded by any means available to them but rarely had an answer to armoured cars and machine guns.

The state invested ever more heavily in defence. The security forces also employed a sinister web of African activists who instigated vigilante movements against political opponents of the regime. These reactionary groupings, nominally set up to protect people and property from attack in response to boycott breaking, extended their work to include assaults upon anti-apartheid protestors. In this way, the state was able to get civilian agents to do its work for it, and as black turned on black, the violence became more than just politically motivated.

The actions of paramilitary bands, black or white, and the breakdown of law and order meant that South African society became more characterised by violence during the 1980s. Figures show that by the middle of the decade one in eight black deaths in Cape Town, Johannesburg and Pietermaritzburg was as a result of homicide. Social deprivation and degradation created the conditions in which extreme violence became something of a norm. The further breakdown of social institutions, and the lack of educational and job opportunities, also had the effect of persuading greater numbers into a criminal way of life.

Despite such lawlessness, by late 1987 the security forces, aided by emergency legislation, could claim to have re-established order across the country. A high-level security presence was able to contain the situation in most townships and homelands. Pressure had also been brought to bear on political organisations, which curtailed the ability of the UDF to operate freely. Thousands, meanwhile, languished in prison with little prospect of their cases going to trial. Most detainees were physically abused to some extent and some were picked out for torture. Cases have been recorded of children as young as ten being subjected to electric shock treatment.

STALEMATE

With the army in occupation of large areas of the country, a seemingly unbreakable stalemate had come into existence. While on the one hand the forces of opposition were not strong enough to dislodge the government from power, on the other, the regime could not entirely quash dissension or political unrest. Along the line somewhere, something would have to give.

INKATHA UNREST

In Natal a further factor was introduced to an already volatile situation. This emanated from the KwaZulu homeland and centred on chief Mangosotho Buthelezi's (1928–) Inkatha movement.

Inkatha was formed in the 1920s as an organisation to further and preserve Zulu culture. In 1975, Inkatha was revived by Buthelezi, who was a high Zulu chief, as a means of furthering the cause of Zulu nationalism, and also his own power base within KwaZulu. Initially an

Chief Mangosotho Buthelezi, President of the Inkatha Freedom Party

ardent opponent of the South African government, over time Buthelezi modified his stance as he was encouraged by the leaders of white South Africa in his attempts to revive Zulu culture and reinvigorate nationalist aspirations within the homeland. Inkatha was thus transformed from a merely cultural organisation into a more overtly political movement.

Buthelezi attracted followers to Inkatha by extending patronage to its members. In a highly impoverished society, this guaranteed him a mass following. However, Inkatha was quick to use intimidation and violence against its opponents. By the early 1980s, KwaZulu was a dangerous and repressive place. In response to its policies and increasingly accommodating stance in relation to the apartheid regime, Inkatha was dismissed as a collaborationist party by the Black Consciousness movement and lambasted by the ANC for its rejection of direct action and condemnation of economic sanctions. Buthelezi therefore came to be seen as at worst a stooge of the South African government, and at best, no more than the mere defender of Zulu, as opposed to African rights. He had stated a desire to carve out for himself a role as a conciliator among the country's African communities but had managed simply to alienate himself from most of them.

Inkatha clashed with the UDF after 1983, as it attempted to stop the Front from extending its political actions throughout Natal. There followed a widening of the gulf between Inkatha and ANC activists in the mid-1980s which quickly developed into open confrontation. With allegations that the police did less than enough to confront or prosecute the violence of Inkatha members, battles rapidly evolved into a state of near civil war in parts of Natal. Attacks and counter-reprisals became more indiscriminate and women and children became caught up in the violence. The government, which was keen to see the UDF weakened by any means, materially supported Inkatha in a conflict that served to entrench notions of Zulu nationality. The struggle, which was very much connected to the right to control African politics in Natal, would continue for some time to come. The ultimate suppression of the UDF in 1988 did nothing to stem the war.

THE ENDING OF CROSS-BORDER CONFLICTS

In 1988 the South African army in Angola was defeated by a joint Cuban–Angolan force. A subsequent peace accord acted as something of a face-saver for the South African government, which agreed to withdraw its forces at the same time as the Cubans. It also pledged to end its support for opposition forces in Angola. During the same year it was agreed that South Africa would recognise previous UN Security Council resolutions and end its long-standing occupation of Namibia. That country's independence would come on stream in 1990. Thus ended a costly and misguided attempt by the South African government to impose its will on neighbouring states, whose right to self-determination it had undermined for as long as they adhered to ideologies that did not converge with its own.

A New President

Amid simmering unrest across the country, and a perceptible loss of confidence among the white electorate, health problems forced Botha to step down in 1989. He was replaced by the Transvaal-based lawyer F.W. de Klerk (1923–), an unremarkable cabinet minister since 1978, and, on the face of it, a hard-line apartheid advocate. Less authoritarian than Botha, few realised that this pragmatist had the wherewithal for unlocking the political deadlock that gripped South Africa.

De Klerk assumed power at a time when repression was beginning to fail and the forces of political opposition were once again making headway in the cities and villages of South Africa. A highly organised campaign of mass civil disobedience run by the Mass Democratic Movement (MDM), the direct descendent of the suppressed UDF, was proving effective as it confined its protests to the realities of life under the State of Emergency. A series of peaceful marches, held in every major town and city across the country, took place in September and October of 1989. Aimed purely against the continuing emergency legislation, these protests attracted a notable number of white people who had come to realise that apartheid was no longer justifiable or tenable. The security forces were instructed to allow the demonstrations to run their course. No instances of violence were recorded.

There were some who argued that the government had handed the initiative to the MDM. If this was the case, De Klerk acted to claim it back early the next year when he removed the ban on the ANC, the PAC, the Communist Party, the MK and thirty-one other illegal organisations. On the same day, 2 February 1990, he also announced the unconditional release of all political prisoners, including Nelson Mandela, after twenty-seven years in prison.

This, indeed, was an act of momentous significance for South Africa that resonated around the world. Nine days later and in full view of the world's media, the distinctive figure of Mandela, now with ashen hair, walked away from a holding prison near the town of Paarl and was driven to Cape Town. Here he addressed a huge crowd that had assembled to hear him speak from a balcony of the town hall. Millions watched on television sets around the world as he declared: 'I stand here before you not as a prophet but as a humble servant of ... the people. Your tireless and heroic sacrifices have made it possible for me to be here today. I therefore place the remaining years of my life in your hands.' It was a highly charged moment from which there could be no turning back.

The Transition Begins

De Klerk's act was a determined attempt to change for the better the structures of political power in South Africa. Over the next few months he backed it up with further legislative changes that inaugurated a period of transition during which apartheid was dismantled.

By the end of 1991 the framework of apartheid legislation concerning land and amenities had been repealed. Most significantly, the Population Registration Act, which had been in force since 1950, was revoked. In practice this ended the racial classification of South Africans and meant that individuals could no longer be deprived of rights on the basis of their ethnicity. In reverse, it also signalled the ending of white social and political privileges.

The State of Emergency was ended that same year. The more

pernicious divisions of the security forces were disbanded and many covert operations halted. Violence, however, continued unabated in many places, and the change of course by the regime did not bring to an end anti-activist activities or sponsorship of Inkatha in Natal. Unidentifiable bands attacked, and in some cases murdered, Africans commuting to and from Soweto. Nor was the detention of political dissidents immediately stopped. There could be no sea change on the ground or in the minds of thousands of people who had important personal interests to defend.

The question is often asked as to why De Klerk acted in the manner that he did and at the time he did. There was no immediate threat to the longer-term position of the government and repressive measures, although costly and unpopular, could still have been made to work. The answer would appear to lie in the fact that De Klerk was acting to pre-empt the inevitable collapse that would be brought on by the culmination of a number of fairly evident trends.

The increasing international condemnation of, and protests against, apartheid had strong moral and severe economic implications for South Africa. The collapse of Soviet communism also dissolved fears of a Marxist plot to overthrow the established order, and radically changed white South African political views of the country's place in the world. There was also a realisation that popular protests within South Africa were never going to go away and would become more difficult to contain over time. In truth, however, De Klerk's actions were only partly influenced by such considerations. His decision was based rather upon the prevailing economic reality.

The longer sanctions were in place the more precarious became the state of South Africa's economy, which had gone into a period of considerable decline and showed no signs of recovery. This affected the material prosperity of white South Africans, and therefore, was a direct challenge to the NP's hold on power. The increasing influence of the reactionary Conservative Party illustrated the need not only to reform, but also actively to turn around the faltering economy. This, however, could only be achieved by dismantling at least some of the structures of apartheid which did not allow for the education of a competitive labour force. In an era of fast technological change, there were few enough jobs for whites, let alone Africans. Capital investment and industrial diversity needed to be encouraged to address unemployment and inflation, but this could not happen under apartheid rule. De Klerk realised the extent of this quandary and acted to break out of it.

The risks involved, from the government's point of view, were huge. However, by acting quickly, De Klerk felt certain that he could control the process of change while, at the same time, upholding essential NP interests and keeping the party in power. This was a fair assumption, given that those who had turned to the Conservative Party were just as likely to return to the NP once the economic climate improved. Furthermore, the ANC would need time to adjust to its new-found legal status, and De Klerk, who had the backing of Buthelezi, believed that Inkatha would act as the perfect counterweight to the African nationalists. In the end, all of these calculations were to backfire.

NEGOTIATIONS

Formal negotiations between the government and an array of non-governmental bodies, over a future multi-racial constitution for South Africa, began in earnest in December 1991 following a white referendum that voted unanimously in favour of just such a process. The Convention for a Democratic South Africa (Codesa) was representative of a wide variety of the country's political interest groups, although the militant PAC and ultra-right Conservative Party both refused to attend. The initial meetings were hampered by mutual suspicions and took place in a highly charged atmosphere. Only after the ANC leaders agreed to call a halt to the armed struggle was there a lightening of tensions.

The meeting of Codesa caused an increase in violent conflict across the country. The conflict between Inkatha and the ANC also spread from Natal and was played out in hostels and cheap hotels on the Rand. The fact that governmental secret forces were still at work in Johannesburg and other urban centres also increased suspicions over the true intentions of the state. All of these tensions were exacerbated by the reality that tens of thousands of impoverished Africans were migrating to the cities. Everywhere huge social and economic problems were in evidence.

The Convention nevertheless proceeded with its work. The basis for talks first had to be agreed and the government insisted on a guarantee of constitutional continuity. In other words, whatever was agreed by Codesa could only be enacted through legal means and by the South African parliament and any new government could only come into being as the legal successor of De Klerk's regime.

Five working parties were formed, each to discuss a particular area of governance and they were briefed to reach 'sufficient consensus' on every proposal they made. In practice this was difficult to achieve in the first months of Codesa as there was not much trust and good will remained in short supply. Petty squabbling took up a lot of the time of each working party and sub-committee; there was disagreement over procedure and a number of poorly timed public utterances by members of Codesa threatened to wreck the entire undertaking.

The NP's demand for future protection of minority safeguards and insistence on the control of an interim government designed to last for a decade were incompatible with ANC demands for the institution of a freely democratic government at the earliest opportunity and a refusal to countenance any sort of racial weighting. The NP were bolstered by favourable opinion poll ratings and tried to force these issues, but could not attain anything approaching consensus from the Convention.

Meanwhile, the ANC was struggling to transform itself into a legitimate political party and was troubled throughout the earliest phases of Codesa by the continuing conflict with Inkatha. Men like Mandela, Thabo Mbeki (1942–) and Joe Slovo (1926–95) could weather accusations, levelled by the PAC, that the ANC had sold out the African masses; the blatant support of the sitting government for Inkatha forces against ANC followers they could not stomach. The ANC called for a halt to the violence, threatening to walk out of Codesa and launch a campaign of mass action if De Klerk did not rein in the security forces.

The mandate De Klerk felt he had, and which he attempted to exploit during the first months of Codesa, disappeared in January 1992. A by-election at Potchefstroom, a traditional NP stronghold, was won with a sweeping majority by the Conservative Party, whose candidate used the campaign to condemn the negotiations in no uncertain terms. This transformed the atmosphere of Codesa and appeared to hand the initiative to the government's opponents.

However, Codesa's days were numbered. It collapsed in May 1992, amid much bitterness and having made little tangible progress, due to the escalating social disorder and uncertainty prevalent throughout the country. Nadir was reached in June when forty-five ANC supporters, including women and children, were murdered by residents of an Inkatha hostel in the Vaal township of Boipatong. The strong suspicion of police involvement (or at the least, collusion) in the massacre provoked the ANC to call a countrywide mass action. A general strike in early August brought the country to its knees. De Klerk threatened a return to repression if the ANC stirred up unnecessary unrest. He was, in turn, reminded by Nelson Mandela of the grave implications of any such actions.

This exchange suggested that the government and the ANC were a long way from returning to the negotiating table. In fact, the opposite was true. Secret negotiations aimed at getting Codesa back on line were held between Cyril Ramaphosa (1952–), the general secretary of the ANC, and Roelf Meyer (1947–), on behalf of the government, which managed to iron out many major issues of contention. This was a painstaking process and compromise was only reached slowly. However, the two men were able to reach consensus on behalf of those they represented over both the nature and form any transitional administration would take. Although nothing was formalised, there was now a reasonable agenda for discussion and government leaders agreed to meet ANC representatives to sign a Record of Understanding that would form the basis for a further round of discussions.

This new sense of tentative mutual trust was compounded by the ending of economic sanctions by the European Community, a lead quickly followed by the United States. Almost as quickly, the cultural boycotting of South Africa was lifted, and in 1992, a South African team was invited to the Olympic Games in Barcelona. It was thirty-two years since this invitation had last been extended.

UNDERSTANDING REACHED

The Record of Understanding, signed by De Klerk and Mandela in late September 1992, allowed for the resumption of open negotiations in April 1993. The Understanding was a pragmatic solution to an intractable situation and allowed both sides to admit to certain limitations. The NP, for example, quietly dropped its insistence upon the constitutional protection of minorities. Simultaneously, the ANC came to realise that it could not effect a complete revolution of South African society and understood that if it was to form a working government it would need to keep existing administrators and governmental mandarins on its side.

The real breakthrough was achieved in late 1992 and early 1993 when the government and the ANC entered into secret bilateral talks ahead of further open discussions. Proposals suggested by Joe Slovo, the white communist stalwart who had spent decades in exile directing MK and who, in consequence, had been vilified by the apartheid establishment as *the* symbol of all evil, were a realistic response to the prevailing political climate and largely appeased NP sceptics. These were the so-called Sunset Clauses, pushed through the ANC's Executive by Mandela, which allowed for a power-sharing government of National Unity, that would sit for a fixed term, and in which the largest political parties could expect fair representation at the highest level. An amnesty was also to be extended and existing government worker contracts would be fully honoured.

When open negotiations recommenced, they were boycotted by Buthelezi who was opposed to proposals for a unitary form of government. He held out for a federal constitution that would favour Inkatha. The white ultra right also refused to be drawn into the negotiations, believing that Afrikaner interests were not being properly addressed. Meanwhile, there was still unrest and violence across the country from both disaffected African youths and extreme right-wing paramilitary groups.

Regardless of the disquiet that existed, and of all forms of resistance to the negotiations, in June a date was set for South Africa's first multi-racial democratic elections: 27 April 1994. By the following month an interim constitution had been agreed by all parties privy to the negotiation process. This constitution, which included a wide-ranging Bill of Rights, the promise of universal suffrage and the ending of the homelands, provided for the creation of the Government of National Unity, to be formed by all parties who won a sufficient proportion of representation in the National Assembly of 400 delegates. Each party which claimed 5 per cent of the total votes would be entitled to a seat on the cabinet. The President would be drawn from the party that had elected the majority of members to the Assembly. Any party winning eighty or more seats in parliament would be allowed a Deputy President. There were to be no further weightings or minority safeguards.

The new government's main focus would be writing a new constitution that would need the approval of two-thirds of the National Assembly. A further Bill of Rights would guarantee human rights and liberty regardless of race, religion or sex. Nine new provinces were also agreed although federalism was categorically rejected.

Extreme white groups such as Eugene Terre'Blanche's (1941–) AWB, formed in 1973 in reaction to perceived 'liberalism' within the ranks of the Vorster administration, threatened to provoke a race war although this did not materialise. More seriously, Inkatha supporters, whose leaders refused to accede to the new interim constitutional agreement, went on the offensive across Natal, forcing the government to proclaim a State of Emergency across the region. Buthelezi, meanwhile, was becoming an increasingly marginalised figure. He was only persuaded to contest the election a mere week before it was due to take place.

Democracy

Prior to the election, Nelson Mandela and F.W. de Klerk were jointly awarded the Nobel Peace Prize. This was important as far as the election campaign was concerned, as both men attempted to put the past behind them and present a professional image to the electorate. Their two personalities dominated the campaign and all other parties trailed in the wake of the ANC and NP.

The result of the election was never in doubt. There were widespread concerns that the four polling days would see instances of violence, or worse, politically motivated killings. In the event, the election passed off peacefully but not without difficulties. The sheer logistics involved in getting millions of people to the polls for the first time, in every corner of the country, were massive and the especially created Electoral Commission oversaw a blatant shambles. This was outweighed, however, by the sheer euphoria that accompanied South Africa's first-ever freely held democratic elections.

In the event not everyone got to vote, some polling stations could not be opened due to security fears or a shortage of manpower, and not all ballot boxes could be accounted for. Nevertheless, people waited for hours to cast their vote. Men and women who had been denied the vote all their lives thought nothing of queuing for a day or more. Of the estimated twenty million voters, that is some 86 per cent of the electorate, who participated in the 1994 South African election, the majority were doing so for the first time in their lives.

The ANC won the poll by a landslide and the NP was voted out of power for the first time since 1948. Although the ANC did not quite achieve the two-thirds of the vote required to enable it unilaterally to write the new constitution, it nevertheless swept the board in six of the nine provinces. The NP polled a little over 20 per cent of the total vote, allowing for De Klerk's appointment as Deputy President alongside the ANC's Thabo Mbeki. Inkatha's vote held up in its Natal stronghold where the party recorded 10.5 per cent of the vote and Buthelezi accepted the offer of a cabinet position as Minister of Home Affairs. As

Nelson Mandela, South Africa's first democratically elected President, with his two Deputies, Thabo Mbeki and F.W. de Klerk

these statistics prove, the majority of South Africans had voted along racial lines.

On 10 May 1994, the Government of National Unity assumed power and Nelson Mandela was inaugurated as South Africa's first democratically elected President. Tens of thousands of people assembled outside the Union Buildings in Pretoria to see him take the oath of allegiance. As the new President proclaimed the election result 'a common victory for justice, for peace, for human dignity', the scars of the previous 300 years faded, if only temporarily.

CHAPTER NINE

Truth and Reconciliation

The dismantling of apartheid and the relatively peaceful transition to democratic rule was an achievement of genuine magnitude that was rightly applauded around the world. Most South Africans felt a sense of pride in their new government. However, the harsh economic and social realities of life throughout the country meant that the period of euphoria was only short-lived. The Government of National Unity was required to address the serious problems it faced with the utmost haste. In every conceivable field – health, education, welfare, housing, land distribution and urban regeneration – there was much work to be done.

The New South Africa

In every aspect of government an immediate and strong emphasis was placed upon reconciliation. There were great efforts made to reach understanding and to bridge ideological differences. The 'new' South Africa, it was hoped, would be built upon a consensus of diverse, yet united groupings. As if to illustrate the fact, the new South African flag combined the old colours of the apartheid regime with the black, gold and green of the ANC. The former national anthem, *Die Stem van Suid Afrika* (The Voice of South Africa), was amalgamated with the liberation hymn *Nkosi Sikelela iAfrika* (God Bless Africa), to create a new national anthem for the new South Africa.

SOUTH AFRICA ON THE WORLD STAGE

South Africa's reacceptance into the international community of nations was illustrated by the range and number of world political

251

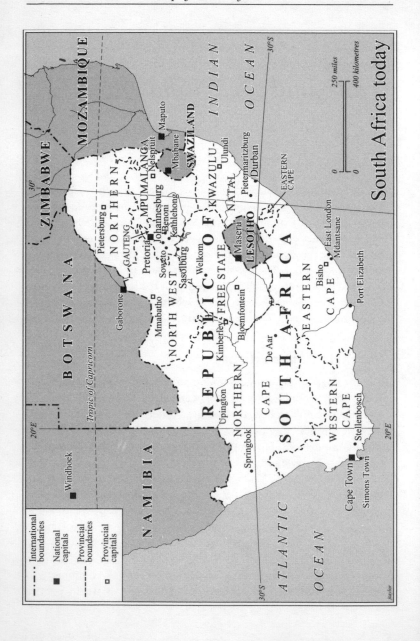

South Africa today

leaders who attended Nelson Mandela's presidential inauguration. Immediately welcomed into the Organisation of African Unity, and readmitted to the British Commonwealth of Nations, South Africa emerged as a powerful and immediately respected state. In this respect it was greatly helped by the person of Mandela, who was cherished as a symbol of dignity and fortitude the world over. Before his retirement from politics in 1999, Mandela was perhaps South Africa's biggest asset and he did much work to reverse the damage done to the country's reputation by the apartheid state. He also encouraged investors and visitors back to his country, supporting government schemes to improve customer service and conservation as a means of enticing to South Africa increasing numbers of tourists from around the world.

A NEW CONSTITUTION

The new constitution was agreed only after much time and negotiation. A Constitutional Assembly, chaired jointly by the ANC and the NP, encouraged submissions from the general public and opened its meetings to anyone who wanted to attend them. By fusing new ideas with a list of principles pre-agreed as part of the interim constitution, a draft document was ready for discussion in May 1996. After some revisions, the President was able to sign the final text at Sharpeville in December that year. Early in 1997, parliament swore allegiance (having approved the constitution by 421 votes to two, with few abstentions), thereby bringing the constitution into force.

This constitution was one of the most liberal in the world and encompassed wide-ranging safeguards to protect the rights of individuals. These pertained not only to political rights, but as importantly, to socio-economic rights such as free education and clean air. The deliberate provocation of hatred and violence was also outlawed. Custodial and judicial rights and privileges were enshrined in the law and capital punishment was abolished. Employee, as well as employer, rights were also laid down.

Eleven official languages (Afrikaans, English, Ndebele, North Sotho, Siswati, South Sotho, Tsonga, Tswana, Venda, Xhosa and Zulu), each protected in status, were recognised. Wherever practical, children could receive educational instruction in their language of choice. The nine provinces of the interim period (Northern Province, North-West Province, Gauteng, Mpumalanga, KwaZulu-Natal, Free State, and Northern, Eastern and Western Cape) were to remain in place, with a strong partly elected, partly appointed National Council of Provinces acting as the upper house of parliament. The National Assembly, selected under a system of universal suffrage and according to proportional representation, acted as the lower house and was to be elected for terms of no more than five years.

The Reconstruction and Development Programme

The Government of National Unity was faced with the massive challenge of trying to right the social and economic wrongs of the apartheid era and to improve the lives of millions of impoverished people in a practical manner. The will to do this existed, and there were many capable people either in or aligned to the government prepared to give their all in transforming the state of the nation. Unfortunately, there was not enough money to make much more than a marginal difference to the vast majority of the population in the immediate term.

The ANC's election manifesto, *A Better Life For All*, after the election was used as the basis for the government's Reconstruction and Development Programme (RDP), which was to be the political vehicle for bringing about socio-economic change. According to Mandela, the RDP aimed

> ... to create jobs through public works; to build a million houses with electricity and flush toilets; to extend primary health care and provide ten years of free education to all South Africans; to redistribute land through a land claims court; and to end the value-added tax on basic foodstuffs.

These were high ideals indeed, and even before the end of 1994, some commentators were doubting the feasibility of the RDP. Certainly, the programme aroused hopes that, in reality, could not be immediately fulfilled.

Nevertheless, the programme was instituted under a minister without portfolio, and following an inflation-cutting budget, the government began to prioritise its workload. Primary health care was introduced in deprived areas, partly paid for by cutting subsidies in other sectors. The education system was overhauled to replace the (racially) tiered structure of the apartheid era, and multi-racial schools were opened with a narrower teacher/pupil ratio. A programme of urban renewal was launched with a project to build a million new homes within five years, which would be supplied with electricity and running water. The land claims court was established, although few people managed to complete successful claims. Where land could not be restored and claims were validated, alternative land or cash was offered. Local authorities were also reformed into singular, democratic institutions to drive through reconstruction and development.

But there could be no quick fixes. By 1997, the government could claim to have made some progress in terms of providing better health care facilities and housing in some of the most deprived regions of the country. However, the RDP was clearly falling short of its very high goals, and the administration, which was careful not to move too fast too soon, became susceptible to the criticism that it was more concerned with courting local and international big business than attacking the root cause of the country's social ills. This was unfair in as far as the RDP could not be made to work without some privatisation of the public sector and a large amount of non-governmental investment. Nonetheless, many promises made in the run up to, and immediately following, the 1994 election came back to haunt the Government of National Unity (most notably in the area of land redistribution, where by the time of the 1999 election, only 230 out of some 63,000 claims had been granted).

In 1997 Thabo Mbeki took direct responsibility for the RDP. The programme was modified in terms of its goals and deadlines for delivery of targets. A more concerted effort was made to bring private enterprise into various schemes for improving the provision of education, health care, housing and electricity. In this instance, some notable successes were achieved. By March 1999, 748,000 new homes (75 per cent of the original government target) had been constructed and electricity and running water had been provided for a large section of the rural and urban populations. But the government remained committed to strict economic principles and continued to refuse to borrow sums that it could not afford to pay back.

Economic growth remained sluggish throughout the time of the Government of National Unity. This situation was not helped by the relatively low price South African gold could fetch on the world market. The technical realities of gold mining in South Africa meant the country could not compete with more efficient concerns in Australia and the United States. Nonetheless, gold remained central to the economy, and mining goods (mostly gold and related products) accounted for about half of South Africa's exports in the 1990s.

The overall economic outlook was not helped by the inability of industry and business to compete on equal terms with foreign competitors. The labour force, in general, remained poorly trained. Legislation guaranteeing a minimum wage was a further disincentive to businesses. A series of parsimonious budgets also did little to encourage diversification of the economy or investment. Many firms looked to places other than South Africa, while the so-called 'brain drain', which was a feature of the last three decades of the apartheid era, showed no signs of reversing. Meanwhile, unemployment continued to run at an abnormally high rate and public service provisions were, if anything, deteriorating.

South Africa at the End of the Millennium

The estimated population of South Africa in 1996 was just under 41 million, growing at a rate of 2.5 per cent a year (it was expected to top 66 million by 2020). Of this population, 55 per cent lived in designated urban areas, another trend that was fast rising year on year. When asked, three out of every four South Africans claimed to be a member of a Christian denomination and many other religions, notably Islam, are followed by increasing numbers. Unemployment in 1996 was running at 30 per cent of the adult population. Since then this figure remained the same and millions of people are still forced to make an income in the 'black' economy or through crime. In South Africa the inequalities of wealth distribution are as marked as in many Latin American or other emerging nations in Asia. According to a 1996 United Nations report, the richest 20 per cent of the South African population earned as much as twenty times more than the poorest 20 per cent. Over half of the population accounted for only 10 per cent of the total yearly economic consumption within the country. Such a wealth gap is not easily closed and is reflected in the strains put upon the country's health and education services. Those who can afford the best regularly receive it. The rest, that is the overwhelming majority of the population, simply have to make do. By the end of the twentieth century, over half of all South Africans were living below the poverty datum line, with an average income in 1998 of US\$ 60 per month or less. Sixty per cent of the population were estimated to be living in extreme poverty, a figure that rose to two-thirds of the infant population. In 1995, before the RDP had a chance to effect change, eight in every ten African households did not have running water or a toilet, while 60 per cent of all people had no electricity supply to their homes. Homelessness was so rife at one stage during the late 1990s that there were more South Africans without a house than there were white citizens. Clearly, the government and local authorities were struggling to provide even the most basic of services. This situation has improved in the past couple of years but such deep-rooted problems cannot be eradicated at a stroke. South Africa today is a country slowly on the mend.

Such poverty, of course, has serious implications for the social welfare of a nation. In terms of health, the government is now able to provide basic preventative medicines and vaccines to the country's young but is less well placed to deal with the AIDS epidemic that has afflicted the community at large (there are today in South Africa over five million HIV sufferers, predominantly African; deaths from AIDS are expected to reach six million by 2009). Crime, also, is endemic. Rape is believed by some observers to be more prevalent in South Africa than anywhere else in the world, although exact comparisons are hard to draw as the majority of cases go unreported. Gangs and criminal syndicates run amuck in places like Cape Town and Johannesburg to the extent that the latter has been described as one of the world's most unsafe cities. In 2001, some 27,000 people were murdered, usually for a wallet or as part of a carjacking or serious assault. Most murders are committed in the home by intruders. An estimated one in nine deaths in South Africa is from unnatural causes and the South African murder rate is an average 10 per cent higher than in the United States. The police force is only slowly beginning to address this problem. Educational standards are also only slowly improving. Tests of basic numeracy and literacy carried out in 1995 were failed by 80 per cent of adult African participants and 40 per cent of whites, proving the point that quality of education is linked to race. Further education courses were launched to redress such appalling statistics. The extension of universal free education should mean that they are never repeated again.

THE NP GOES INTO OPPOSITION.

F.W. de Klerk bowed out of political life in 1997, a year after he had resigned the office of Deputy President and withdrawn the NP from the government. The move was made in response to the fact that the NP was having little enough influence in an administration that was, in all reality, dominated by the ANC. This led to a serious reassessment of the party by its membership and leaders as it tried to carve out for itself a distinctive role in post-apartheid South African politics. As yet the NP, now renamed as the New National Party, still has not emerged out of the shadows of its past and its followers are decreasing all the time. In the 1999 general election, the New NP's share of the vote plummeted to a mere 7 per cent, forcing the party's hierarchy to reconstitute the organisation in an attempt to escape its historical legacy.

NATIONAL DIS-UNITY?

By the half-way mark of its term in office, the government of National Unity was under attack for its failure to deliver on promises made prior to the 1994 election, and further, for its slowness in formulating concrete policies. It was fumbling or re-thinking in many crucial areas of government such as education, housing and policing in response to the size of the task in hand. It was only after the re-formulation of the RDP under Mbeki that definite statements of intention were made in these and other areas of policy. The truth of the matter was that the government and its ministers were learning the hard way, while in power. Mandela often conceded this point, while reiterating that permanent cures for the country's ills could only be found given the grace of time.

THE TRUTH AND RECONCILIATION COMMISSION

The Government of National Unity understood one fundamental truth: that unless South Africans of all races addressed the past there could be no hope for the future. Mandela continually spoke of the need for reconciliation and took every opportunity to promote the cause (most famously, by donning a Springbok rugby jersey as he watched the South African team win the 1995 World Cup in Johannesburg). In consequence, the Truth and Reconciliation Commission (TRC) was established in 1995 under the auspices of the former Anglican Archbishop of Cape Town, Desmond Tutu (1931–), a long-standing opponent of apartheid who, in 1984, was awarded the Nobel Peace Prize in recognition of his non-violent campaigning against the South African state.

Based loosely on similar commissions that had sat in Chile and East Germany, the TRC was designed to open up the crimes of the past. Realising that individuals or ex-institutions would be unprepared to incriminate themselves, amnesty was offered on political crimes and human rights violations committed between 1960 and 1993, in return for the giving of a frank and public testimony. Desmond Tutu opened the hearings of the Commission by stating that only in the wake of the truth would reconciliation be possible. The country seemed to agree

Desmond Tutu, the former Anglican Archbishop of Cape Town

with him, although there were some people, notably P.W. Botha, who refused to speak to the commissioners or acknowledge the role they were playing in attempting to right the wrongs of the past.

The TRC was constituted of seventeen people from each of South Africa's major racial groupings. It comprised three committees, one each to consider human rights abuses, amnesty claims and reparation payments, that met in public and had the powers to subpoena witnesses. Confessions were heard from both the defenders and opponents of apartheid: security officials, political activists, local and national politicians. These testimonies were a confirmation of the violence and brutality inherent in the apartheid system. As the truth was uncovered, it became clear that this was characteristic not only of the state, but also of the liberation movement. In total, 7,000 people applied for amnesty.

The TRC could not be called an unqualified success. Those who faced the Commission were, essentially, freed of any or all culpability. Furthermore, many of the old wounds that were reopened could not be closed again. Many relatives of victims became distraught at the fact that justice would not be done. Indeed, there was some sense that some of the most evil figures and institutions of the apartheid era used the Commission to buy themselves freedom. Perhaps as a result of this, in June 2002, some families of apartheid victims launched a campaign against large multinational companies in an attempt to gain recompense from businesses that, they argued, had funded the apartheid state.

Despite these shortcomings, and its failure to provide answers to all the myriad questions it raised, few would deny that the TRC, which took three years to complete, was a cathartic experience for the whole nation, a necessary stepping stone to a better future.

THE 1999 ELECTION

In 1997 Nelson Mandela retired from the presidency of the ANC and, his job done, announced he would not be standing for re-election in 1999. His position as President of both the party and the country was filled by Thabo Mbeki, who had been especially groomed for the role, and had effectively overseen the daily running of the administration since 1997.

Mbeki's father Govan (1910–2001) had been an ANC activist since the mid-1930s and was imprisoned along with Mandela in 1964. The young Thabo had followed in his father's footsteps by joining the ANC's Youth League at the age of fourteen. Ordered into exile by his family following the Rivonia arrests, Thabo lived first in Tanzania, before moving to Britain, where he obtained a Masters degree in economics. Thereafter he became active as a member of the ANC in exile, travelling to Russia for military training, before assuming representative roles in various African states. In the late 1980s, Mbeki was part of the ANC delegation that negotiated with the Botha and De Klerk administrations. He returned to South Africa after the ban on the ANC was lifted and participated in all the negotiations leading up to the adoption of the interim constitution. During the time of the Government of National Unity, he was an active and studious Deputy President.

The election of 1999 was the first to be fought under the new constitution, and saw the ANC assume office with a small increase in the share of the vote at both national and provincial level. With overall control of seven of the country's nine provinces, an almost two-thirds majority in the National Assembly, and the backing of much of the national media, Mbeki was strongly placed to build on Mandela's legacy and take South Africa into the twenty-first century.

Mbeki had a hard act to follow and maintained a low-key approach to both national and international politics in the first year of his presidency. He did, however, attempt to assert South Africa's role as a regional super power and was dedicated to spearheading an 'African Renaissance'. He was able to prove himself in this respect when, during the turbulent Zimbabwean election of 2002, he mediated between Robert Mugabe and the rest of the world, handling a possibly fraught situation with a calmness that diffused, perhaps only temporarily, the possibility of much bloodshed.

At home, Mbeki does not enjoy the kind of close relationship his predecessor had with the population. The fact that, close on a decade after the introduction of democratic rule, South Africa is still an overwhelmingly poor country racked by serious social problems does little to endear a seemingly distant President to the people, despite his stated commitment to 'a caring society ... capable of extending sustainable and equitable benefits to all our people'. His sometimes confused utterances also do him no favours. His controversial views on AIDS – he has stated that HIV is not the cause of immune system collapse – have cast doubt over his suitability for the premiership and made him a figure of some ridicule, drawing stinging criticisms from his mentor, Mandela. Nevertheless, few commentators doubt he will be returned to a second term in office in 2004.

Today, for all its faults and problems, South Africa is a vibrant country, struggling to put the past behind it and move in a forward direction. It is not, nor will it ever be, a staid or uniform place. Its people and culture are too diverse for that. However, after decades of schism and imbalance, South Africa is finally at one with itself. This is not only remarkable, but a testament to mankind's nobility. On the eve of his retirement from politics, Nelson Mandela told the nation that it could do 'much, much better'. It was a fair analysis of a society that has come a long way in a short period of time and will continue to go forward. South Africa still lives in the hope of a brighter, fairer future.

Notes

Notes

List of Abbreviations

ANC	African National Congress
APO	African Political Organisation (after 1919, African Peoples' Organisation)
AWB	Afrikaner Weerstands Beweging
Boss	Bureau of State Security
Codesa	Convention for a Democratic South Africa
HNP	'Purified' National Party
ICU	Industrial and Commercial [Workers'] Union
MDM	Mass Democratic Movement
MK	Umkhonto We Sizwe; Spear of the Nation
NEUM	Non-European Unity Movement
NNC	South African National Native Congress
NP	National Party
OB	Ossewabrandwag; Ox-Wagon Sentinels
OFS	Orange Free State
PAC	Pan Africanist Congress
RDP	Reconstruction and Development Programme
SANAC	South African Native Affairs Commission
SAP	South African Party
SAR	South African Republic
TRC	Truth and Reconciliation Commission
UDF	United Democratic Front
UP	United Party
VOC	Vereenigde Ooste-Indische Compaigne; Dutch East India Company

Chronology of Major Events

Prior to c.1000 BC	Ancestors of Khoi–San living within boundaries of modern southern Africa
c.1000 BC–c.AD200	Pastoralist herders move into the region of southern Africa
c.AD300–1000	Bantu-speaking mixed farmers migrate into southern Africa
1487	Portuguese explorer Dias rounds the Cape of Good Hope
1652	VOC establishes station at the Cape; beginnings of colonial expansion into interior and conquest of Khoi–San population
1658	VOC imports first slaves into the Cape
1795	British occupy the Cape
1799	Khoi–Xhosa rebellion on eastern frontier of the colony (to 1803)
1803	The Dutch Batavian Republic regains control of the Cape
1806	British re-take the Cape and establish permanent control of the colony (confirmed 1815)
1811	First British attempts at settling Xhosa–settler conflict in east of colony; Xhosa expelled west of Fish River
1816	Emergence of nascent Zulu kingdom under Shaka
1820s	Expansion of Zulu nation leading to *Mfecane*; great turmoil and dislocation across the southern African interior
1820	5,000 British migrants settled in Albany
1834	Abolition of slavery; emancipation of indentured labourers throughout the Cape
1835	Xhosa defeated by British–settler forces
1836	Beginnings of Great Trek – Afrikaners head out of the Cape
1838	Trekker commando defeats Zulu force at Battle of Blood River; Republic of Natalia founded
1843	British annex Natalia (Natal)
1847	Xhosa annihilated by colonial forces

1852	Through Sand River Convention, British recognise independent Boer state of Transvaal, in region north of the Vaal River
1854	British recognise independence of Orange Free State; representative government introduced at the Cape
1856	Xhosa cattle killings
1860	First indentured Indian labourers arrive in Natal
1866	Cape annexes region known as British Kaffraria
1867	Discovery of diamonds at Griqualand West; establishment of Kimberley
1871	British annex Griqualand West
1872	Responsible government introduced at the Cape
1875	British plans for confederation announced
1877	Transvaal annexed to Britain
1879	After initial set-back, British defeat Zulus; Pedi defeated by British forces
1881	British defeated by Transvaal forces at Majuba; Transvaal independence reinstated by British government
1886	Discovery of gold on Witwatersrand
1887	British annex Zululand
1894	Responsible government extended to Natal
1895	Jameson Raid fails to topple Transvaal government
1899	South African War (to 1902); British army defeats Afrikaner forces and annexes OFS and Transvaal
1902	Peace treaty signed; Milner starts his 'reconstruction' programme of southern Africa
1903	SA Native Affairs Commission meets (to 1905)
1904	First Chinese labourers brought to Rand
1906	British government restores autonomy to defeated Boer republics; 'Bambatha' rebellion is ruthlessly crushed
1910	Union of South Africa (Cape, Natal, Transvaal, OFS)
1911	Mines and Works Act – colour bar imposed on Rand
1912	Formation of SA Native National Congress (forerunner of ANC)
1913	Native Land Act – African land ownership restricted to segregated 'reserves'; start of policy of segregation
1914	SA enters First World War (to 1918)
1920	African industrial unrest on the Rand; Native Affairs Act – separate administration for Africans
1922	Rand Revolt – white strikers crushed by government under a state of emergency
1923	Native (Urban Areas) Act – segregation of Africans in urban areas and introduction of movement controls

1924	Labour–Nationalist 'Pact' wins general election
1925	Afrikaans recognised as an official language
1926	Extension of colour bar to private business
1929	Wall Street crash followed by Great Depression (to 1933); SA leaves gold standard 1932
1934	Smuts–Hertzog 'Fusion' government comes to power
1936	Area of land 'reserved' for Africans doubled; Cape franchise revoked; Africans placed on separate roll
1937	Marketing Act protects white farmers
1939	SA fights with allies in Second World War (to 1945)
1946	African miners strike on Rand; 12 shot dead
1948	NP wins election; beginning of apartheid
1949	ANC Youth League publishes Programme of Action
1950	First apartheid era legislation – Popular Registration Act; Group Areas Act; Immorality Act; Suppression of Communism Act. Government assumes wide-ranging controls over people and political organisations
1952	Pass Laws extended; defiance campaign against government launched
1953	Bantu Education Act; Separate Amenities Act; Criminal Law Amendment Act
1955	Freedom Charter adopted by Congress of the People
1956	Congress leaders charged with treason and tried (to 1961)
1959	Pan Africanist Congress founded
1960	Non-white representation in parliament ended; promotion of Bantustan homeland scheme; massacre at Sharpeville; 67 demonstrators are shot by government forces; State of Emergency declared; ANC, PAC and other political organisations are outlawed
1961	SA leaves the Commonwealth; ANC and PAC begin underground guerrilla movements
1963	Detention without trial permitted
1964	ANC and PAC leaders imprisoned for life
1973	Beginnings of African strike wave
1976	Soweto uprising spreads to other townships
1977	Murder of Black Consciousness leader Steve Biko
1978	PW Botha becomes Prime Minister and instigates policy of 'Total Stategy'; African trade unions recognised (1979) and colour bar relaxed in some industries
1983	United Democratic Front is formed in opposition to apartheid
1984	Tricameral constitution is introduced giving coloureds and Asians, but not Africans, a say in central government;

elections are widely boycotted; beginnings of unrest in townships and counter-repression by the state; Botha assumes role of State President and offers amnesty to Mandela and others if they refute violence as a political weapon

1986   State of Emergency declared and security forces deployed in townships; thousands are detained without trial; pass laws are repealed; international sanctions are stepped up; beginnings of Inkatha–ANC unrest in Natal and Rand (to 1995)

1989   FW de Klerk replaces Botha as President; programme of mass civil disobedience launched

1990   ANC, PAC and other banned organisations are decreed lawful; Mandela is freed from prison after 27 years

1991   Core apartheid legislation is revoked; State of Emergency is ended; Codesa formed by 18 parties to negotiate transition to democracy

1992   White referendum votes in support of Codesa, which breaks down due to spiralling conflict between Inkatha and ANC supporters; SA team competes at Olympic Games in Barcelona

1993   Negotiations reactivated and interim constitution is approved by Codesa; date set for election

1994   Nelson Mandela elected President of Government of National Unity after ANC majority victory in election; beginnings of Reconstruction and Development Programme; SA rejoins the Commonwealth; remaining sanctions are lifted

1995   SA team wins Rugby World Cup

1996   Truth and Reconciliation Commission starts (to 1998); mixed-race SA team wins football African Nations Cup

1997   Permanent Constitution comes into effect via Constituent Assembly; Mandela announces he will not stand for re-election in 1999

1999   ANC wins election and Thabo Mbeki succeeds Mandela as President

2000   NP reconstitutes itself after merging with Democratic Party

2001   Brewing political crisis in Zimbabwe has knock-on effect in SA; Mbeki negotiates with Mugabe

2002   Zimbabwe election held April; AIDS crisis in SA spirals; Mbeki is forced by courts to accept use in SA of drugs he believes cause immune system failure; UN World Summit on Sustainable Development held in Johannesburg (August–September); NP ends its alliance with the Democratic Party to form an alliance with ANC, winning control of the Western Cape province and the city of Cape Town

Estimated Population of South Africa, 1910–1996 (millions)

	1910	1936	1960	1980	1996
African	4.0 (67%)	6.6 (69%)	10.9 (68%)	20.8 (72%)	31.1 (77%)
Coloured	0.5 (9%)	0.8 (8%)	1.5 (9%)	3.6 (9%)	3.6 (9%)
Indian	0.2 (3%)	0.2 (2%)	0.5 (3%)	0.8 (3%)	1.0 (3%)
White	1.3 (21%)	2.0 (21%)	3.1 (19%)	4.5 (16%)	4.4 (11%)
Total	6.0 (m)	9.6 (m)	16.0 (m)	29.7 (m)	40.1 (m)

Note: These figures are approximate

Heads of State (selective) 1652–present

VOC RULE *1652–1795*

Governors
J. van Riebeeck   *1652–62*
S. van der Stel   *1679–99*
W.A. van der Stel   *1699–1707*
M.P. de Chavonnes   *1714–24*
H. Swellengrebel   *1739–50*
R. Tulbagh   *1751–71*
J. van Plettenberg   *1771–84*

THE BATAVIAN ADMINISTRATION *1803–05*

J.W. Janssens (Governor); J. de Mist (Commissioner)

BRITISH ADMINISTRATION OF THE CAPE *1795–1801* AND *1805–47*

Governors
Gen. J.H. Craig   *1795–97*
Earl of Caledon   *1807–11*
Gen. Sir J.F. Cradock   *1811–13*
Gen. Lord Charles Somerset   *1814–26*
Gen. Sir B. D'Urban   *1834–38*
Gen. Sir P. Maitland   *1844–47*

HIGH COMMISSIONERS AND GOVERNORS OF THE CAPE *1847–1910*

Gen. Sir H.G. Smith   *1847–52*
Sir G. Grey   *1854–56*

Sir P. Wodehouse   *1862–70*
Sir H.B.E. Frere   *1877–81*
Sir H. Robinson   *1881 & 1895–97*
Sir A. [Lord] Milner (HC for SA, and also, Governor of Orange River Colony
   and Transvaal)   *1897–1905*
Lord Selbourne   *1905–1910*

NON-BRITISH HEADS OF OFS PRIOR TO UNION

J.P. Hoffmann   *1854–55*
J.H. Brand   *1864–88*
F.W. Reitz   *1889–96*
M.T. Steyn   *1896–1900*

NON-BRITISH HEADS OF THE TRANSVAAL PRIOR TO UNION

M.W. Pretorius   *1856–60*
T.F. Burgers   *1872–77*
S.J.P. Kruger   *1883–1901*
L. Botha   *1907–10*

UNION OF SOUTH AFRICA *1910–61*

(i) Governors-General

Viscount Gladstone   *1910–14*
Viscount Buxton   *1914–20*
Earl of Athlone   *1924–31*
Earl of Clarendon   *1931–37*
Sir P. Duncan   *1837–43*
E.G. Jansen   *1951–60*

(ii) High Commissioners (as separate from Governor-General after 1931)

Sir W.H. Clark   *1935–41*
Sir E. Baring   *1944–51*
Sir J. le Rougetel   *1951–55*

(iii) Prime Minsters

Gen. L. Botha   *1910*
Gen. J.C. Smuts   *1919*

Gen. J.B.M. Hertzog   *1924*
Gen. J.C. Smuts   *1939*
Dr D.F. Malan   *1948*
J.G. Strijdom   *1954*
Dr. H.F. Verwoerd   *1958*

THE REPUBLIC OF SOUTH AFRICA *1961–PRESENT*

(i) Prime Ministers as Heads of State

Dr. H.F. Verwoerd   *1961*
B.J. Vorster   *1966*
P.W. Botha   *1978*

(ii) Presidents as Heads of State

P.W. Botha   *1984*
F.W. de Klerk   *1990*
N. Mandela   *1994*
T.M. Mbeki   *1999*

Public Holidays

1 January	New Year's Day
Easter	Good Friday and the following Monday (Family Day)
21 March	Human Rights Day
27 April	Freedom Day
1 May	Workers' Day
16 June	Youth Day
17 June	Public Holiday
9 August	National Women's Day
10 August	Public Holiday
24 September	Heritage Day
16 December	Day of Reconciliation
25 December	Christmas Day
26 December	Public Holiday

Further Reading

DAVENPORT, R. & SAUNDERS, C. *South Africa: A Modern History* (Macmillan, London; 5th edition, 2000)

DENOON, D. & NYEKO, B. *Southern Africa Since 1800* (Longman, London; new edition, 1984)

HALL, M. *The Changing Past: Farmers, Kings and Traders in Southern Africa, 200–1860* (D. Philip, Cape Town, 1987)

MALAN, R. *My Traitor's Heart* (Vintage paperback, London, 1991)

MANDELA, N. *Long Walk To Freedom* (Little Brown, London, 1994)

PARSONS, N. *A New History of Southern Africa* (Macmillan, London, 1982)

ROSS, R. *A Concise History of South Africa* (CUP, Cambridge, 1999)

THOMPSON, L. *A History of South Africa* (Yale UP, New Haven; revised edition, 1995)

VAN HARTESVELDT, F. *The Boer War* (Sutton, Stroud, 2000)

VAN ONSELEN, C. *The Seed is Mine: The Life of Kas Maine, A South African Sharecropper 1894–1985* (James Currey, Oxford, 1996)

VENTER, L. *When Mandela Goes* (Doubleday, Johannesburg, 1997)

WELSH, F. *A History of South Africa* (HarperCollins, London; revised edition, 2000)

WORDEN, N. *The Making of Modern South Africa: Conquest, Segregation and Apartheid* (Blackwell, Oxford, 2000)

Historical Gazetteer

Numbers in bold refer to main text

Note: The nine provinces that constitute South Africa today – Gauteng, Northern Province, North-West Province, Mpumalanga, Northern Cape, Western Cape, Eastern Cape, Free State and KwaZulu-Natal – have not been separately included in this gazetteer in their modern guises.

Albany District of the Suurveld annexed by the Cape in 1809 following an expedition led by Colonel Graham, the eastern Commissioner of the colony. The settlement of Graham's Town (qv.) was founded in the district, although land continued to be contested by local Xhosa farmers. 5,000 hand-picked British migrants were settled in the area in 1820, although the experiment quickly failed and most of the settlers migrated to local towns. Today, the region is incorporated into the Eastern Cape province. **63, 73–4**

Alexandra Township adjacent to Johannesburg. It was the centre of protests against high transportation costs during the Second World War and again in the late 1950s, when boycotting of public buses by township residents (during which workers would rise early and walk to work) led to a lowering of fares and the introduction of subsidised transport into the city. Like all townships, Alexandra was established in response to segregation era policies that forced Africans, coloureds and Indians out of cities across South Africa. Its residents were increasingly impoverished during the apartheid years. **186**

Bantustan Homelands Legislation was passed in 1959 that was designed to turn locations reserved for Africans into 'homelands', denying black South Africans citizenship of the republic. The Bantustans were far removed from areas of agricultural productivity, and suffered from a lack of funding, underdevelopment and overcrowding. In the early 1960s, millions of people were forcibly removed from 'white' South Africa to lands they had never seen before but which they were classed as citizens in accordance with notions of indigenous ethnicity.

No state other than South Africa ever recognised the nominally independent status of the four biggest homelands, which all remained heavily dependent on South Africa, especially in economic terms. Resistance and revolt, especially against local chiefs appointed by the apartheid regime, became common features of the homelands from the 1960s.

Technically independent Bantustans were: Transkei (from 1976), Bophuthatswana (1977), Venda (1979), Ciskei (1981). KwaZulu and KwaNdebele resisted being granted the same status during the 1980s. **213–18, 233–38**

Basutoland Basutoland emerged in the 1820s under the guidance of Moshoeshoe and its population was comprised mostly of refugees from the *Mfecane* and other groups of mainly Sotho speakers. Based in the central Drakensburg region, the state grew at a fast rate, bringing it into conflict with white settlers. In 1868, Basutoland was annexed by the Cape and later incorporated into the colony. The area remained outside South Africa after union, and was instead ruled by the British as a High Commission territory. It became the independent state of Lesotho in 1965. However, the country is reliant on South Africa economically, and many Sotho work within the republic. **54, 59–60, 150, 155**

Bloemfontein Provincial capital of the Free State and South Africa's judicial capital. Founded on farm land it was the base of a local Cape agent prior to the withdrawal of the British under the terms of a convention signed on the site in 1854, which

recognised the area as an independent state. In the second half of the 1800s the town was built up into a respectable interior settlement. Captured by the British during the South African War, Bloemfontein resumed its role as capital of the OFS in 1906. Situated in the middle of the country, today it is a quiet and pleasant place, well situated for exploring the Maluti Mountains and Lesotho. **7, 92, 93, 95, 96, 136, 143, 154, 156, 160, 180**

Boipatong Vaal township, scene of the 1992 massacre in which forty-five ANC supporters were massacred by residents of an Inkatha hostel. **246**

Boomplats Settlement in Griqua territory where forces of the Orange River Sovereignty, led by Pretorius, were defeated by the British, who were determined to quell unrest across the Orange River. Thereafter, Pretorius was forced back across the Vaal River. **93**

British Kaffraria See Ciskei.

Cape Colony Colony established around Cape Town (qv.) following the establishment of a station by the VOC in 1652. The colony expanded initially in a northerly direction, but by the early 1800s it had reached the Fish River in the east. In view of unrest in Europe following the French Revolution, and as a means of securing a strategically sensitive communications point, the British occupied the colony from 1795 until 1803, when the Dutch Batavian administration regained control of the region. The British reoccupied the colony in 1806, a gain subsequently upheld by the 1815 Vienna peace settlement. The area was to benefit economically from the change of regime, and a number of agricultural industries began to expand at a fast rate.

The British attempted to stabilise the eastern frontier of the colony by settling migrants in the east of the region (see Albany). Conflict with local Xhosa communities continued until the middle of the nineteenth century.

The abolition of slavery in 1833 led to an exodus of Dutch speakers from the colony. Nevertheless, the Cape was politically secure, and the British introduced representative government (in 1853) and responsible government (in 1872). The colony's boundaries, meanwhile, were extended to include British Kaffraria (1866), Basutoland (1871), Griqualand West (1880) and Bechuanaland (1895).

The Cape was one of the four provinces of South Africa after the Act of Union came into effect in 1910 and Cape Town became the seat of parliament. After 1994, the province was split into three smaller provinces of the Western Cape, the Eastern Cape and the Northern Cape. **23–6, 32–42, 47–8, 70–72, 74–8,** *passim*

Cape Town South Africa's second largest city after Johannesburg, but undoubtedly one of the country's most beautifully located settlements, at the northern end of the Cape peninsula, beneath Table Mountain, and surrounded by marvellous beaches that stretch for miles.

The San, and later Khoi, pastoralists lived at this location for thousands of years prior to the arrival at Table Bay of the Portuguese explorer Dias in 1487. In 1652, encouraged by the local climate, Jan van Riebeeck chose Table Bay as the location for the VOC's southern African refreshment station.

Van Riebeeck oversaw the difficult formative phase of the colony and laid the foundations of the city and encouraged local agriculture. It was not long before the station was able to serve its designated purpose of supplying visiting Company ships. During the course of the 1700s, there developed at Cape Town a nascent colonial society that went from strength to strength under British tutelage. It also became home to an increasingly diverse and cosmopolitan population, and until the 1870s, was the undisputed hub of southern Africa's economic, social and political life.

Today, Cape Town remains the seat of the South African parliament (although there are plans to move it to Pretoria). Despite evident social fractures, tourism is increasingly a vital industry to the city, reflecting the fact that it is an ideal holiday destination. **23–6, 70–71,** *passim*

Ciskei Area between the Keiskamma and Great Kei Rivers on the eastern frontier of the Cape colony, annexed by the British in 1847 as British Kaffraria. Following the cattle killings of 1856–57 the African population of the area fell greatly, and white settlers moved into the region in increasing numbers. The area was incorporated into the Cape colony in 1866.

During the apartheid era, the area, now known as Ciskei, was established as a Bantustan homeland (qv.), accepting independent status in 1982. The homeland was severely over-crowded (due to forced relocations) and economically dependent on South Africa. After the fall of apart-heid, Ciskei was incorporated into the new province of the Eastern Cape. **65, 68, 216, 217**

District Six   A thriving area of cen-tral Cape Town, home to a variety of ethnic groupings and a large coloured population. The area was demolished during the 1960s after it was rezoned by the government as a white area. There was a concerted effort to resist this process by the inhabitants of the district, but ultimately, they were forced to relocate. Internationally, the clearance became symbolic of the inequities of the apartheid system, especially as the land was left vacant for some considerable time. Former residents of District Six have applied for restitution in terms of land legis-lation but these claims are yet to be settled. **196**

Drakensberg Mountains   Dominat-ing mountain range, mostly in the province of KwaZulu-Natal. Separ-ating the veld plateau from the southern escarpment, the mountains run for over 200 miles, with an average height of 3,300 metres above sea level. An area of out-standing beauty and home to multi-tudinous examples of San rock painting. **4, 82**

Durban   Originally built up by British settlers as Port Natal, Durban was named after an 1830s British Governor. Razed by the Zulus in the 1830s, the port survived owing to its strategic and economic importance to the Cape colony and the British.

Today, it is South Africa's third largest city and still the country's busiest port. Its sandy beaches and sheltered bay act as a beacon to tourists from South Africa and abroad. Durban is also the home to South Africa's largest South Asian commu-nity, centred in the west end of the city and neighbouring hills. **7, 84, 87, 90, 91, 153, 187, 196, 218**

East London   Port in the Eastern Cape province, built up in the late 1840s to support the colonial–settler forces in their efforts to overcome the local Xhosa population. A small city, somewhat off the beaten track, East London is still a busy port and important internal communications point. **7**

Graaff-Reinet   The settlement of Graaff-Reinet was founded as an outpost of the Cape in the 1780s. It is one of the country's oldest European interior towns, and today much of its history can be seen through its architecture. It was the centre of the Patriot uprising against VOC rule in 1795. **44, 48, 62, 84**

Grahamstown   Garrison town developed after the annexation of the Albany district (qv.) by the Cape colony in 1809. It was military out-post until the arrival of British migrant settlers in 1820, who helped turn the town into an important trading centre. Later in the 1800s, it was the centre of an increasingly lucrative ivory trade.

Part of the city has retained its English character and is home to one of South Africa's largest English-speaking universities (Rhodes), as well as an annual arts festival held in July. **63, 64, 81, 225**

Griqualand West Area of the Northern Cape settled by the Griqua community in the early part of the 1800s. It was in this area that diamonds were discovered in the 1860s, an event that transformed the region from a sleepy backwater into a thriving magnet for prospectors. Annexed by the British in 1871, Griqualand West was thereafter incorporated into the Cape colony in 1880. **103–5**

Johannesburg The City of Gold: South Africa's largest city and Africa's second most populous was built up after the discovery of gold in the 1880s. Johannesburg is at the heart of South Africa's industrial belt, a vast conurbation, so sprawling that today it almost runs into Pretoria (technically, some thirty-five miles away). Many of the city's characteristics have been with it since inception: a high crime rate, great wealth and extreme poverty, a mixed and transient population (thousands of whom still live in one of the numerous 'temporary' townships that circle the place). Money is and always has been the driving force in Johannesburg, and as any visitor will soon find out, the majority of the city's five million inhabitants do not have enough of it. **7, 123–7**

Kalahari Over 700 miles from Cape Town, the Kalahari Desert in the northern extremities of the country is not easily accessible. A vast area that stretches across the borders into Namibia and Botswana, the Kalahari is home to the last few bands of independent San. Vast sandlands are broken by scrub and the occasional acacia tree, although the spartan landscape belies the fact that the region is home to some unique wildlife. Temperatures soar in the summer months, making the winter the best time to visit the region. **4**

Karoo The Great Karoo, which dominates the centre of the country, is an area of semi-desert which, like the Kalahari, initially acted as a natural barrier to colonial expansion in the early 1800s. The deep-lying water supplies were later tapped, and a number of small farming communities were established in the region. It has captivating landscapes and skies, baking hot days and clear, cold nights. **4, 34, 39, 42**

Kimberley In the northern Cape, Kimberley was founded following the discovery of diamonds in Griqualand West in the late 1860s (qv.) and became the centre of the subsequent boom. Within a matter of years, Kimberley was southern Africa's second largest town and accounted for some 80 per cent of the region's exports. The town became an important railway junction as a result of the diamond industry. On the outbreak of the South African War in 1899, Kimberley became the focus of a siege by Boer forces that lasted for 124 days.

Today, Kimberley is still the centre of South Africa's diamond industry, and the world headquarters of the De Beers conglomerate is in the town. There is also a thriving industry centred on the site of the siege and surrounding battlefields. **103–7, 138, 139, 141, 143**

Kliptown Kliptown, on the outskirts of Johannesburg, was the location where the Congress of the People met in June 1955, to voice opposition to the apartheid regime and to sign the Freedom Charter. The meeting was dispersed after two days by the security forces and, the following year, 156 leaders of the Congress were tried for treason. The Charter, however, remained a focus for opposition to the apartheid regime until the advent of democracy in 1994. **201**

Ladysmith Small settlement in KwaZulu-Natal, most famously besieged by Boer forces for 118 days in 1899–1901. **141–3**

Lesotho See Basutoland.

Mafikeng (formerly Mafeking) Town in north-eastern extreme of the Cape colony, it was the settlement longest under siege by Boer forces in 1899–1901 (217 days in total). Mafeking was later used by the British as the administrative centre for Bechuanaland, even though it was outside the boundaries of the territory. **143**

Majuba Majuba Hill, literally meaning 'hill of doves', was the site of the British defeat at the hands of Transvaal forces on 26 February 1881. As unexpected as it was humiliating, the reverse caused the British Prime Minister, Gladstone, to retract the 1877 annexation of Transvaal (qv.). **121, 129**

Mossel Bay The place at which the first recorded European explorer to set foot on southern African soil, Bartolomeu Dias, landed in 1487. He did not stay for long but proceeded

further along the coast. In Dias' footsteps came Vasco da Gama, close on a decade later, stopping at the point for a week. Portuguese shipping continued to use Mossel Bay into the 1600s although its popularity waned once the Dutch base was established at the Cape. **19, 21**

Natal Situated between the Drakensberg Mountains (qv.) and the Indian Ocean, the area of Natal was settled by migrant Bantu-speaking mixed farmers after AD 300. A small number of white migrants moved into the region in the early 1800s, settling around the port of Durban (qv.). These migrants were later joined by *trekker* communities, who in 1837 established the republic of Natalia. In view of concerns regarding the *trekker* use of slaves, but also as a means of protecting strategic and trading interests in the region, the British annexed the republic, renaming it Natal, in 1843. Further waves of white migrants flowed into the area and the local African population was subjugated and forced from much of the land, eventually being segregated on specially created reserves.

The economy of the region was boosted after the 1860s following the success of sugar plantations that relied on indentured labour imported from India. Conflict over land persisted, however, especially with the Zulus, resulting in the incorporation of Zululand into Natal in 1897.

Natal was granted responsible government in 1893 and was one of the four provinces of South Africa after the Union of 1910. Today, the province has been renamed

KwaZulu-Natal. **88–92, 98–9, *passim***

Orange Free State   Region between the Orange and Vaal Rivers. Inhabited by Sotho and Tswana speakers, it was later occupied by migrants on the Great Trek. A far from stable place after the advent of these white migrants, in 1848 it was annexed by the Cape colony and named the Orange River Sovereignty. Perpetual conflicts between the settlers and colonial forces, and the Sotho and local white population, resulted in a British withdrawal, and under the terms of the 1854 Bloemfontein Convention, the British acknowledged the independence of the region as a settler republic (the Orange Free State).

Conflict with the Sotho continued throughout the 1850s and 1860s, until Basutoland was annexed by the Cape (qv.). The OFS sided with the Transvaal against Britain during the South African War, but was overrun by British forces in 1900, and reoccupied. Its independence was restored in 1906, and in 1910, the OFS was one of the four provinces of the Union (Bloemfontein becoming South Africa's judicial capital). These boundaries remain to this day, although the province is now known simply as the Free State. **93–9, *passim***

Pietermaritzburg   The joint capital of KwaZulu-Natal, Pietermaritzburg was originally a Zulu settlement, located in the midst of a wooded valley. Small and isolated, after 1838, the settlement was taken over by *trekkers* who named the town after two leaders of the Great Trek – Piet Retief and Gert Maritz. Settled by British migrants following the annexation of Natal in 1843 (qv.), Pietermaritzburg is marked out by some fine Victorian-era architecture. **7, 152**

Port Elizabeth   The 'windy city', situated in the Eastern Cape, is South Africa's fifth largest city and one of the country's oldest ports. Originally an outpost of the Cape colony during the early years of British administration, the settlement was named after his wife by the British Governor Sir R. Donkin. Today the city is climbing out of a recession, which was the consequence of the closure of many locally based car factories, and is decidedly on the up, thanks in no small part to a vibrant student population.

Port Natal   See Durban.

Potchefstroom   A small community established by *trekkers* in the 1830s in the south-west Transvaal. One of the more stable frontier communities of the time, Potchefstroom became attached to Natalia, but ceded from the region once it was annexed by the British. Later incorporated into the republic of Transvaal, during the course of the 1900s the town became a NP stronghold until the late 1980s and home to a deeply conservative university which produced some of the leading academics of the apartheid era. **82, 91, 92, 245**

Pretoria   Named after Andries Pretorius and in memory of the *trekker* victory over the Zulus at the Battle of Blood River in 1838, Pretoria was the capital of the republic of Transvaal after 1860 and has been the seat of the

South African government since 1910. A quiet city that is dwarfed by its neighbour Johannesburg, Pretoria is a strangely uniform place, dominated by a mass of government buildings. **7, 156**

Robben Island   An island seven miles off the coast of Cape Town, it has been used by successive white regimes in southern Africa as a prison, and also as an asylum for the insane and a leper colony. After the Second World War the island was used to hold political prisoners, including Nelson Mandela, and so became a focal point for the anti-apartheid movement.

After the release of political prisoners in 1990, Robben Island ceased to be used as a prison, and today houses a museum dedicated to recording the struggle against apartheid. It is also home to a small nature reserve. **37**

Sharpeville   Township near Vereeniging where police shot at a crowd demonstrating against the pass laws in March 1960. Sixty-nine people were killed. In the aftermath of the massacre, the anti-apartheid struggle was characterised by more direct action, and a wave of unrest spread across the country forcing the government to declare a State of Emergency. There was much international condemnation of the shootings and calls for stringent sanctions against the South African government.

The anniversary of the Sharpeville shootings was unofficially observed as a day of mourning throughout the remainder of the apartheid era. In 1995, the Government of National Unity declared the anniversary a public holiday (known as Human Rights Day). It was at Sharpeville that Nelson Mandela signed South Africa's new constitution in December 1996. **207–10, 253**

Simonstown   A naval base near Cape Town, it was established and developed by the British navy after they occupied the Cape. It was taken over by the South African navy in 1955, and thereafter a British–South African defence pact was concluded. **104**

Sophiatown   A one time multi-racial suburb of Johannesburg. By the 1940s, the district was overcrowded and suffering from deteriorating conditions and a run-down local infrastructure. After the passing of legislation by the government in 1950, Sophiatown was classified a white area and its African inhabitants were forcibly moved despite strong local resistance. The area was flattened and a new white suburb called Triomf, or Triumph, was built on the site. **196**

Soweto   A township close to Johannesburg that absorbed much of the population forced out of Sophiatown. A grim, utilitarian place, Soweto (an abbreviation for south-western township) was, by the early 1970s, a hotbed of discontent and dissatisfaction about the terrible squalor in which its residents were forced to live. A demonstration by students in June 1976 was shot at by the police; two children were killed. This sparked a wave of unrest throughout Soweto and, indeed, the rest of the country, which would account for hundreds of lives.

Condemnation   of   the   state's

actions in Soweto during 1976 was strong, although the regime merely ignored all such criticisms. Nevertheless, the Soweto rising marked a new era of militancy in anti-apartheid activity within South Africa. In the longer term, the established order could not overcome the threat to its stability that this presented. **224–8**

Spion Kop Site of South African War battle, January 1900. On the way to relieve the besieged town of Ladysmith, British commanders attempted to take the dominant position of Spion Kop. A series of miscalculations enabled the Boers to thwart the British advance. It was a catastrophic defeat for the British, resulting in 1,700 dead. **141–3**

St Helena Bay Seventy miles north of Cape Town, this was the point at which Vasco da Gama first alighted in southern Africa, on 4 November 1497. **21, 40**

Sun City The South African Las Vegas? Certainly, a major attraction to South African and foreign visitors alike, offering gambling, entertainment and top sporting events. Opened in the 1970s by the nominally independent homeland government of Bophuthatswana, Sun City initially operated outside the remit of the republic, but since 1994, it has entered the mainstream culture of South Africa. **217**

Swaziland An autonomous nation within the boundaries of South Africa, it was established around Swazi ethnicity. The Swazi in the late 1800s were susceptible to attack by other African polities, notably the Zulu, and settlers from the Transvaal. The British incorporated Swaziland into the empire in 1907 as a High Commission territory. It remained outside the Union and achieved independence in 1968. **3, 14, 129, 150, 155**

Swellendam Once the northern

Sun City and its exotic hotel Palace at the Lost City

outpost of the Cape under the VOC, Swellendam rebelled against the Company in 1795 and proclaimed itself a republic. Order was later restored under the first period of British administration. It is one of South Africa's oldest European settlements. **34, 40, 44, 48**

Table Bay Site of the VOC station established in 1652 (qv.). See also Cape Town. **22, 23, 48**

Thaba Bosiu The Mountain of the Night, a defensive table-top base from where in the 1840s Moshoeshoe expanded his control over Basutoland. **59–60**

Transkei A region between the Kei River and Natal, inhabited by Xhosa farmers and, during the late 1800s, brought under the control of the Cape colony. After 1913, the Transkei was set aside as an African reserved location. During the apartheid era, the area was transformed into a Bantustan (qv.) and accepted nominal independence in 1976. Today, Transkei is incorporated into the Eastern Cape province. **43, 122, 216**

Transvaal During the latter stages of the Great Trek, increasing numbers of white settlers came into the area, which is sandwiched between the Vaal and Limpopo Rivers. After the British withdrew from the region north of the Vaal River in 1852, it was established as an independent settler republic (known as the South African Republic). Conflict with local African communities characterised the early years of the SAR, a situation that resulted in British annexation in 1877. Following a short war and victory at Majuba (qv.), independence was restored in 1881, although the republic remained a rather unruly, backward place until the discovery of gold on the Witwatersrand (qv.) during the 1880s. This transformed the region from an agricultural backwater into the economic focal point of southern Africa. An influx of capitalist interests resulted in rising tensions between the Transvaal government headed by Paul Kruger, which was increasingly the focus of Afrikaner nationalist aspirations, and the Cape administration. The ensuing South African War saw the occupation of the Transvaal by the British as a crown colony.

Independence was restored to the Transvaal in 1906. In 1910, it was a founder province of South Africa and Pretoria became the country's capital city. After the advent of democratic rule in 1994, the Transvaal province was split into four smaller provinces (North-West Province, Gauteng, Mpumalanga and Northern Province). **94–9, 123–6,** *passim*

Vereeniging The town south of Johannesburg where the treaty ending the South African War was signed in May 1902. **147–8**

Witwatersrand Commonly referred to as the Rand, this rocky ridge is where gold was discovered in vast quantities in the 1880s. It also contains rich deposits of manganese and coal. Despite the recent slump in gold production, the Rand and adjacent Johannesburg (qv.) is today the chief industrial area of South Africa. **123–6, 223–5**

Index